Here Comes your King!

Copyright 2020 Kenneth R. Ross

All rights reserved. No part of this publication may be reproduced, stored in a retrieval system, or transmitted in any from or by any means, electronic, mechanical, photocopying, recording or otherwise without prior permission from the publishers.

First Published by Kachere Series in 1998.
Second Impression with new Introduction 2020

Published by
Luviri Press
P/Bag 201 Luwinga
Mzuzu 2

ISBN 978-99960-66-34-4
eISBN 978-99960-66-35-1

Luviri Reprints no. 12

Luviri Press is represented outside Malawi by:
African Books Collective Oxford (order@africanbookscollective.com)

www.luviripress.blogspot.com
www.africanbookscollective.com

Printed in Malawi by Baptist Publication, P.O. Box 444, Lilongwe

Here Comes your King!
Christ, Church and Nation in Malawi

Kenneth R. Ross

Luviri Press

Luviri Reprints no. 12

Mzuzu

2020

Foreword

More than twenty years have passed since this book was first published yet its themes remain vital for understanding the way in which Christian faith is coming to expression in a context like Malawi. It begins with Christology, with the question of the identity of Jesus Christ that is perennially at the centre of the Christian theological task. For a century and more Malawians have been hearing the proclamation, "here comes your king!" This has struck a chord in millions of hearts as individuals, families and communities have named Jesus Christ as Lord. It has also posed the challenge of discovering what this Lordship means in every dimension of life. Much of the rest of the book pursues this question as it explores how church identity has been formed and consolidated, how the faith has been a resource for the nation at critical moments, and the ways in which the faith has shaped national identity and helped to meet political challenges.

The book was a fruit of the fresh opportunity for contextual theology that came with the end of the thirty years of one-party rule in Malawi during which it was scarcely possible to develop socially critical theology. As Malawi during the mid-1990s sought to redefine itself in the post-dictatorship era, the initiatives in research, conference and publication that were fostered by the Department of Theology and Religious Studies at the University of Malawi's Chancellor College provided one forum in which key questions could be addressed. It was in this particular crucible that the essays collected in this book were conceived and constructed. Looking back with the benefit of hindsight I am grateful for the stimulating environment and supportive community that enabled me to cut my teeth as a contextual theologian and offer the essays that were brought together to make this book.

History does not stand still. As we enter the 2020s those who attempt to do contextual theology in Malawi will need to consider a set of realities that differ from those that prevailed in the 1990s. Nonetheless, I hope that the essays collected in this book will retain some value both by offering methodological hints and by opening up lines of analysis that remain relevant. Therefore I am deeply grateful to Luviri Press for including this book in their reprint series and for the pleasure of collaborating together once again. If the reprint can be of any assistance to those who seek to bring theological perspectives to bear on contemporary realities in Malawi or elsewhere, the effort will have proved its worth.

Kenneth R. Ross

Zomba

Easter 2020

For Hester

and the people of Malawi who freely shared

their life and wisdom with us 1988-98

with thanksgiving and in hope

Contents

Foreword	4
Series Editors' Preface	8
Acknowledgements	10
Introduction	11
1. The Christological Task in Africa Today: Nicene Methodology Reconsidered	14
2. "Who do you Say that I Am?" Popular Christology in Northern Malawi	38
3. Contested Identity: Ecclesial Self-Understanding in Northern Malawi	59
4. Crisis and Identity: Presbyterian Ecclesiology in Southern Malawi 1891-1993	85
5. The Renewal of the State by the Church: the Case of the Public Affairs Committee	107
6. Partnership in Mission and Postcolonial Politics: the Case of the Church of Scotland and the CCAP	131
7. Where were the Prophets and Martyrs in Banda's Malawi? Four Presbyterian Ministers	154
8. Christian Faith and National Identity	175
9. After Freedom: Christ's Kingdom and Malawi's Second Republic	197
Bibliography	224

Series Editors' Preface

The Kachere Series is an initiative of the Department of Theology and Religious Studies at the University of Malawi. It aims to promote the emergence of a body of literature which will enable students and others to engage critically with religion in Malawi, its social impact and the theological questions which it raises. An important starting point lies with the publication of essays and theses which until now have been inaccessible to all but the most dedicated specialist. It is also hoped, however, that the development of theological scholarship in Malawi will stimulate the writing of many new books. General works with popular appeal can be published as Kachere Books. Documents and essays, which are of value as sources for the study of religion in Malawi, can be published as Kachere Texts. Full-length treatises, the fruit of sound primary research which meet rigorous academic standards, are published as Kachere Monographs. The Editors intend the Series to contribute substantially to the growth of a body of knowledge in the area of theology and religious studies in Malawi. As important resources for study related to this field, we are confident that they will come to be prized not only within Malawi but in every academic centre concerned with religion and society in Africa.

This book by Kenneth Ross is the first in this series to tackle the issue of theological method and in particular method in Christology. Ross joins the Christological debate in the African context. In this respect he calls theologians involved in a quest for an African Christology to revisit the theological method of the Nicene Fathers. In addition to basing their Christology on involvement in Church life and the Bible, the Nicene Fathers believed that a scientific and properly critical Christian theology must be built on the apprehension of the divine revelation of Jesus Christ. *Christ, Church and the Nation* is a fitting subtitle to this book.

The identity of the Church and the Church's engagement with the state are based on the proper understanding of Jesus Christ and the implications of following him as King. This study is specific to Malawi but its implications will certainly have a great impact on the wider Christological debate in Africa and abroad. It is in this spirit that we offer the book to our readers.

Kachere Series Editors
Zomba, Sexagesima 1998

Acknowledgements

Some of the chapters of this book were published in earlier versions in various journals. A version of chapter 2 appeared in the *Journal of Religion in Africa,* of chapters 4 and 7 in *Missionalia,* of chapter 5 *in Religion in Malawi,* of chapter 6 in the *Records of the Scottish Church History Society* and of chapter 8 in the *Journal of Theology for Southern Africa.* I am grateful to the editors of these publications who gave permission for the material to be revised and edited so as to be included in the present volume. Chapter 1 originated as a Seminar presentation at the Centre for the Study of Christianity in the Non-Western World, University of Edinburgh, on 3 December 1996. Most of the others had an airing at one of the conferences or seminars of the Department of Theology and Religious Studies at the University of Malawi between 1995 and 1997. I am therefore greatly indebted to faculty and students who participated in these discussions and contributed to the formation of the material which is presented here. Most of all, I must record my thanks to my colleagues in the Kachere Series - Joe Chakanza, Felix Chingota, Klaus Fiedler, Celeste Geddes, Hilary Mijoga, Fulata Moyo, Martin Ott, Isabel Apawo Phiri and James Tengatenga. Their sharp insights, unfailing encouragement and constructive criticism immeasurably strengthened the book. For its remaining deficiencies, of course, I alone am responsible.

Kenneth R. Ross, Zomba, February 1998

Introduction

Surely something tremendous was happening in Malawi in the early years of the twentieth century when Peter Thole, *ng'ombwa ya zingtombwa* (king of minstrels), wrote:

> Leap up, my soul; leap up and sing;
> Take heart again, *here comes your king.*
> Redemption done by God's right hand
> Is breaking forth through all the land.
>
> God has spread before our face
> Wondrous salvation, love and grace;
> Lifted you up and set you free.
> Now he is beaming forth in light,
> Driving away the clouds of night;
> Praise him, my soul, exultantly.[1]

Today, towards the end of the twentieth century, this hymn continues to be sung very meaningfully in Malawian Christian congregations, even at a time when society is experiencing severe difficulties. What is offered in this book is an attempt to gather resources for a deeper apprehension of the king at the centre of the song: hence the Christological focus of the first two chapters. Our understanding of the king, however, depends much on what we experience of the kingdom taking effect in human life. Chapters three to nine. therefore, examine different aspects of Malawian experience in church and in nation. Neither of these can be identified with the kingdom of Christ yet both are integrally related to it and

---

[1] For the full text of the hymn in Tumbuka with English translation, see Kenneth R. Ross ed., *Christianity in Malawi: A Sourcebook.* Gweru: Mambo Press, 1996, p. 67. For further discussion of Peter Thole and his contemporaries, see Gift Nkunika, "Hymns of Early Christian Converts of the Livingstonia Synod of the Church of Central Africa Presbyterian," BEd, University of Malawi, 1996.

provide the context in which that kingdom breaks into human life. Some of the studies are more historical, others more contemporary. Some are heavily based on primary research, others more on theological reflection. Some are ecumenical in scope, others more concentrated on the Presbyterian tradition which has been particularly influential in Malawi. What unites the essays is that they seek to bring to light aspects of the "redemption done by God's right hand" which "is breaking forth through all the land." Since all were written and presented in various fora between 1995 and 1997, their context is, very firmly, Malawi in the early years of the Second Republic.

A common thread running through the book is concern with method: how can we most effectively do theology in Malawi today? What are the resources at our disposal and how can they best be used? What are the methodological wrong turnings of which we should beware? What directions promise to be fruitful in theological construction? These questions are tackled head-on in the first chapter in reference to the central issue of how we may form an accurate and authentic understanding of Jesus Christ. Reference is made to the way in which this question was approached in the fourth century with a view to finding clues which could guide the churches in Africa today. One clue is that the lived experience of ordinary Christians, in worship and discipleship, is a key source for Christological construction. Chapters two and three report on primary research which seeks to tap into "grassroots" Christian experience and suggest how the research results might open up new directions for theological enquiry. These two chapters are directly engaged with contemporary experience. Chapter four turns to the past and provides a sample of how the historical experience of a particular church community may be ecclesiologically formative. The case in point is the Blantyre Synod of the Church of Central Africa Presbyterian and examination is made of four historical crisis points, each of which played an influential role in the formation of a distinct and robust ecclesiological identity.

In chapter five the focus shifts from the church's own identity to the role of the churches in shaping the life of the nation. A close examination of the part played by the Public Affairs Committee in Malawi's transition from dictatorship to democracy in 1992-94 reveals the extent, as well as the limitations, of the contribution of the churches to the renewal of the state which ushered in the Second Republic. One feature of that process was that it brought into view the nature of Malawian churches' partnerships with churches elsewhere. In the sixth chapter we examine the oldest of such partnerships - that between the CCAP and the Church of Scotland. Even in a post-colonial context this proved to be an influential relationship and one which revealed important aspects of the nature of the church and its role in national life. This consideration of international partnership in mission also highlights weaknesses in the witness of the churches in the period of the Banda dictatorship. The fact that things were allowed to go so terribly wrong in the Malawian political order poses sharp questions for the churches. Where were the prophets and martyrs who would expose the evils of society and point to a better way? Chapter seven attempts to answer this question by turning again to the CCAP Synod of Blantyre and examining its social witness during the one-party era. The eighth chapter probes the question of national identity in Malawian history and attempts to show how a Christian understanding of national life may have much to contribute to sustaining and nourishing a healthy sense of nationhood at a time when fragmentation threatens. Finally, the ninth chapter attempts an examination of the political order in Malawi's Second Republic in light of the coming kingdom of Jesus Christ. As may be expected in contextual theology, the essays are more suggestive than conclusive and the book is offered in the hope that it will provoke an ever more intensive theological engagement with church and society in Malawi.

1. The Christological Task in Africa Today: Nicene Methodology Reconsidered

The Agenda for Christology in Africa Today

At the heart of the quest for authentic African Christian identity has lain the question of Christology. In societies where much of life revolves around kinship it is not at all obvious that the man from Nazareth, who has been for so long accommodated in Greek philosophy and European culture, should be given the definitive role in establishing what it means to be human. "Why should an Akan," asked John Pobee, "relate to Jesus of Nazareth, who does not belong to his clan, family, tribe or nation?"[1] Hence a sense of alienation marked much of early Christian experience in Africa and the primary theological task was one of indigenization. The question, as Benezet Bujo put it, was: "In which way can Jesus Christ be an African among the Africans according to their own religious experience?"[2] To this agenda the first generation of African theologians addressed themselves with vigour. Over against an understanding of Jesus Christ where he seemed to be enclosed in alien categories, answering questions which Africans had never asked, a determined effort was made to think through the identity of Jesus Christ in terms of African categories and in response to African realities.

The programme was vigorously set out in the 1960s by E.B. Idowu: "We set ourselves the task of finding an answer to the delicate question of whether there is any correlation between the Biblical concept of God and the African concept of God, between what God has done and is doing according to the Biblical record and teaching

---

[1] John Pobee, *Towards an African Theology,* Nashville: Abingdon, 1979, p. 81.

[2] Benezet Bujo, *African Theology in its Social Context,* New York: Orbis, 1992, p. 12.

and what God has done and is doing according to African traditional beliefs.... We seek, in effect, to discover in what way the Christian faith could best be presented, interpreted and inculcated in Africa so that Africans will hear God in Jesus Christ addressing Himself immediately to them in their own native situation and particular circumstances.[3] Accordingly, themes such as ancestor, chief, *nganga*, life, initiation, were adopted as new frameworks within which the reality of Jesus Christ might be understood. Such an exercise was long overdue since it is apparent that, in accepting Jesus Christ, Africans *could* respond only in the categories of their own religion and culture. It was therefore entirely proper that thorough examination should be made of how Jesus Christ may be understood in the mind of someone whose spiritual universe is composed of the ancestors, the *nganga*, the chief, the master of initiation and so on. Academic theologians throughout Africa have applied themselves to this task and have shown how the message of Jesus Christ has resonance within the categories of a traditional African worldview.

Curiously, however, this endeavour has had rather little effect within the African church at large. In his recent survey of African theology John Parratt concludes: "Perhaps the most important question is what such adaption of aspects of African religion into Christian theology actually accomplishes at the level of Christian experience. Does it, on the ground, help towards the experiencing of the Christian faith in a more authentic way, or is it an academic exercise of little practical value?"[4] Charles Nyamiti frankly acknowledges that: "none of the existing African Christologies has had any appreciable influence in the life of the African churches."[5] This unfortunately leaves the efforts of academic theologians at Christological

---

[3] E. Bolaji Idowu. "Introduction," in Kwesi A. Dickson & Paul Ellingworth eds., *Biblical Revelation and African Beliefs*, London: Lutterworth Press, 1969, p. 16.

[4] John Parratt, *Reinventing Christianity: African Theology Today*, Grand Rapids: Eerdmans & Trenton: Africa World Press, 1995, p. 202.

[5] Charles Nyamiti, "African Christologies Today," in Robert J. Schreiter ed., *Faces of Jesus in Africa*, London: SCM, 1992, p. 18.

construction looking rather artificial and contrived since they are not owned or recognized to any significant extent by their natural constituency. As Aylward Shorter observed: "Christology in Africa ... has been a notional theology and not couched (to use Cardinal Newman's terminology) in the grammar of real assent – the imaginative expression of popular faith."[6]

Cecie Kolie is one scholar who has questioned the motives and procedure of fellow African theologians who have been active in Christological reconstruction: "Since their communities cannot name Christ personally without going to the Bible and the catechisms, they do just the opposite, and attribute to Christ the traditional titles of initiator, chief, great ancestor, and so on, that they would *like* to see him given in their communities. Once more we impose on our fellow Africans the way of seeing that we have learned from our Western masters."[7] The paradoxical situation arises where the conscious attempt to "Africanize" Christology results in nothing other than a further alien imposition! "What are we to say," asks Benezet Bujo, "of an African theology which never gets beyond the lecture halls of universities and congresses, mostly outside Africa? ... African theologians can easily turn into eager proselytizers whom you keep meeting in international gatherings but whom you never see in the bush... "[8]

Meanwhile, however, there has occurred, "in the bush," in countries like Malawi, a vast and profound apprehension of the Christian faith. In approaching the question of Christology today, it is of paramount importance to notice that the great change which has occurred since the agenda was first mapped out in the 1960s is that the Bible has been read in African languages for 30 more years, Christian worship has taken place in African communities for 30 more years and the

---

[6] Aylward Shorter, "Folk Christianity and Functional Christology," *AFER* Vol. 24/3 (June1982), pp. 133-137 [135].

[7] Cecie Kolie, "Jesus the Healer," in Schreiter, *Faces of Jesus,* pp. 141-42.

[8] Bujo, *African Theology,* pp. 70, 72.

Christian self-understanding of many of the African peoples has been nurtured for 30 more years. In the 1990s this reality became dramatically evident at a political level. In the movement for democratization churches throughout Africa were active "challenging political structures, urging reform, advocating political change, and even presiding over the change itself."[9] This reflects a very different scenario from that prevailing in the 1960s when the initiative lay with the nationalist movements. As Terence Ranger has observed: "Even while church leaders kept their heads down, their moral standing had grown indigenous. The churches came to be seen as the only surviving institutions which ordinary people still trusted. Political institutions have lost all credibility, but ecclesiastical institutions have been gaining it."[10] Clearly the churches would not enjoy such public confidence if their message was not taken very seriously by the population at large. The political reality suggests that a massive indigenization of Christian faith has, in fact, occurred in the generation from the 1960s to the 1990s.

The question is whether constructive theology has taken adequate account of this religious shift at the popular level. The danger is that African theologians continue to burden themselves with the task of reconciling the Christian tradition and the African heritage[11] when this dilemma is every day diminishing in importance within the empirical reality of popular Christianity. In this context it may be time for those concerned with understanding Jesus Christ in Africa today to re-examine the agenda. Towards that end I will now turn to some aspects of the theology of the Nicene fathers of the 4th century. My concern at this point is not so much with the *content* of

---

[9] Paul Gifford, "Introduction: *Democratisation* and the Churches," in Paul Gifford ed., *The Christian Churches and the Democratisation of Africa,* Leiden: E.J. Brill, 1995, p. 3.

[10] Terence Ranger, "Conference Summary and Conclusion," in Gifford ed., *The Christian Churches and the Democratisation of Africa,* p. 19.

[11] See, e.g., Bujo, *African Theology,* p. 75; Parratt, *Reinventing Christianity,* p. 194.

this theology, enshrined in the well-known Nicene Creed, as with the *method* by which the theology was constructed.

The Nicene Methodology

1. Church Life and Academic Theology

The first point to be noted in respect of the methodology of the Nicene fathers is that they constructed their theology out of a committed engagement with the life of the church of their time. In particular, they sought to be true to the Christian experience of salvation in Christ as this was evident in the congregations in whose life they participated. This, it is commonly acknowledged, is what tilted the balance in the struggle between "orthodoxy" and Arianism.[12] Only the fully divine Jesus Christ of the Nicene faith could adequately correspond to what Christian believers had experienced in their salvation. As H.R. Mackintosh explained: "The Church refused, on purely religious grounds, to be put off with a Saviour who turned out on examination to be only an inferior cosmological principle."[13] This was the point which Athanasius had grasped through his participation in the life of the church in Egypt and which, once it had been articulated in the Nicene Creed, was passionately upheld by the monks in the Coptic-speaking Egyptian church among whom the bishop was able to slip into hiding during periods of exile from Alexandria. Very important for a proper understanding of Athanasius is the awareness that, as Kannengiesser explains: "he spent the best of his time during the first six years of his episcopate among the monastic circles and among the far distant Christian communities spread through the deserts and along the Nile, as well as along the Libyan border. These pastoral visits led him as far as Upper Egypt near the frontier of modern Sudan....

---

[12] See, e.g., J.N.D. Kelly, *Early Christian Doctrines*, (5th rev. ed.), London: Adam & Charles Black, 1977, pp. 233-247.

[13] H.R. Mackintosh, *The Doctrine of the Person of Jesus Christ*, Edinburgh: T. & T. Clark, 1912, p. 178.

[Athanasius] established the durable authority of his forty-five years in office on the ground of his spontaneous solidarity with Coptic Christianity."[14] In this context Athanasius not only cast biblical Christology in a new Hellenistic key but also communicated his theological commitment to a church in Egypt which immediately and enduringly adopted it. The extent to which Africa was the cradle of Christian theology in the fourth and fifth centuries is an important consideration at a time when the non-Western character of the faith is being recovered.

Hilary of Poitiers, a champion of Nicene Christology in the Latin-speaking West, likewise did theology out of the life and worship of the church. As he himself explained his methodology: "we must believe in him, understand him, adore him, and by such actions we shall make him known."[15] The worship of the church was in this way made the spring and the source for systematic theology. The Nicene understanding is that, as T.F. Torrance explains: "the revealed truth of God is grounded in and built into human life and society as it is proclaimed and believed, known and taught by the Church in a way that promotes godliness."[16] This means that orthodoxy is integrally linked to orthopraxis. For Athanasius it was axiomatic to connect the good works and holy countenance of the monk Antony with his theological orthodoxy.[17] Conversely, the error of the Arians he found

---

[14] Charles Kannengiesser, "Athanasius of Alexandria vs. Arius: The Alexandrian Crisis," in B.A. Pearson & J.E. Goehring eds., *The Roots of Egyptian Christianity*, Philadelphia: Fortress, 1986, pp. 204-215 [211-212].

[15] Hilary, *De Trinitate*, 2.7; *Saint Hilary of Poitiers: The Trinity*, trans. S. McKenna, Washington: Catholic University of America Press, 1954, p. 42.

[16] Thomas F. Torrance, *The Trinitarian Faith: the Evangelical Theology of the Ancient Catholic Church*, Edinburgh: T. & T. Clark. 1988, p. 30.

[17] See Athanasius, *Vita S. Antoni*, pp. 69, 82: P. Schaff & H. Wace ed., *Nicene and Post-Nicene Fathers of the Christian Church*, Vol. IV, Grand Rapids: Eerdmans, 1971 [1891], pp. 214, 217-8.

to be apparent in their lack of care for the poor.[18] The actual knowledge of God from which theology may be constructed is not an idealist or mystical form of knowledge but rather one which is worked out in personal discipleship and social praxis. The life of the community was thus made fundamental to the task of theological construction. There emerged the principle of *lex orandi lex credendi* (the law of worship is the law of belief) to express the conviction that it is what is apprehended in worship which must govern what is formulated as doctrinal belief. The extent to which this process actually occurred in the Nicene period is indicated by H.J. Carpenter: "The outcome of the fourth- and fifth-century controversies can only be understood as the result of a perpetual pressure exercised by popular Christianity in its Western and some Eastern forms which forced the speculations of the theologians into channels which they would not naturally have followed."[19]

2. The Bible as the Currency of Theology

The Nicene theologians proceeded on the basis of confidence that, as Athanasius stated: "the sacred and divinely inspired Scriptures are sufficient for the exposition of the truth."[20] They constantly referred to biblical texts, either exegetically or by citing scripture as "epitome" of theological argument. Their commitment to the Bible had a twofold reference. First, it referred to the biblical text. "It is our confidence in the Scriptures," wrote Athanasius, "that encourages us to write to you: when you read them you will be able to trust what we say."[21] "For Hilary," George Newlands observes, "theology

---

[18] See Athanasius, *Historia Arianorum,* 61, 62; *Nicene and Post-Nicene Fathers,* Vol. IV, pp. 292-3.

[19] H.J. Carpenter, "Popular Christianity and the Theologians in the Early Centuries," *Journal of Theological Studies,* NS Vol. 14 (October 1963), pp. 294-310 [310].

[20] Athanasius, *Contra Gentes, 1; Contra Gentes and De Incarnatione* (ed. and trans. R.W. Thomson), Oxford: Clarendon Press, 1971, p. 3.

[21] *Contra Gentes,* 45; ibid, p. 124.

without the direction of the biblical text is impossible.... The text has its own spiritual significance and mediates the knowledge of God in Jesus, who is the object of its witness, to the reader."[22] Secondly, there is reference to the "read" Bible, to the scriptures as absorbed and believed in the community. Much of Hilary's theological work clearly arose out of the devotional and homiletic context of church life. It was the Bible as it was read and internalized and found application in the life of the community which created the field within which the theologian could operate. "In addition to the study and true knowledge of the Scriptures," wrote Athanasius, "are needed a good life and pure soul and virtue in Christ, so that the mind, journeying in this path, may be able to obtain and apprehend what it desires, in so far as human nature is able to learn about God the Word."[23]

An innovative step taken by Athanasius, as Kannengiesser explains, was that he "dispensed with the intellectualist and learned theory of knowledge presupposed in biblical exegesis by his Alexandrian predecessor [Origen], and offered access to the whole truth of divine Scripture as living now in the hearts of the faithful and as incarnate in the community's liturgy."[24] This claim requires, however, the qualification offered by Maurice Wiles that, "the instinct of worship which helped Athanasius to triumph over Arius was not the pattern of ordered liturgical development but the pattern of popular devotion."[25] In both patterns the Coptic Bible occupied a prominent

---

[22] George M. Newlands, *Hilary of Poitiers: A Study in Theological Method* Bern, Frankfurt am Main, Las Vegas: Peter Lang, 1978, pp. 131, 62.

[23] Athanasius, *De Incarnatione,* 57; Thomson, p. 275.

[24] Charles Kannengiesser, "Athanasius of Alexandria: A Paradigm for the Church of Today," *Pacifica 1* (1988), pp. 85-99 [98]; repr. in Charles Kannengiesser, *Arius and Athanasius: Two Alexandrian Theologians,* Hampshire: Variorum, 1991.

[25] Maurice Wiles, *The Making of Christian Doctrine: A Study in the Principles of Early Doctrinal Development,* Cambridge: Cambridge University Press, 1967, p. 88.

place. The Nicene theologians, with this twofold reference, sought to express their theology as far as possible in biblical vocabulary and conceptuality. Their dispute with the Arians was conducted, to a great extent, as a contest as to the proper interpretation of biblical texts.[26] They made the Bible the currency of their theology.

3. Knowledge of Christ and Scientific Theology

The daring project undertaken by the Nicene fathers was to articulate the completely new understanding of God and the world which was emerging in the Christian community. The discipline to which they subjected themselves was one where their theology had to be rooted and grounded in the objective reality with which they were concerned, namely the revelation of God in Jesus Christ. This, they found, was accessible to them in and through the experience of the church as its members discovered the reality of Jesus Christ and reformed their thinking and indeed their whole way of life accordingly. As is well evidenced in the history of the 4th century, this was a bruising business yet faithfulness to the central realities made evident in the worshipping life of the church demanded it. As Torrance observes, the incarnation and resurrection of Christ, to which the church bore witness, "forced themselves upon the minds of Christians from their own empirical and theoretical ground *in sharp antithesis* to what they had believed about God and *in genuine conflict* with the framework of secular thought or the world view of their age.... They took root within the Church only through a seismic restructuring of religious and intellectual belief."[27] It was their engagement with the ultimate reality of God's revelation in Jesus Christ as that was known and experienced in the life of the church which gave the Nicene theologians the courage and the intellectual

---

[26] See, e.g., Athanasius, *Oratio contra Arianos*, i37 - iii58; P. Schaff & H. Wace ed., *Nicene and Post-Nicene Fathers of the Christian Church*, Vol. IV, Grand Rapids: Eerdmans, 1971 [1891], pp. 327-425.

[27] Thomas F. Torrance, *Space, Time and Resurrection*, Edinburgh: Handsel Press, 1976, p. 17.

impetus to place the philosophy and culture of their time on a new basis.

Christian theology, when truly scientific, cannot simply accommodate its data to a conceptual framework which is already well established and accepted. The strength of the Nicene theologians was that they refused to make use of the (Arianizing) structures of thought which were already in place but instead reconceived the Hellenistic conceptual categories so that they could be true to the central reality of Jesus Christ whom they found to be revealed in the Bible, the apostolic tradition and the contemporary life of the church. The fundamental intuition of Nicene theology, as Charles Kannengiesser has noted, was "*against* all religious cosmology posited before the exposition of faith, according to a pattern inherited from Gnostic theology and more generally according to classical Hellenism."[28] Their theology was constructed on the basis that, as Athanasius wrote, "Just as when the sun is present darkness no longer has any strength, but even if there is some darkness left anywhere it is put to flight, even so, since the divine manifestation of God the Word has occurred, the darkness of idols has no more strength but all parts of the world everywhere are illumined by his teaching."[29] We may now turn to an exploration of the relevance of this profile of Nicene methodology to the Christological task in Africa today.

Church Life and Academic Theology

Even a brief consideration of the method adopted by the Nicene fathers alerts us to a source for the Christological task in Africa today: the worshipping life of the community of faith. Nowhere in southern Africa today could one go far without encountering the

---

[28] Charles Kannengiesser, "Athanasius of Alexandria and the Foundation of Traditional Christology," *Theological Studies* 34 (1973), pp. 103-113 [112], my italics.

[29] Athanasius, *De Incarnatione* 55; Thomson, p. 271.

empirical reality of Christian worship. Yet the experience of the believers in their faith has been little tapped in the business of Christological construction. After noting that there is in the African churches a "latent," "oral" and "unsystematic" Christology, Charles Nyamiti comes to the remarkable conclusion that: "As far as I know, systematic scientific investigation in this topic has not yet been made.[30] The 4th century fathers remind us that it is the life of the church which provides access to the ultimate reality with which all authentic Christian theology must be concerned, i.e. the actuality of the risen Christ. In the case of Africa at the end of the 20th century this points us to an extraordinarily rich field. Throughout the continent at the heart of countless communities is the encounter with Jesus Christ which finds expression in the life of the church. It is out of this encounter that academic theologians may attempt to construct a viable African Christology.[31] This is what gives Christian theology its authenticity, dynamism and energy. It then arises out of the empirical field of force within which African people are encountering and apprehending the risen Jesus Christ.

Failure to sufficiently connect with this existential reality leaves African theologians working in a rather wooden way with the terms and concepts of Christian and African traditions. It is no wonder that the resultant Christology seems to arouse little enthusiasm among the people at large. It is in danger of becoming no more than an intellectual game, very absorbing to the participants, but of scarcely any relevance to the way ordinary people understand themselves and live their lives. Arianism, Kannengiesser has suggested, "revealed more than anything else the deepest cause of the crisis in Alexandrian Christianity: a century-long estrangement between learned theology and the Christian self-consciousness of the man in the street."[32] In

---

[30] Nyamiti, "Contemporary African Christologies," pp. 67-68.

[31] For a recent example of such an attempt see James R. Cochrane, "Christ from Above, Jesus from Below," *Journal of Theology for Southern Africa* No. 88 (September 1994), pp. 3-14.

[32] Kannengiesser, "Athanasius of Alexandria," p. 92.

order to avoid this fate, current African Christology must be rooted anew upon its proper ground in the life of the church and the experience of salvation.³³ As Kwame Bediako has written: "Being an articulation of an apprehension of Jesus 'where faith has to live' at 'the living roots of the church', this sort of grassroots or oral theology can deliver the academic theologian from the burden of imagining that it is his or her task 'to construct an African theology' unaided."³⁴

In 1965 John Mbiti, one of the pioneers of African theology, noted this point: "We cannot artificially create an 'African theology' or even plan it; it must evolve spontaneously as the Church teaches and lives her Faith and in response to the extremely complex situation in Africa.³⁵ Yet thirty years later there is little evidence of theology which has sprung from the grassroots of Christian experience and consequently carries the confidence of the community at large. There seems to have been a lack of engagement on the part of academic theologians with the whole area to which Mbiti was drawing attention and which the Nicene theologians had earlier found to be so fruitful for disciplined theological work. Consider, e.g., the influential Final Communique of the Pan African Conference of Third World Theologians held at Accra, Ghana in December 1977. Here five sources of theology were identified: the Bible and Christian heritage, African anthropology, African traditional religions, African

---

[33] See further John W. de Gruchy, "From Cairo to the Cape: the Significance of Coptic Orthodoxy for African Christianity," *Journal of Theology for Southern Africa,* No. 99 (November 1997), pp. 24-39.

[34] Kwame Bediako, *Christianity in Africa: The Renewal of a Non-Western Religion,* Edinburgh: Edinburgh University Press & Maryknoll: Orbis, 1995, pp. 59-60.

[35] John Mbiti, 'The Ways and Means of Communicating the Gospel," in C.G. Baëta ed., *Christianity in Tropical Africa,* London: Oxford University Press, 1968, p. 332; cit. Bediako, *Christianity in Africa,* p. 117.

Independent churches and "other African realities."[36] Only in regard to the African Independent churches is attention drawn to the "worship, organization and community life" through which faith in Jesus Christ is given expression. Otherwise the tendency is for the Christian faith and African reality to be understood as separate entities which must somehow be reconciled through the intellectual endeavour of the theologian. What is being missed is the massive reality of Africans' encounter with Jesus Christ which, on the Nicene pattern, forms the integral centre from which authentic theology unfolds. Confidence in contemporary African Christian experience as resting on the objective reality of God's revelation in Jesus Christ may be the key to the achievement of viable Christology.

Will the resultant Christology, however, be truly African? Will it bring about the much longed-for indigenization of Christianity? Or is this a further attempt to impose on Africans a faith which was constructed elsewhere and which fails to meet the deepest needs of the African soul? Such questions often betray a rather static concept of indigenization where there is the given data of the Christian faith on the one hand and the settled structure of African culture on the other. The African theologian's task appears then to be the tricky one of reconciling two partners in a marriage who are living together but have little in common! This is to miss the profound reality that there is at the heart of contemporary African life and culture an apprehension of Jesus Christ as he is received in faith by the people in their millions. To understand what is occurring at this decisive point it is necessary to appreciate that neither the Christian faith nor the African culture are fixed, impermeable systems of belief and

---

[36] Kofi Appiah-Kubi & Sergio Torres ed., *African Theology en Route*, Maryknoll: Orbis, 1979, pp. 192-93.

practice. In fact, African culture is hospitable and adaptable while Christianity is distinguished by its "translatability."[37]

This creates a situation on the ground where Jesus Christ enters as a participant into the vernacular world of an African community, is accepted there, becomes known there, and steadily comes to occupy a central place in the spiritual and moral universe of the people. In the nature of the case, a fully African understanding of Jesus Christ comes to be formed. Of course, Christ must be understood using the concepts and categories which are available to the people within their own culture. This can lead to the conclusion, reached by Absalom Vilikazi and others, that "all the separatist churches - and even the African sections of mission churches - are syncretistic.... All their Christian ideas are edited by the religious ideas they bring with them from their cultural upbringing."[38] A process of editing does occur but to describe it in terms of syncretism is to miss the fact that it is a two-way process. Not only is there a conceiving of Jesus Christ in terms of traditional African culture, there is also a reconception of African culture in terms of the new reality encountered in the Christ of the Bible and the apostolic tradition.

The Bible as the Currency of Theology

By any standards an extraordinary phenomenon on the continent of Africa today is the engagement, possibly unprecedented in scale and intensity, of wide sections of the population with the biblical text. Recent studies have demonstrated the massive importance of the

---

[37] See Lamin Sanneh, *Translating the Message: the Missionary Impact on Culture,* New York: Orbis, 1989; Andrew F. Walls, *The Missionary Movement in Christian History,* Edinburgh: T. & T. Clark & New York: Orbis, 1996.

[38] Absalom Vilikazi et al., *Shembe, the Revitalization of African Society,* Braamfontein: Skotaville Publishers, 1986; cit. J. Matthew Schoffeleers, "Folk Christology in Africa: The Dialectics of the Nganga Paradigm," *Journal of Religion in Africa,* XIX/2 (1989), p. 157.

Bible in shaping the religious life and understanding of the people.[39] In the Malawi context, e.g., the centrality of the Bible to public worship may be gauged by a 1992 study of Christian preaching where research assistants were required to assess how closely the sermon was related to the Bible reading: "For the CCAP [Presbyterian] sermons, 91% were said to be very closely related, 7% to be slightly related, and 3% to be not at all related to the Bible reading. For the Roman Catholic sermons, 88% were said to be very closely related, 6% to be slightly related and 6% to be not related at all.[40] This suggests that direct biblical exposition lies at the heart of contemporary Christian worship in Malawi, both Catholic and Protestant!

In the next chapter we will show how a sample of Christians in Malawi showed a marked preference for the biblical titles for Jesus Christ, such as "Saviour" or "Messiah," as opposed to titles derived from the African tradition such as "ancestor" or "chief." Such data *could* be interpreted as evidence of the docility of the Christians, that they simply accept and repeat what is prominent in the Bible and the church tradition. On the other hand, it could be interpreted in terms of a community being drawn to biblical vocabulary and conceptuality as a means of accurately stating what it has to say about the reality of Jesus Christ. A comparable development in patristic theology would be the way in which the initial natural inclination to understand Jesus in terms of the "Word" (*Logos*) gradually gave way to the more biblical "Son" as it was found that only in this way could justice be done to the relational understanding of God which was found in the Gospel of Jesus Christ. So in African Christology it may well be that the categories which at first seem to make sense of Jesus in African terms gradually give way to the more biblical categories which are preferred, e.g., by respondents to the Christology survey in northern

---

[39] See, e.g., John S. Mbiti, *Bible and Theology in African Christianity,* Nairobi: Oxford University Press, 1986.

[40] Kenneth R. Ross, "Preaching in Mainstream Churches in Malawi: A Survey and Analysis, " *Journal of Religion in Africa* Vol. XXV/1 (1995), pp. 3-24 [7-8].

Malawi. As the Bible comes to occupy an increasingly formative place in the life of the community, its vocabulary and conceptuality may come to displace or revise the terms and categories which initially were predominant. It may be that we are entering a time when biblical vocabulary and concepts are *no less* indigenous than those derived from the African tradition!

A further area where the Nicene methodology may be of relevance is in its twofold reference to the text of the Bible and to the "read" Bible, i.e. the Bible in the community. A proper indigenization will take account of the pronounced African tendency to take the Bible at face value. John Mbiti has astutely noted that "[the Bible] exerts greater impact on Oral Theology than what can be gathered in the ... published material."[41] Is it not high time this imbalance was corrected? Confidence in the text itself will be a hallmark of an African theology that is true to its roots. Yet it will not be the kind of theology which handles the text with icy detachment for it will have continuous reference also to the reading of the Bible in African communities. It will work out of a recognition that, as Stuhlmacher has put it: "the biblical texts can be fully interpreted only from a dialogical situation defined by the venture of Christian existence as it is lived in the Church."[42] This opens theology to the extraordinarily lively interface between the Bible and every facet of African life at a time of massive upheaval and transition. The Nicene theologians took up this challenge in a no less turbulent era and constructed Christology which was viable because it had resonance with the Bible-reading life of the believing community. So today, in this field where people are engaged with the text of the Bible, the life of their community and the discipleship of following Jesus, there may be

---

[41] John S. Mbiti, "The Biblical Basis in Present Trends in African Theology," *Africa Theological Journal*, Vol. 7/1 (1978), pp. 77-85 [83].

[42] P. Stuhlmacher, *Historical Cricticism and Theological Interpretation of Scripture*, p. 89; cit. Lesslie Newbigin, *Foolishness to the Greeks: The Gospel and Western Culture*, Geneva: WCC, 1986, p. 57; see also Newbigin's discussion, pp. 55-61.

found the component parts for a Christology that is both truly African and true to the ultimate reality of which it speaks.

Knowledge of Christ and Scientific Theology

The Nicene premise is that a scientific and properly critical Christian theology must be built on apprehension of the divine revelation in Jesus Christ. Cultural considerations are often relevant in this exercise but its central critical principle is its reference to the actuality of Jesus Christ. The Nicene theologians were gripped by the confidence that, as T.F. Torrance explains: "Through the Word made flesh, we human beings with our created minds are enabled by the Spirit to know and think of God in such a way that our knowledge and thought of him repose upon his divine reality, or, to express it the other way round, that his divine reality through Jesus Christ and in his Spirit determines the way in which we know and think truly of him."[43] "In subjecting his theological inquiry to this kind of discipline, Athanasius was guided by Alexandrian scientific method with its drive towards "rigorous knowledge according to the inherent structure or nature ... of the realities investigated, together with the development of the appropriate questions and the apposite vocabulary demanded by the nature of the realities as they have become disclosed to us.[44]

Would such scientific rigour be of value to the Christological task in Africa today? Relating Christian faith and "Africanness" has been the urgent and necessary task undertaken by the first generation of African academic theologians. This was a necessary corrective to the earlier failure to take African culture seriously as a source for Christian theology. As Bujo remarks: "Contemporary African theology arose out of the feeling of black people that they had not been taken sufficiently seriously by white people, including

---

[43] Thomas F. Torrance, *Theology in Reconciliation*, London: Geoffrey Chapman, 1975, p. 239.

[44] !bid, p. 240.

missionaries. African theology is a reaction."[45] A necessary reaction yet, like all reactionary movements, it carries the danger of over-reacting. For contemporary African theology this would mean becoming trapped in existing religious frameworks and traditional culture. Christian theology finds its critical edge not by adopting an existing religious and cultural framework as it stands.[46] It was the Nicene determination to ground all theology in the given reality of Jesus Christ which provided the impetus for rethinking the received understanding of God. The project of such theologians as Athanasius and Hilary was to renew the ancient understanding of God on a trinitarian basis.

As Christian faith has today crossed a further frontier and is being re-thought in relation to African religion and culture, it is possible to assume that Christianity is simply a new superstructure on a religious foundation which remains unchanged. This confidence was expressed with unusual clarity twenty years ago by Samuel Kibicho: "the God preached and worshipped in Christianity is the same God *(Ngai, Nyasaye, Asis, Mungu* etc.) who was fully-known, to the extent that any humans can know God, worshipped and trusted by their fore-fathers in the traditional religions of ancient times.... As far as the converts or non-converts to Christianity were concerned, God *(Ngai)* was never an issue. Despite the strange doctrine about the Son of God who became man, died and rose again ... the *Ngai* the missionaries preached was the same *Ngai* whom the Kikuyu had

---

[45] Benezet Bujo, *African Theology,* p. 49.

[46] We may notice that a similar concern underlay another powerful movement of theological renewal, the Reformation of the 16th century. When Martin Luther rejected a "theology of glory" in favour of a "theology of the cross," his concern was that the biblical message should be interpreted in its own terms, however paradoxical, rather than on the basis of the predetermined conceptual framework which he detected in much of medieval religion. For a recent discussion see Alister E. McGrath, *Luther's Theology of the Cross: Martin Luther's Theological Breakthrough*, Oxford: Basil Blackwell, 1985, pp. 95-181.

always known and worshipped.[47] Of course, Kibicho was right to note the vast and profound continuity between "the God of ATR" and "the Father of our Lord Jesus Christ."[48] Such a confidence is integral to the theological task in Africa today. Yet where this continuity is made the central principle of theological construction it tends to interpret Christianity in terms of the inherited cultural and cosmological system of understanding. This is the approach *against which* the Nicene theologians were sure they must stand! Their methodology challenges any complacency in regard to an inherited understanding of God and provokes nothing less than a revolutionary restructuring of all religious belief and action in light of the reality encountered in Jesus Christ.

This poses a challenge to contemporary African theology where, as Charles Nyamiti observes: "most writers start from the African reality in order to see how this reality can be utilized to present Christian teaching on Christ in an African way."[49] It is this starting point which is called in question by the Nicene methodology. On the Nicene model, the Christian theologian must always work under the constraint of what Richard Hanson describes as "the ineradicably Christocentric nature of Christianity, the concept of Christ as the Last Act of God, the eschatological pressure that his figure exerted on Christian thought."[50] The rethinking of belief and conceptuality provoked by this pressure involves a differential and discriminating

---

[47] Samuel G. Kibicho, "The Continuity of the African Conception of God into and through Christianity: a Kikuyu Case Study," in Edward Fasholé-Luke et al. eds., *Christianity in Independent Africa*, London: Rex Collings, 1978, pp. 388, 384; cf. G.M. Setiloane, "How the Traditional World-View Persists in the Christianity of the Sotho-Tswana" in ibid, pp. 402-412.

[48] Kibicho, "Continuity," p. 370.

[49] Charles Nyamiti, "Contemporary African Christologies: Assessment and Practical Suggestions," in R. Gibellini ed., *Paths of African Theology*, London: SCM, 1994, p. 65.

[50] Richard P.C. Hanson, *Studies in Christian Antiquity*, Edinburgh: T. & T. Clark, 1985, p. 239.

approach to inherited tradition. As Oliver O'Donovan explains: "revelation in Christ does not *deny* our fragmentary knowledge of the way things are, as though that knowledge were not there, or were of no significance; yet it does not *build on* it, as though it provided a perfectly acceptable foundation to which a further level of understanding can be added."[51] The biblical, ecclesial and scientific imperative to make knowledge of Jesus Christ the fulcrum of constructive theological endeavour provokes critical engagement with, rather than easy acceptance of, the inherited frame of mind.

The same scientific constraint applies when it comes to theological engagement with contemporary social issues What is said must be strictly in accordance with the objective reality with which it is concerned. In the case of Christology this means that the theologian is not at liberty to construct an understanding of Jesus Christ that is based on any criteria other than that of faithfulness to the reality given in God's revelation as this is accessible to us in the biblical text and in the life of the church where Christ is known and apprehended. To do so would be to fall into projectionism where our understanding of Christ is formed on the basis of *our* needs and wants, rather than a disciplined attempt to allow our whole frame of thought to be shaped by the objective reality with which we are concerned. Within the currently prevailing approach to the construction of African Christology it is all too easy to fall into this trap, as may he illustrated in the following passage of another Kenyan theologian Teresa Hinga:

> For Christ to become meaningful in the context of women's search for emancipation, he *would need to be* a concrete and personal figure who engenders hope in the oppressed by taking their [women's] side to give them courage and confidence to hope and persevere. Secondly, Christ *would also need to be* on the side of the powerless by giving them power and voice to speak for themselves. Thirdly, the Christ *whom*

---

[51] Oliver O'Donovan, *Resurrection and Moral Order: An Outline for Evangelical Ethics,* Leicester: IVP, 1986, p. 89, author's italics.

women look for is one who is actively concerned with the lot of victims of social injustice and the dismantling of unjust social structures. Christ would, therefore, *be expected to be* on the side of women as they fight for the dismantling of sexism in society, a sexism that has oppressed them through the ages.[52]

The concerns expressed by Hinga may well be valid and urgent but to construct Christology in terms of what "Christ would need to be," what "we look for," and what he would be "expected to be," is to fall into the trap of projectionism. Christ is here (re)constructed in terms of our agenda, in terms of what we think he ought to be like.

The problem is that it is then our cultural context and our current concerns which shape our understanding of Jesus. Christ becomes a mere cipher to which we are responsible to impart content. In taking this path African Christology runs the risk of following in the footsteps of the European liberal theology of the 19th century where the "quest for the historical Jesus" was finally revealed to be bogus since the theologians pursuing it saw only what amounted to their own reflection "at the bottom of a deep well."[53] If the theologian first decides what kind of Christ "is needed" then it is clear that it is his or her assumptions and aspirations which will be the decisive criteria in the task of Christological construction. It is important to be aware that the matter with which theology is concerned is, in the words of Colin Gunton, "the decisive self-relating of *God* to lost humankind in Christ" rather than "*our* relatedness to a God who has no shape other than that which our language happens, from time to time, to confer upon him"[54] Scientific theology depends for its

---

[52] Teresa M. Hinga, "Jesus Christ and the Liberation of Women in Africa," in Mercy A. Oduyoye & Musimbi R.A. Kanyoro eds., *The Will to Arise: Women, Tradition and the Church in Africa,* Maryknoll: Orbis, 1992, pp. 191-92, my italics.

[53] G. Tyrell, *Christianity at the Cross-Roads,* London: Longmans, Green & Co., 1909, p. 44.

[54] Colin Gunton, "Proteus and Procrustes: A Study in the Dialectic of Language in Disagreement with Sallie McFague," in Alvin F. Kimel ed., *Speaking the*

integrity on its commitment to eschew all projectionism and articulate the intrinsic intelligibility of the revelation of God. Failure at this point means lapsing into what Athanasius would call "mythology, for it is not theology. Far from it!"[55]

Such scientific discipline will not be alien or intimidating for the African theologian. For there is to be found, at the heart of countless African communities, an engagement with the biblical text and the life of the church through which there occurs an apprehension of the living Christ. Here Jesus Christ is already earthed in African reality, understood in terms of traditional categories while at the same time extending and transforming them through the impact of the biblical proclamation. It is within this dynamic field of force that African theologians can find the necessary materials for the construction of a viable Christology. As Harold Turner has shrewdly pointed out: "Theology as a science depends upon access to its appropriate data in their most authentic and vital forms.... Here at the growing edges of Christianity in its most dynamic forms, the theologian is encouraged to do scientific theology again, because he has a whole range of contemporary data on which to work. It is not that these dynamic areas of the Christian world are free from imperfection; but being full of old and new heresies they need theology and offer it an important task."[56]

The strength of the Nicene theology of the 4th century lay not only in its philosophical coherence but equally in the ecclesial context from which it arose. The fact that among the Copts of Egypt, e.g., the biblical proclamation of Jesus Christ was being received and

---

Christian God: The Holy Trinity and the Challenge of Feminism, Grand Rapids: Eerdmans, 1992, p. 71.

[55] Athanasius, *Contra Gentes* 19; Thomson, p. 55.

[56] Harold W. Turner, 'The Contribution of Studies on Religion in Africa to Western Religious Studies," in Mark Glasswell & Edward Fasholé-Luke eds., *New Testament Christianity for Africa and the World,* London: SPCK, 1974, pp. 177-78; cit. Bediako, *Christianity in Africa,* p. 255.

absorbed in such a way that the experience of salvation became the central reality of communal life, gave to Athanasius and others the critical reference point for their Christology. Every intellectual attempt to state the identity and significance of Jesus Christ had to be measured in terms of how far it did justice to this reality found at the heart of the life of the church. It was on this basis that Arianism was decisively rejected and the Creed of Nicaea adopted and defended at all cost. What does this mean for African Christology at the end of the twentieth century? Given the vitality of African Christianity on the ground, the African theologian is enviably well equipped to bring forward a Christology which is true to the context, true to the Bible and which will be received with acclaim by the churches.

Conclusion

The achievement of the Nicene theologians, at the level of method, was to appreciate that Christology does not depend primarily upon our constructive endeavour but, rather, is a matter of articulating a reality which is actually *there* and which finds expression in the life of the church. This may be an immensely liberating methodology for African theologians concerned to offer a viable Christology. They are not required, on the one hand, to present a pre-packaged Christ who remains wrapped up in terminology and conceptuality that has been constructed elsewhere. Nor are they required, on the other hand, to work out their own Christology on the basis of their own assessment of what will be relevant to the African situation. Their task is, in fact, to bring to the clearest possible expression a reality which is already powerfully evident within African life, namely God's revelation in Jesus Christ. This will involve neither adherence to an exotic Christological tradition in all its details and nuances nor acceptance of the categories of African traditional religions as if these could never be subject to any significant modification or renewal. It will arise out of the vernacular world where African peoples have given to Jesus Christ the central place, where all their tradition is concentrated upon the task of understanding his identity and significance, and where the biblical message is a force powerful to reform and renew all kinds of vocabulary and conceptuality. It will arise equally out of the concrete historical contexts in which African believers seek to follow Jesus as they meet the social, political and economic challenges of the day. The remainder of this book is devoted to analysis of personal, ecclesial and national experience which may contribute to such positive theological construction.

This involves going beyond the relatively complacent approach of "slotting" Jesus into African categories and doing theology, rather, out of the transformative process arising out of the African encounter with the biblical message. Where language is being stretched and renewed under the impact of the reality of Christ, as is the case in African life today, then the theologian has the materials at hand to state the identity of Jesus Christ in a way that is at once biblical and indigenous, catholic and creative, apostolic and contemporary. When Charles Nyamiti ponders the question of how "African Christologies could penetrate the churches," the matter is being considered quite the wrong way round.[57] The question is, rather, how the life of the churches could penetrate African Christologies! At a time when African peoples are locked in a passionate embrace with the biblical message, the challenge for constructive theologians is whether they can do their work out of that passion! In a battered continent it may be difficult to believe that the experience of ordinary believers could be the central source for Christological construction. Yet examination of the Nicene methodology suggests that confidence in contemporary African Christian experience as resting on the objective reality of God's revelation in Jesus Christ may be the key to the achievement of viable Christology.

---

[57] Nyamiti, "African Christologies Today," p. 18.

2. "Who do you Say that I Am?" Popular Christology in Northern Malawi

The life and worship of the people of God is always an important formative factor in theological reconstruction *(lex orandi lex credendi)*. As we argued in the first chapter, it is a necessary source for the theological task required in Africa today. One starting place for Malawian Christology, then, is to develop a clearer picture of the prevailing understanding at the "grassroots." We may venture the confidence that, as Charles Nyamiti has written, "Serious scientific research of (Christology) in African Christian communities would reveal authentically African Christologies from which all could profit in many ways."[1] In order to make a small contribution to such "serious scientific research" this chapter focuses on popular Christology in northern Malawi.

The methodology used in the research was that of questionnaire and interview, using University theology students as interviewers.[2] All the interviews were completed during the Easter vacation in 1995. The results were then entered into a computer programme which was designed to summarize the statistical trends of the responses. Some questions offered a limited number of possible answers from which the respondent had to choose, while others were "open" questions for which it was necessary to form broad categorization for the

---

[1] Charles Nyamiti, "African Christologies Today," in Schreiter, *Faces of Jesus*, p. 19.

[2] This research was funded by a grant from the Research and Publications Committee of the University of Malawi. Particular thanks are due to Ms Rosie Fearn, of Chancellor College Department of Mathematical Sciences, who designed the computer programme and produced a statistical analysis of the results of the research; to Rev Akim Chirwa who worked very effectively as a data processor; and to the twenty-one undergraduates who spent part of their Easter vacation working for the project as research assistants.

answers. The research aimed to survey a representative sample of Catholic and Presbyterian Christians in the Northern Region of Malawi. These are the largest churches in the Region and both have an extensive and well-organized network of parishes.

Research assistants were assigned to all the Districts of the Northern Region: four to Chitipa, four to Karonga, four to Rumphi, four to Nkhata Bay, and five to Mzimba, ensuring a fairly broad geographical spread. The interviews were conducted among the following language groups: Tumbuka, Chichewa, Tonga, Nkhonde, Chinyika, Lamya and Sukwa. Of the 417 interviewees, 197 were Catholic while 220 were Presbyterian; 202 were women while 215 were men; and 214 were over 30 years of age while 203 were under 30. As regards levels of education, 40 had had no formal education, 168 had been to primary school, 199 had been to secondary school, and 9 had tertiary education.

Noting these demographic differences gave the opportunity to draw comparisons in the computer analysis. However, what the statistics reveal is that there is a remarkable consistency of understanding and experience which crosses these demographic divisions. Where there are occasional differences which may be significant, these will be noted. The principal results of the research are the statistical trends which are indicated below. All figures are in the form of percentages. However, there is also a body of anecdotal evidence in the form of comments offered by respondents and recorded by the interviewers. Such comments will be cited occasionally to illustrate the trends which are demonstrated by the statistics. The study was conducted in full awareness that only quite limited results may be expected from such a crude approach to so profound a subject as Christology. However, if it does succeed in indicating some trends in the Christological thought which is current in northern Malawi at the end of the twentieth century then it may serve to open up a subject which merits further, and more refined, study.

Sources of Christology

When respondents were asked "of the following means of experiencing the presence of Jesus tick the three which you find most important," the percentages were:

Personal prayer and Bible reading	70
Listening to sermons in church	59
Prayers in the family	50
Visiting the sick and needy	37
Receiving the sacrament in church	34
Working for justice in society	21
Singing with fellow Christians	19
Being taught the catechism of the church	8

These figures clearly indicate, first of all, the priority of the Bible as a source for Christology. 70% of all respondents indicated that their own personal Bible reading and prayer was a most important means of experiencing the presence of Jesus. The percentage of Catholics is slightly lower - 62% compared with 77% of Presbyterians - but this was still the most frequently chosen option among the Catholic respondents. Listening to sermons in church was the second most frequently chosen option with 59% (Presbyterians 66%; Catholics 50%). Here it should be bourne in mind that sermons in Malawi, both in Presbyterian and in Roman Catholic churches, are generally very closely related to the Bible. We may also surmise that the "prayers in the family" which was chosen by 50% of respondents normally include Bible reading as a central feature. The Bible, then, stands out as the principal source of Christology. Other resources offered by the Christian tradition, such as sacraments, hymns, catechisms and charitable works, are not so highly valued as the Bible. This underlines the massive importance of the text of the Bible in contemporary African Christianity, in this case in the central area of the construction of a Christology. It is striking that "singing with fellow Christians," which appears to be a central expression of Christian faith in Africa, is relatively little valued when the question of experiencing the presence of Jesus is being considered. Formal catechetical instruction is much the least valued among the options offered. On the other hand, the charitable works of caring for the sick and needy, which have been a hallmark of Christianity since its earliest beginnings, are here chosen by more than one third of respondents as a most important means of grace. A similar number opt for receiving the sacrament, with Presbyterians (29%), interestingly, not far behind Roman Catholics (40%) in taking this option. For Catholics the number opting for the sacraments (40%) is less than for personal prayer and Bible reading (62%), prayers in the family (56%), and listening to sermons in church (50%). It is very clear that the conventional divide in which the Bible was the means of grace for Protestants and the sacraments the means of grace for Catholics does not apply in Northern Malawi today.

A critical question when it comes to assessing sources of Christology in the Malawian context is how far Christians draw on the teaching of the expatriate missionaries who have played a major role in the implantation of Christianity during the past one hundred years and how far they draw on their own indigenous traditions. Respondents were asked: "to know the truth about Jesus should we read the Bible in light of (a) the teaching of European missionaries, (b) African wisdom, or (c) both of the above. 30% opted for the teaching of European missionaries, 19% for African wisdom and 49% for both. These results suggest that missionary teaching still has a normative role for around one-third of respondents but almost one-half appear to be seeking some kind of integration of what they have learnt from expatriate missionaries and what they derive from their own African tradition. Only a 19% minority opt for the more radical approach of constructing a Christology on the basis of indigenous African wisdom. It may be worth noting that there is a marginally greater inclination towards this approach among Catholic respondents (22% compared with 17% of Presbyterians) but otherwise the responses of the two communities suggest that they are closely in parallel on this issue. A final point worth noting is that the high number of respondents indicating that they found "family prayers" important in experiencing the presence of Jesus suggests that this is an aspect of religious practice which would merit further investigation. In a later question on the message of Jesus and family life many respondents drew attention to the importance of daily prayers in the home. Not only the ecclesiastical but also the domestic expression of Christian faith and worship must be taken into account in order to reach a full understanding of Christianity in contemporary Africa.

Predominant Christological Categories

The first question on the questionnaire simply required respondents to choose, out of eight possible titles, which three "best describe who Jesus is." The results were as follows:

Saviour	82
Messiah	65
Lord	50
God	50
Healer	25
Conqueror	19
Chief	10
Brother	8
Ancestor	4

It is clear that by far the most commonly chosen categories are the biblical "umbrella" terms "Saviour" and 'Messiah" which speak strongly of the function of Jesus Christ as the bringer of salvation. A remarkable 88% of Presbyterian respondents opted for "Saviour." Next come the terms God and Lord which speak of the divinity and authority of Christ. Last come the terms which speak more specifically of Christ's sharing in our humanity and bringing redemption to human life. Again the powerful influence of the Bible is apparent. 65% opted for the biblical category "messiah" - a category unknown to traditional African religion while few opted for categories which might be expected to have a particular resonance in the African context such as "chief" or "ancestor." These results could be read as substantiating Charles Nyamiti's claim that "none of the existing African Christologies has had any appreciable influence in the life of the African churches."[3] Yet it is worthy of consideration that substantial minorities of respondents are working with the categories of "Healer," "Conqueror," "Chief" and "Ancestor" in constructing their Christology. While the functional biblical categories of "Saviour" and "Messiah" appear to be primary, there is evidence of considerable diversity and experimentation in understanding the meaning of Christ as Saviour in relation to human experience. The preference for functional biblical categories was reflected also in the "open" final question which invited respondents to express in their own words what Christ meant for them. A 71% majority responded to this question in terms of such functional biblical categories as Saviour, Messiah and Redeemer.

Another question which aimed to reveal some basic orientation in Christology was "Do you think of Jesus mostly as (a) someone who lived long ago, (b) someone who is active in our world today, or (c) both of the above?" Only 9% thought of Jesus primarily as someone who lived long ago. 44% thought of Jesus primarily as someone active in the world today. 46% opted for both of the above. It is very clear that the great majority relate to Jesus Christ as a contemporary rather than as a historical figure. It is the "Christ of faith" rather than the "Jesus of history" who predominates. However, almost half of the respondents appear to attach importance to holding together the historical Jesus and the Christ whom they know by faith. This tendency is particularly evident among the Presbyterians, of whom 57% opted for "both of the above" compared with 34% of Catholics.

---

[3] Nyamiti, "African Christologies Today," p. 18.

Another fundamental question which was asked was "Do you think of Jesus mostly as (a) the suffering servant who died on the cross, (b) the powerful conqueror of death and evil, or (c) both of the above. 15% opted for the suffering servant, 27% for the powerful conqueror, and 57% for both. Interestingly, the number opting for the suffering servant was higher among those under 30 years of age, of whom 23% took this option, compared with only 8% of those over 30 years. The general trend is that, of those with a clear preference on this question, almost two-thirds opt for the powerful conqueror and one-third for the suffering servant. However, more than half of the respondents clearly express the need to include both of these components in their Christology.

The Function of Jesus Christ

Central to any understanding of Christology is the function which Jesus Christ is perceived to have in human life. Respondents were asked: "of the following benefits promised by Jesus which three do you find most precious?" Results were as follows:

Eternal life after death	79
Forgiveness of sins	71
Daily fellowship with God	60
Reconciliation - making good relationships between people	36
Defeat of evil forces	34
Power to become a better person	14
Power to transform society	6

These figures reveal very clearly that the primary benefits with which the respondents are concerned are the personal and spiritual matters of eternal life after death, forgiveness of sins and fellowship with God. The place of "eternal life after death" as the most frequently chosen benefit may offer corroboration to the thesis that

Christianity's appeal in Africa owes much to the answer it offers to the problem of death. It is worth noting that this option was preferred especially by men (86% compared with 72% for women). At the other end of the scale, the least favoured option is "power to transform society" which was chosen by only 6% of respondents. It is what Jesus Christ offers at the personal rather than the social level which clearly predominates. It may also be observed that issues which might be expected to be given prominence in an African context, such as reconciliation within the community or the defeat of evil forces, are in fact secondary to the issues which are central in the biblical proclamation, such as eternal life after death and the forgiveness of sins.

Another approach to the same issues was to ask respondents: "of the following evils which three do you think Jesus helps you to overcome the most?" Results were as follows:

The Devil	53
Envy and Hatred	48
Fear of Death	44
Sexual immorality	42
Witchcraft	29
Evil Spirits	28
Pride	27
Injustice in society	26

We may observe, first, that all of the suggested evils attracted serious consideration since all were chosen by between one quarter and one half of the respondents. Significantly, the only option to attract more than half of the respondents is the devil. This was the most frequently chosen option among both Catholics and Presbyterians but this preference was particularly marked among the latter (58% compared with 47% for Catholics). It may also be noted that 70% of those with no formal education chose this option. It appears that the biblical understanding of evil in terms of the devil is more influential than such traditional categories as witchcraft and evil spirits. The theme of the devil is not one which has attracted very much attention in the emerging theological literature in Africa but, in view of its prominence in this study, it may require more thorough study not only in Christology but in other attempts to accurately understand the character of African Christianity. Another pertinent observation is that "envy and hatred" figures highly as one of the evils which faith in Jesus overcomes, despite the fact that the corresponding benefit of "reconciliation – making good relationships between people" was not so frequently chosen. On the other hand, just as "power to transform society" was the least commonly chosen benefit, so "injustice in society" is the least commonly chosen evil. The social significance of Christology clearly plays second fiddle to issues of personal spirituality and morality, though the 26% who did opt for "injustice in society" demonstrate that it is by no means a concern which is entirely neglected.

Jesus Christ - Divine and Human

In order to test how far Christians in Northern Malawi hold a Chalcedonian balance (fully divine *and* fully human) in their Christology the questionnaire offered two propositions which are false and three which are true in terms of classical orthodoxy. Respondents were required to indicate whether they found these statements to be true or false. The results can be summarized in tabular form: statements to be true or false. The results can be summarized in tabular form:

	True	False	Don't know
Jesus was a human being who became divine after his resurrection	41	52	6
Jesus was a divine being who just looked like a man	83	12	5
Jesus' Humanity was the same as ours (except he did not sin)	82	13	5
Jesus in heaven today is still a real human being	20	49	30
There never was a time when God was without Jesus	68	16	15

It must be conceded that respondents found these highly abstract questions difficult to answer and the figures suggest that they provoked a measure of confusion. Nevertheless, it is possible to discern a clear trend in that there is greater confidence in the divinity of Jesus Christ than in the humanity. On the litmus test of belief in the full humanity of Jesus Christ - "Jesus in heaven today is still a real human being" - only 20% affirmed this to be true, while almost half (49%) stated that it was false. Significantly, this was also the question which provoked the most uncertainty, in terms of 30% of respondents answering "don't know." On the other hand, on the (anti-Arian) litmus test of belief in the full divinity of Jesus Christ - "There never was a time when God was without Jesus" - 68% affirmed it to be true, only 16% stated that it was false and 15% answered "don't know." On this test of orthodoxy the respondents were very much firmer in upholding the divinity than in upholding the humanity of Jesus Christ. On the trick (Adoptionist) statement - "Jesus was a human being who became divine after his resurrection" - 41% "fell for it" while 52% found it to be false. On the other hand on the trick (Docetist) statement - "Jesus was a divine being who just looked like a man" - 83% "fell for it" while only 12% found it to be false.

Given that Docetism was an over-emphasis on the divinity of Christ and Adoptionism was an over-emphasis on the humanity of Christ, these findings suggest that the Christology of the respondents is much more vulnerable to Docetism than to Adoptionism. Though 82% uphold the fundamental affirmation that "Jesus' humanity was the same as ours (except he did not sin)," the responses to the other statements demonstrate that there is a considerable lack of confidence in the full humanity of Jesus Christ. It is worth noting that the differences between Catholics and Presbyterians in their response to these statement are negligible. The only exception is that the Presbyterians had a bigger minority who affirmed the truth of "Jesus in heaven today is still a real human being" - 26% as opposed to only 15% of Catholics. Otherwise their responses are remarkably parallel. The lack of emphasis on Christ's humanity was also reflected in the answers given to the "open" final question: "State in your own words what Jesus Christ means to you." As noted above, the overwhelming majority (72%) opted for a functional category such as Saviour, Messiah or Redeemer. Most of the remainder of the respondents expressed themselves in terms which emphasized either the divinity or the humanity of Christ. However, while 14% expressed themselves in terms of Christ's divinity, only 3% used language which laid emphasis particularly on Christ's humanity.

Christology, Soteriology and Pre-Christian Ancestors

The strong sense of solidarity with the ancestors which is evident in Africa gives a sharpness to the question of the fate of those who never heard the message of Jesus Christ. Are they excluded from the salvation which Christ brings to those who believe the gospel? Very contemporary for Christian Africans is the question which the philosopher Symmachus put to Ambrose of Milan in 384: if the

Christian God is indeed a God of love who desires all to be saved, why did that God wait so long to send the saviour? Why have human beings been allowed to seek God along so many different paths for such a long time?[4] The questionnaire included two questions which attempted to enter into this question. The first asked: "Is Jesus the only way to God? Explain your answer." Only 3% answered "no" and suggested that there might be other ways of knowing God. Those advocating a pluralistic approach to the question of revelation and salvation are few. On the other hand, 97% affirm that Jesus is the only way to God - the closest to unanimity among the respondents in response to any of the questions! Of these, 21% justified their position by a direct appeal to biblical teaching, while 76% argued on the basis of Jesus' status as the Son of God and therefore the only authentic Mediator. This indicates a massive confidence in the uniqueness of Jesus Christ as the revelation and salvation of God.

The second question asked: "What about our ancestors who lived before the message of Jesus came - were they able to know God and be saved?" 21% answered "no" - they had no hope that there could be true knowledge of God and experience of salvation among their pre-Christian ancestors. "They did not know God and never shall they be saved" is a representative answer for this group. However, a 76% majority answered in the affirmative - they did have the confidence that their pre-Christian ancestors did know God and experience salvation. To justify this position 22% appealed to the experience of Old Testament believers, such as Enoch, Noah, Abraham, Moses and Elijah, who lived before Christ and yet who, according to the Bible itself, had an authentic knowledge of God and experience of salvation. 54% argued on the basis of the validity of African Traditional Religion and demonstrate confidence that traditional religious beliefs and practices did mediate a true

---

[4] Cit. Paul F. Knitter. *No Other Name?: A Critical Survey of Christian Attitudes Towards the World Religions*, New York: Orbis, 1985, p. 18.

knowledge of God and an experience of divine salvation. A typical response was: "My grandmother told me that our ancestors before us did know God and did pray to him in the mountains and forests. So, even if they did not know Jesus, they will be saved, for they lived in a generation when the message of Jesus was not there." There is a deep respect for the way of life of the ancestors, as evidenced in a comment like: "Yes, they were able to know God. They will be saved because their way of life then was more upright than our present way of life." However, while in general terms this confidence is strongly held there is also evidence of a principle of discrimination, as suggested by the comment: "Our ancestors knew God and they are going to be saved. This does not mean that all the ancestors are going to be saved, only those who were good are going to be saved, not the witches."

Taking the responses to these two questions together it is apparent that the majority regard Jesus Christ as the only way to God and, at the same time, hold that their ancestors who lived before the message of Christ was preached in Malawi were able to know God and be saved. *Prima facie* this may appear to be a self-contradictory position but there is the possibility of explaining it in terms of the *logos spermatikos* Christology first suggested by Justin Martyr and other early Christian Fathers. The thrust of this Christology is that Jesus Christ as Logos has been active in human life and history from the beginning and that all people have access to God in Christ through the best of their own tradition. The incarnation brings not something totally discontinuous with previous experience but, rather, the fulfilment of the antecedent traditions which reflect the presence of the *logos spermatikos*. The responses outlined above indicate that there is, at least implicitly, a Christology of this type in the minds of the respondents when they consider the question of salvation in relation to their pre-Christian ancestors. Some responses suggest this quite explicitly, e.g: "Jesus was already there as God although he was not yet in this flesh." Or, "they knew Jesus as the Holy Spirit. Jesus existed as the Holy Spirit." There is clearly no inclination to relativize Christ as Saviour. Jesus *only* is the way to God. Yet there is also the confidence that, though Jesus Christ was not named in Northern Malawi until the 1870s, those who lived before that time did have a knowledge of God and an experience of salvation which is in continuity with that found among their Christian descendants today.

Christology and Gender

Rosemary Radford Ruether has observed that "of all Christian doctrine, it has been the doctrine of Christ that has been most frequently used to exclude women from full participation in the Christian Church."[5] In light of this, the quite specific question was asked: "Jesus was a man. Therefore only men, not women, should be ordained as priests/ministers in the church.' Do you agree with this statement?" 39% indicated agreement; 60% indicated disagreement. In a context where there have never been any women Presbyterian ministers nor women Catholic priests, this is a remarkable finding. Within the Presbyterian Livingstonia Synod there have been some moves in the direction of ordaining women to the ministry which may partly explain why a 71% majority of Presbyterians indicated disagreement with maintaining a male-only ministry on Christological grounds.[6] The figure for Presbyterian women is higher at 77% but even Presbyterian men favoured this position by a 63% majority. Nevertheless, in a socially and ecclesiastically conservative constituency it is surprising that such a large majority of ordinary church members would express support for such a radical innovation as the ordination of women to the ministry.

Perhaps even more remarkable is the 48% of Roman Catholics who indicated support for the ordination of women. Though a 52%

---

[5] Rosemary Radford Ruether, "The Liberation of Christology from Patriarchy," in A. Loades, *Feminist Theology: a Reader,* London: SPCK, 1990, p. 138.

[6] In November 1994 Livingstonia Synod presented an overture to the CCAP General Synod seeking approval in principle of the ordination of women to the ministry. Papers of CCAP General Synod, Chongoni, November 1994.

majority of Catholics expressed agreement that ordination to the priesthood should be reserved for men, it is striking that barely half of Catholic respondents maintained this position which is strongly emphasised in official church teaching. Indeed among Catholic women respondents, only 40% supported the traditional position while 60% rejected the exclusion of women from the priesthood on Christological grounds. At least in this sample of Roman Catholics in northern Malawi, there is a substantial body of opinion favouring the ordination of women to the priesthood. Perhaps less surprisingly, it can be observed that support for women's ordination is stronger among women respondents who are in favour by a 71% majority. Even the men, however, were almost equally divided with 50% in favour and 49% against. Another factor revealed by the statistics is that the more educated a person is the more likely it is that they will be in favour of the ordination of women. Of those with no formal education 48% are in favour, of those with primary education 59% are in favour, of those with secondary education 63% are in favour, and of those with tertiary education 78% are in favour.

The comments offered in answer to this question suggest that convictions are strongly held on both sides of the question and that there is lively debate at the grassroots level. We may offer some samples of agreement with the statement that "Jesus was a man. Therefore only men, not women, should be ordained as priests/ministers in the church."

> Only men should be ordained priests because Jesus himself chose his disciples who were men only. The same trend should be maintained.

> Only men because when God created them, he gave men more authority than a woman.

> Women are not worthy to stand at the altar and .preach because of what happened to Adam and Eve under the influence of Eve.

> Only men because women can't manage all those works and duties performed by men.

If she is expectant then she cannot lead the congregation.

Only men and not women should be ordained as priests because even in the Bible it is stated that women should not stand before men.

Only men must be ordained as priests because women have more sins.

Women are sinful. They like aborting when they have unwanted pregnancies. As such most of the time they are unclean (from a woman respondent).

There was no apostle of Jesus among the twelve who was a woman

When God sent Jesus he gave us a picture that it is only men who can be priests.

We may also offer some samples of comments offered in disagreement with the above statement:

I think both men and women should be ordained as priests because both are equal in the eyes of God and have the same gifts from God.

Though Jesus was a man he came on earth for the sins of all people so there should not be any separation between men and women.

As a woman and as God's own creation, I have a part to play in the house of God.

There are some women who know much better than men. A woman can preach and still you can be converted!

The Word of God is not for the chosen nor does it depend on sex but only on dedication to the Lord's service. The death of Jesus brought both sexes into union with him.

Ladies too can be brave for when Jesus was being taken to Golgotha, we see only ladies being brave and courageous enough to go with him.

It is a woman who experienced the birth pangs. It is women who stood near the cross of Jesus. It is women who first experienced the resurrection of Jesus.

On the day of Pentecost the Holy Ghost in the form of tongues of fire fell on women as well, thus giving them the go-ahead to become witnesses.

In serving the Lord there is no gender. Ministers are not Jesus but servants of Jesus. This being the case any person can be a servant of Jesus.

Jesus, as God in human form, only came in one of the two forms a human can be, male or female. It just happened that he was a man, he could as well have been a woman. Hence women as well should be ordained as priests/ministers.

These sample comments indicate that while there are cultural and personal factors to be taken into account, Christological considerations are of central importance in the question of the role of women in the church. Moreover the arguments advanced demonstrate that the issue is approached with a remarkable degree of theological sophistication. Christology is clearly a site of struggle for those concerned with gender issues today in northern Malawi.

Christology and Discipleship

A number of questions were asked to try to elicit a profile of what a knowledge of Christ means for personal self-understanding and conduct, for family life, communal life, national life, and the natural order. When the "open" question "what sort of things do you think Jesus wants you to do?" was asked, 63% of respondents mentioned personal ethical qualities, such as forgiving others or keeping the commandments; 35% mentioned personal spiritual qualities, such as offering praise to God or cultivating holiness; 24% mentioned ecclesiastical activities, such as church attendance or financial offerings; while 23% mentioned action for social justice. The figures suggest that in following Christ there is a greater emphasis on personal morality and spirituality than on what Christology means in terms of church and society, though this more communal dimension is by no means absent. This pattern emerges even more clearly in response to the related question, "what sort of person do you think Jesus wants you to be?" 55% mentioned personal ethical qualities, 47% personal spiritual qualities, and only 6% qualities which relate to action for social justice. Presbyterians more commonly stress personal spiritual qualities - 54% compared with 40% of Roman Catholics.

Turning to family life, 97% understand the message of Jesus to have relevance to their family life. Of these, 80% stress that Jesus is a source of harmony in family life, while 17% lay emphasis on the guidance which Jesus offers to the family. Jesus as the source of harmony has a prominent place in this Christology. Many respondents testified to the peace, forgiveness and reconciliation which Jesus has brought to their families. Some compared the strife and division of their pre-conversion days with the peace and harmony which have prevailed in their families since their conversion to Jesus Christ. The same emphasis is found when it comes to the local community. When asked, "Do you think belief in Jesus has made a difference to life in your community?" many answered in terms similar to this typical response: "Yes, it has helped us, in that in those communities which have belief in Jesus peace and harmony prevail, while in those lacking this belief, only chaos, quarrels and anarchy reign throughout."

Looking more widely to the nation as a whole, the question was asked: "Do you think the message of Jesus applies to politics in Malawi today? If so, how'?" Here 30% answered a straightforward "no." Almost one third, then, did not see any relation between their belief in Jesus and national political life. A typical answer would be: "Politics are worldly things. Jesus is not concerned with them." The remaining 68% did note some political application of their Christological faith. 40% expressed a concern that Christian values should influence political life. 20% drew attention to the recent successful movement for political reform which had been inspired by Christian faith.[7] This group recalled, as one respondent expressed it, that "the Catholic Bishops were filled with God's power which led them to write a Pastoral Letter in 1992 denouncing the evils of the past regime hence paving the way for change in Malawi. Now we are in a democratic system. Praise Jesus!" 8% stressed the importance of Christians engaging in prayer for national political life. There is little variation from these percentages when comparison is drawn between Catholics and Presbyterians, male and female, young and old or differing levels of education.

A more specific question asked: "Did knowing Jesus help you to know how to vote in the national referendum and the General Election? If so, how?" (After thirty years without meaningful elections under the one-party system, Malawians went to the polls in June 1993 for a referendum on the question of one-party or multi-party politics and in May 1994 for the first multi-party General Election of the new political era.) 24% answered in the negative. Some were quite frank, e.g., "No. I went on tribal lines," or "No. I only voted using my own feelings and not by Jesus Christ." However, 71% affirmed that knowing Jesus did help them to know how to vote. Turning to the question of *how* knowing Jesus helped, 48% indicated that through approaching the elections prayerfully they received guidance from Jesus, e.g., "The 'still voice' directed me how to vote for the good of my country." 23% indicated that their faith in Jesus gave them principles of discernment which enabled them to make their decision, e.g., "I voted in light of the love and justice brought by Christ." For most respondents there is a substantial connection between their Christological faith and their engagement in the democratic processes which have recently been introduced in Malawi. A representative response claimed that "without Christians voting, the people would still continue dying under one-party

---

[7] See Matembo S. Nzunda & Kenneth R. Ross eds., *Church, Law and Political Transition in Malawi 1992-94,* Gweru: Mambo Press, 1995, esp. pp. 31-42, 59-74 and 153-70; see also chapter five of the present work.

government, there would be no democracy or freedom of speech and there would be no peace in our motherland."

Looking beyond the human community to the natural order, the questionnaire took up the question of land use. Northern Malawian society is predominantly rural and the vast majority are engaged in either full-time or part-time farming. It was therefore a pertinent question to ask: "Does your faith in Jesus affect the way in which you farm your land? If so, how?" 16% answered "no"; 4% answered "don't know." 76% gave positive answers which can be categorized as follows: 70% answered primarily in terms of reliance on God for fruit for their labours, while 3% emphasised that faith in Jesus led to honesty and integrity in farming practice (avoiding the use of African medicine or witchdoctors and respecting land boundaries), and 3% made the connection that faith in Jesus has implications for environmental stewardship. A more specific question related to the environment asked: "Is tree-planting an expression of your faith in Jesus? If so, how?" Here 40% answered "no" and 8% "don't know." A blunt answer stated: "trees have nothing to do with Christianity." Or, "a tree is just a plant without the Holy Spirit." 50% gave positive answers which can be categorized as follows: 22% answered in terms of reliance on God, 20% offered an allegorical interpretation of the significance of tree-planting (e.g. ("our faith too has to grow like a tree"), while 8% made the connection that faith in Jesus has implications for environmental stewardship.

What is clear beyond any doubt is that there is a seriousness about Christology which manifests itself not so much in abstract theory as in concrete decisions and conduct in times of crisis as well as in the ordinariness of everyday life. Take the example of one woman's decision at a time of crisis: "When two of my children died in succession, following one another, people in my village told me that I must consult witchdoctors to find out the cause but I refused because I believed Jesus's message that God gave me those kids and has decided to take them away himself." Or take the example of one man's description of what Jesus means for his daily life as a farmer:

"Because of my faith in Christ I have always started each day with prayer, standing in the garden with the hoe in my hand. My prayer is for protection from harm, from the implement in my hand which is capable of injuring me, and from snakes which abound in these places. I also pray for daily strength to carry on my work. You will be amazed - Jesus is faithful!" Both in the everyday routine and in the times of crisis people are discovering what it means to know Jesus and working out what it means to be a disciple of Christ.

There is, in northern Malawi today, a vibrant Christological piety which conditions every aspect of personal and social life. This preliminary attempt to sketch the shape of the prevalent Christology has suggested a number of trends. Amongst the most prominent are the massive importance of the Bible as a source for Christology. An important question which emerges is whether the culture has been so much influenced by the Bible that, e.g., "Messiah" is a more meaningful term than "Ancestor." The emergence of an indigenous *logos spermatikos* Christology is another development worthy of careful scrutiny. The tendency to play down Christ's humanity represents a possible imbalance in the emerging Christology which calls for closer study. The question of Christology and gender appears to be a potential site of struggle as many Christians are forming a Christology which is favourable to the ordination of women, in contrast to traditional belief and practice. While some find that their faith in Christ has little relevance for thought and conduct in family, community, nation and environment, there are many who are actively thinking through what following Jesus means in each of these areas of life. A notable trend is the convergence of Catholics and Protestants in Christological thinking in northern Malawi. The statistical analysis revealed how closely parallel were the responses from the two communities. It is to be hoped that this rough sketch of some leading trends will provoke more detailed and revealing studies of the Christology emerging in northern Malawi today.

3. Contested Identity: Ecclesial Self-Understanding in Northern Malawi

Having outlined important trends in the contemporary understanding of Jesus Christ, we now consider popular understanding of the nature of the church. Ecclesiology, the way in which a church community understands its own nature and character, is a constantly shifting and contested reality. Recent scholarship has revealed the extent to which differing ecclesial traditions, theological interpretations and social contexts give rise to contrasting ecclesiologies.[1] In the African situation, where the churches are at a relatively early stage in their engagement with new cultures and involvement in new societies, ecclesiology may be expected to be a dynamic and fast-changing sphere of life and thought. Particularly since identity has been singled out as a central theological issue,[2] it might be expected that the community-identity issue of ecclesiology would attract considerable attention from theologians. In fact, few scholars have addressed this question in a sustained or systematic way.[3] At a time when the

---

[1] A ground-breaking study was Avery Dulles, *Models of the Church,* Dublin: Gill & Macmillan, 2nd ed., 1988 [1974]. A useful summary of modern debate may be found in Peter C. Hodgson & Robert C. Wlliams, "The Church" in Peter C. Hodgson & Robert King ed., *Christian Theology: An Introduction to its Traditions and Tasks,* London: SPCK, 1983, pp. 223-47.

[2] See especially Kwame Bediako, *Theology and Identity: The Impact of Culture upon Christian Thought in the Second Century and Modem Africa,* Oxford: Regnum, 1992; and Bediako, *Christianity in Africa.*

[3] A recent Annotated Bibliography of African Theology, found in the *Bulletin for Contextual Theology,* University of Natal, Vol. 3/2 (June 1996) pp. 29-43, contains not one single work on ecclesiology. A survey of the last fifty issues of the *Journal of Theology for Southern Africa* reveals that, while many articles touch on ecclesiological themes, not one article has appeared which specifically addresses the issue of ecclesiology on either an empirical or a theoretical basis. Possibly the only published volume in English addressing the topic is J.N.K. Mugambi & L. Magesa ed., *The Church in African Christianity:*

profound influence of the churches at all levels of African life is coming to be widely acknowledged, it seems to be a matter of some importance to elucidate the self-understanding of churches in Africa. A necessary starting point is the gathering of empirical data on which scientific inquiry may be based. By attempting, on an empirical basis, to discern trends in ecclesiology in one particular area, this study offers a contribution to the task.

Northern Malawi was the site of the study which focused exclusively on the two most influential religious movements in the region, the Presbyterian and Roman Catholic churches. These are the only churches which have an extensive and well-organized network of parishes spanning the Region and both play a central role in the social organization of northern Malawi. However, the recent history and contemporary life of the two church movements has not been subject to much sustained scholarly attention.[4] By identifying current trends in ecclesiology among church members in northern Malawi, this study endeavours not only to fill this gap but to increase our understanding of contemporary Christianity in Africa as a whole.

The points on which the enquiry is concentrated are: the church as institution or fellowship (?), patterns of initiation, church discipline, indigenization and inculturation, church and society, clergy and laity, ecumenism, women and youth. These were all areas where it was expected that church members would be engaged with ecclesiological issues. The methodology used in the research was that of questionnaire and interview, with University theology and

---

Innovative Essays in Ecclesiology, Nairobi: AACC, 1990 (African Challenge Series No. 1).

[4] This deficiency is partly addressed by Anne-Lise Quinn, "Working on the Protestant Ethic: Life in a Presbyterian Community in Malawi," PhD, University of Cambridge, 1993: see also Anne-Lise Quinn, "Holding on to Mission Christianity: Case Studies from a Presbyterian Church in Malawi," *Journal of Religion in Africa,* Vol. XXV/4 (1995), pp. 387-411.

religious studies students as interviewers.⁵ All the interviews were completed during the Easter vacation in 1997. The results were then entered into a computer programme which was designed to reveal the statistical trends in the responses. The research aimed to survey a representative sample of Catholic and Presbyterian Christians in the Northern Region of Malawi. The twenty-two interviewers worked in a variety of social settings in the Districts of Mzimba, Rumphi and Karonga. Of the 423 interviews which they completed, 23 were discarded in an exercise of quality control. Only the best 400 interviews were used in the statistical analysis. Of these, 212 interviewees were Catholic while 188 were Presbyterian, 196 were over 30 while 204 were under 30, and 202 were men while 198 were women. Regarding their level of education, 25 interviewees had no formal education, 149 had primary school education, 199 had secondary school education, and 26 had tertiary education. Noting these demographic categories gave the opportunity to draw comparisons in the results of the computer analysis. Often there proves to be consistency of understanding and experience across the demographic divisions but there are occasions when significant differences emerge. Attention will be drawn to these as the results are presented. The principal results of the research are the statistical trends indicated below. All figures are in the form of percentages. To illustrate the trends, however, reference will also be made to comments which were offered by interviewees.

---

[5] The project was funded by a grant from the University of Malawi Research and Publications Committee which is hereby gratefully acknowledged. Thanks are also due to the 21 Chancellor College students who devoted part of their Easter vacation 1997 to gathering the research data. Also, the project depended for its success on the database design and data analysis undertaken by Mr Gift Nuka of the Department of Mathematical Sciences, and the data entry completed by Ms Hanna Bonzo, research assistant in the Department of Theology and Religious Studies. The high quality work of all of these participants made it possible to unearth the research results outlined in this chapter.

Institution or Fellowship?

A basic difference in perceptions of the church is whether it is regarded by its members primarily as an *institution*, fulfilling a formal role in society, or whether it is regarded primarily as a *fellowship*, with emphasis on its vital and affective character. Three questions were asked to attempt to draw out the perceptions of interviewees on this distinction. The trends revealed by the answers can be indicated in tabular form:

To be a Christian, is it more important (1) to be baptized, or (2) to live a godly life?

	(1)	(2)	Both
Total	41	51	8
Presbyterian	33	60	7
Catholic	48	43	9

To be a true church, is it more important (1) to be under the authority of the church leadership (Synod office, Bishop), or (2) to be a congregation where God's Word is preached and God's Spirit is present?

	(1)	(2)	Both
Total	40	56	4
Presbyterian	35	64	1
Catholic	43	49	7

In church life are the most important decisions taken at (1) Synod/Diocesan level, or (2) Congregational level?

	(1)	(2)
Total	79	20
Presbyterian	71	27
Catholic	85	14

The answers make it clear, first of all, that the community is divided at this point with substantial sections inclining either in an *institutional* direction or in a *fellowship* direction. It may also be noted that the Presbyterians consistently incline more to the fellowship model of the church while Catholics incline more to the institutional model. This is seen most clearly in the responses to the first question above where 60% of Presbyterians emphasize living a godly life while 33% emphasize baptism, whereas the equivalent figures for Catholics are 43% to 48%. Likewise 64% of Presbyterians value the preaching of the Word and the presence of the Spirit more highly than the authority of the church leadership, compared with 49% of Catholics. Finally, while members of both churches tend to look to the "top" for the important decisions affecting church life, this tendency is more pronounced in the Catholic church where 85% look to the top and only 14% to the congregation, while among Presbyterians 71% look to the top and 27% to the congregation. The Presbyterians do have at least a substantial minority which attaches decisive importance to the congregational level, as opposed to the central leadership. Given the ecclesiological histories of the two church movements, it is not surprising that the institutional tendency is stronger on the Catholic side. Perhaps more noteworthy is the fact that in both churches there are substantial numbers of members leaning either way. By the use of cross-tabulation, using the above question on "baptism" or "godly life," I will indicate below some points at which the fundamental divergence between *institution* and *fellowship* affects other aspects of ecclesiology.

Patterns of Initiation

A simple question asked was: how did you become a member of your church? Answers fell into four categories: the influence of family, the influence of friends, personal decision, and influence of clergy:

	Family	Friends	Decision	Clergy
Total	72	6	18	4
Presbyterian	80	4	12	4
Catholic	64	8	24	4
Male	68	5	22	5
Female	76	8	14	3
Over 30	68	6	20	6
Under 30	75	6	16	2

It is clear that a large majority of members joined their church through the influence of their families, reflecting the well-established nature of these two churches in northern Malawi. Significantly, however, this trend is more marked among the longer established Presbyterians (80%) than among the more recently arrived Catholics (64%). Conversely, the number of Catholics (24%) who emphasised personal decision was twice the number of Presbyterians (12%). The fact that more males (22%) than females (14%) emphasised personal decision may reflect patterns of family life in the northern Region. Interestingly, older respondents (20%) emphasized personal decision more often than younger respondents (16%). Conversely, the young (75%) more often than the old (68%) pointed to the influence of family, perhaps suggesting that church growth from direct conversion may be slowing down as more people are born into church families.

Church Discipline

Both Catholic and Presbyterian churches in northern Malawi practise rigorous church discipline.[6] Members who do not conform to the required standards of behaviour, especially in regard to marriage and

---

[6] For a study of the Presbyterian principles and practice, see Paterson K. Nyirenda, "Church Discipline in the CCAP Synod of Livingstonia: An Historical Review," B.A. (Theology) Dissertation, University of Malawi, 1997.

sexual ethics, must expect to find themselves being suspended or excommunicated. This is an aspect of church life of which everyone is powerfully aware. The question was: does church discipline help the church to be truly holy? Answers were as follows:

	Yes	No
Total	65	33
Presbyterian	66	34
Catholic	65	33
Over 30	68	6
Under 30	75	6
No education[7]	76	24
Primary	59	40
Secondary	71	27
Tertiary	42	54

Here it may be observed that two-thirds are favourable to church discipline and one-third is not. This applies equally to Presbyterians and Catholics. Where trends of possible significance may be discerned is in regard to age and educational level. Among young people (below 30 years) 36% are unfavourable to church discipline, compared with 30% among older people. The only section of the sample which has a majority view unfavourable to church discipline is the group which has had tertiary education - 54% think that church discipline does not help the church to be truly holy. The major emphasis in the critique offered by this group is that church discipline promotes hypocrisy: "People pretend a lot in order to protect their reputation in church." This criticism is well understood and has been taken into account at least by some of those who

---

[7] This shorthand phrase is used strictly in the sense of "no formal (school) education" and implies no value judgement whatsoever on how much a person may be educated in the broader sense.

support the system of rigorous church discipline. One Catholic woman explained: "Although it looks as if church discipline implants some sort of pretence in the behaviour of Christians, the long-term results are that members get used to the laws and take them as part of their lives." On such a basis most church members are ready to support the current system of church discipline but there is a strong minority which is quite critical, especially among younger and more educated members. It may also be noted that those with an *institutional* ecclesiology are more favourable to church discipline (72/28) than those with a *fellowship* ecclesiology (64/36).

Indigenization and Inculturation

The issue of indigenization has been, from the early years of the 20th century, the most pressing ecclesiological issue in northern Malawi. It is prominent in the writing of such early leaders as Charles Domingo and Yesaya Zerenji Mwasi, who wrote in 1933: "An exotic Christianity will never take vital root in the lives of the natives.... I wish to *naturalize* and *nationalize* God, Christ, Faith - in short Christianity."[8] Now, at the end of the 20th century, has indigenization taken effect? A straightforward question was: does the church (1) seem rather foreign to you, or (2) would you say that it is truly African? Answers were as follows:

	(1)	(2)	Both
Total	57	39	4
Presbyterian	59	36	3
Catholic	54	41	4

---

[8] Yesaya Zerenji Mwasi, *My Essential and Paramount Reasons for Working Independently*, ed. John K. Parratt, Zomba: University of Malawi, Sources for the Study of Religion in Malawi No. 2, 1979, pp. 2-3; see also Charles Domingo, *Letters of Charles Domingo*, ed. Harry Langworthy, Zomba: University of Malawi, Sources for the Study of Religion in Malawi No. 9, 1983.

Once again, there is a marked division in popular perception. The striking finding is that still a majority of church members find the church "rather foreign," though a substantial minority regards it as "truly African." This minority is slightly stronger among Catholics than among Presbyterians.[9] It may also be noted that the sense of the church being foreign is more marked among those with an *institutional* tendency (63/35) than among those with a *fellowship* tendency (52/44).

A related question was: is it (1) important to maintain the church structures inherited from the missionaries, or (2) can the African church work out its own way to be the church? The answers can be broken down as follows:

	Yes	No
Total	53	45
Presbyterian	56	41
Catholic	49	48
Over 30	57	41
Under 30	49	48
Male	49	48
Female	56	42
No education	56	44
Primary	61	37
Secondary	48	51
Tertiary	35	42

---

[9] It may be noted that many Catholic interviewees spontaneously mentioned the African Synod as having spurred on the process of inculturation in their church. This evidence suggests that the Synod has captured the popular imagination.

Here it may be noted, firstly, that there is a marked division among every section of the sample. The question of whether to maintain the structures of missionary Christianity or to take a more innovative "African" approach is a contentious one, with the community divided almost in half. Those emphasizing the need to conserve the inherited tradition form a slender majority. The minority which is prepared for the African church to work out its own way to be the church is stronger among the youth, among men, and among the more highly educated.

The question where the answers were closest to unanimity was: to understand Christianity properly (1) it must be explained in English, or (2) it can be fully understood in the vernacular.

	(1)	(2)
Total	5	94
Presbyterian	9	90
Catholic	2	97

Confidence in the vernacular language as a vehicle for expressing Christian faith seems to be the point at which indigenization has reached furthest. A typical comment was that of a Presbyterian young man: "The use of Tumbuka, which is my mother tongue, in the church gives me pride and is a traditional value to me. I'm just so happy to have the Bible, hymns and preaching in Tumbuka." It may be noted, however, that confidence in the vernacular is even stronger among Catholics (97%). This finding bears out the stress laid by such recent writers as Lamin Sanneh and Kwame Bediako on the translation of Christianity into vernacular languages as the basis for African Christian self-confidence and the starting point for doing African theology.[10] On other issues of indigenization there remains considerable equivocation among northern Malawian Christians but

---

[10] See Sanneh, *Translating the Message*; and Bediako, *Christianity in Africa*, pp. 109-25.

as to their confidence in their vernacular languages as the vehicle for expressing Christian faith, there can be no doubt as to its width and depth.

Another question on which interviewees were divided was: do you think that church life today embodies the best of African traditional values? Answers were as follows:

	Yes	No
Total	46	52
Presbyterian	45	53
Catholic	46	50
Male	48	48
Female	56	42
No education	56	44
Primary	61	37
Secondary	48	51
Tertiary	35	42

The statistics suggest that this is an issue on which church members are divided. Their perspectives are often diametrically opposed, as in the following two comments from Catholics:

> With this inculturation, many traditional values are incorporated.
>
> No, the church still holds its values without allowing any entry of foreign material.

Interestingly, more women than men answered "no," suggesting that the embodiment of African traditional values in the life of the church is less successful from the women's perspective. It is also apparent that the more educated one is, the more likely it is that one will feel satisfied with the level of inculturation in church life. The only section of the sample showing a high percentage of dissatisfied members (68%) is the group which has had no formal education. The comments offered by interviewees suggest that, to a great extent, their answers depended on how they define "African traditional values." Those who gave prominence to such matters as drumming, dancing, clapping, ululating, clerical vestments, burial rites, women and men sitting separately, or showing due respect to elders, tended to consider that much inculturation had been achieved. On the other hand, those who gave prominence to such matters as polygamy, beer-drinking, *gule wamkulu*, African doctors, or *vimbuza*, tended to look on the church as being antagonistic to African culture. Some respondents could offer critical discrimination on this issue, e.g:

> Although African traditional values are seen in the church today, they are not the best. Even where they are applied, they are applied in an artificial manner.

The relation of church life to traditional culture clearly remains a focal point for critical thought and vigorous debate.

The element of challenge or antagonism came out strongly in the responses to the question: does the church more (1) underline the traditional values of your community, or (2) bring a challenge to a new and different kind of life?

	(1)	(2)
Total	31	66
Presbyterian	30	66
Catholic	31	65

When it comes to a choice between understanding the church as underlining traditional values or as bringing a challenge to a counter-cultural lifestyle, two-thirds opt for the latter, both among Presbyterians and among Catholics. Many expressed themselves strongly on this point, e.g.

> The church should be a mouthpiece of God's Word and not of earthly customs.

> We believe in Jesus Christ and not in traditional values.
>
> The life of the church is not the same as that of the community. There is always a conflict between the two. The people look to the church as alien to them, trying to bring a challenge to a new and different kind of life.
>
> There is a new and different life because true Christians can be differentiated from those following traditional values.
>
> One has to abandon the tradition and take up the cross of Jesus.... One has to do what Jesus did, not following your tradition.

Here is material which must give pause for thought to the African theologian who is attempting to do theology out of the continuities between the African tradition and the Christian experience. Adrian Hastings has observed that, as a matter of history, the primary characteristic of conversion in Africa was "not continuity but challenge, the appeal of otherness, an uncontrollable new loyalty."[11] The above responses, given by northern Malawian Christians in 1997, suggest that what they value in the life of the church is precisely the challenge to, as opposed to the continuity with, traditional culture. It is an ecclesiology of the "contrast community," the counter-cultural congregation, which holds sway among the majority. Even where attention is drawn to the continuity between traditional values and church life, it is often in heavily qualified terms, e.g.

> The church embodies the best African traditional values which are humane and are in line with Christianity. It allows good things only.... It wants to promote a healthy society. As a result, it forbids some traditional values like polygamy or alcohol.

A sense of traditional culture being challenged by the life and values of the church pervades grassroots ecclesiology in northern Malawi.

---

[11] Adrian Hastings, *African Catholicism: Essays in Discovery*, London: SCM, 1989, p. 5.

A final question on how Christian identity is related to indigenous traditions was: do you feel more closely related to (1) ancestors who lived long ago in your community, or (2) Old Testament ancestors like Abraham, Isaac and Jacob?

	(1)	(2)
Total	33	63
Presbyterian	29	67
Catholic	37	59
No education	44	48
Primary	35	63
Secondary	31	65
Tertiary	31	58

For two-thirds, the Christian identity derived from the Bible appears at this point to be stronger than the identity derived from the indigenous community. This tendency is slightly stronger among Presbyterians than among Catholics. The section of the sample where the greatest proportion of people felt more closely related to the ancestors of their own community is the group with no formal education, suggesting perhaps that not having been exposed to formal education increased their chances of remaining closely in touch with the ancestral traditions of the community. For most of the others, they have opted for what Bediako calls the "adoptive past" where their communal identity and meaning is established by reference to what is given in the Scriptures, as opposed to what is inherited within the local society.[12] Since the relation to ancestors has

---

[12] Kwame Bediako, *Christianity in Africa*, p. 227: The Scriptures become *our* story, illuminating our past, reflecting the triumphs of our dependence on God, as well as our failures in disobedience and idolatry. We come to *participate* in the meaning of the scriptural events, as anyone who shares in African Christian worship services knows. The world-view and the religious idiom of the Scriptures themselves, with their ever-renewed stress that the lives and careers of the

often been considered to play a key role in the African universe of meaning, it may be of some significance to notice that most northern Malawian church members feel more closely related to their "adopted" Old Testament ancestors than they do to their "natural" ancestors.

Church and Society

A simple question to open discussion of the social impact of the church was: has the church had a major impact on political life in this country?

	Yes	No
Total	88	11
Presbyterian	82	16
Catholic	92	6
Over 30	85	13
Under 30	90	8

Clearly there is a massive confidence that the church has had a major impact on political life in Malawi, even more marked among Catholics than among Presbyterians, and among the young than among the old. This in itself is an important finding since a study completed early in the 1990s found that church life was very little concerned with the social and political order.[13] The reason for this change in perception is evident in the comments of the many interviewees who made direct reference to the epochal 1992 Catholic Bishops' Pastoral Letter *Living our Faith* and the formation by the churches of the Public Affairs Committee which played a major part in the dismantling of the one-party system in 1992-93 and the

---

'ancestors' - Adam, Eve, Noah, Enoch, Abraham, Isaac, Jacob, Moses, David - have a relevance for every succeeding generation, assuring us that they have something to do with us too."

[13] Ross, "Preaching in Mainstream Christian Churches in Malawi," pp. 21-23.

construction of a democratic political order.[14] This historic engagement of the churches does seem to have had a powerful effect on the popular consciousness in developing a confidence that church life is directly engaged with social and political issues. After all, as one elderly Presbyterian woman put it, "the church helped to eliminate Banda - the greatest dictator the world has ever known!"

Rather more difficult to answer was the reverse question: has the life of the church been shaped by its response to political events? Here it is necessary to introduce a certain amount of refinement to categorize the answers. Of those who answered "yes," some did so with approval and others with disapproval. Likewise, of those who answered "no," some did so with approval and others with disapproval. The results are as follows:

	Yes/approve	Yes/disapprove	No/approve	No/disapprove
Total	35	7	54	5
Presbyterian	38	6	55	1
Catholic	32	7	53	8

From the above data it may be observed that some 60% think that the church should *not* be shaped by its response to political events - 54% said "no" with approval while 7% said "yes" with disapproval. On the other hand, 40% think that the church should be shaped by its response to political events - 35% said "yes" with approval while

---

[14] See Trevor Cullen, *Malawi: A Turning Point,* Edinburgh: The Pentland Press, 1994; *Malawi: A Moment of Truth,* London: CIIR, 1993; Jonathan Q. Newell, "'A Moment of Truth? The Church and Political Change in Malawi, 1992," *The Journal of Modern African Studies,* Vol. 33/2 (1995), pp. 243-62; Nzunda & Ross ed., *Church, Law and Political Transition;* Kenneth R. Ross ed., *God, People and Power in Malawi: Democratization in Theological Perspective,* Blantyre: CLAIM-Kachere, 1996; Kenneth R. Ross, "The Transformation of Power in Malawi 1992-95: The Role of the Christian Churches," *The Ecumenical Review* Vol. 48/1 (January 1996) pp. 38-52.

5% said "no" with a sense of disappointment. It may be of some significance that slightly more Presbyterians noted with approval that the church was responding to political developments while slightly more Catholics noted with regret that it was not responding as they wished it would. Those who noted with approval the impact of political events on the life of the church almost all drew attention to the impact of democratization:

> Christians now do not just receive orders from their leaders; they question some of the decisions affecting them.
>
> People now are able to say their thoughts and convictions aloud to the leaders.
>
> The church has changed from a non-participatory to a participatory basis.
>
> People now demand that decisions should come from the lower levels.

However, the predominant tendency is still to think that the church should not be shaped in any way by its engagement with the political order. There remains a formidable body of opinion that:

> The church should *not* at all costs take part in politics because politics and Christianity are two different things.

Turning to economic matters, and bearing in mind that most northern Malawian Christians are small-holder farmers struggling to make ends meet, the question asked was: does the church help in the struggle against poverty? Again, there needs to be some discrimination in categorizing the answers. Of those who answered "yes," some were thinking primarily in terms of material help while others were thinking more of consciousness-raising. On the other hand, of those who answered "no," some did so because they found the church to be itself caught in the poverty trap while others did so because they considered that the church was unconcerned with such matters. The results of the analysis are as follows:

	Yes/material	Yes/consciousness	No/poor	No/unconcerned
Total	60	22	11	7
Presbyterian	64	15	19	7
Catholic	64	31	7	7

Most respondents do consider the church to be a player in the struggle against poverty but think of this in terms of the material help which the church can offer, such as employment, social services, education, agricultural schemes, emergency food relief etc. Awareness of the role of the church as consciousness-raiser in combatting poverty is more marked among Catholics (31%) than among Presbyterians (15%). On the other hand more Presbyterians (19%) than Catholics (7%) soberly concluded that the church could not help because it was also poor. The main finding, however, is that a large majority of Christians do regard the church as playing a positive role in the struggle to overcome the crippling poverty which grips much of northern Malawi.

Clergy and Laity

The respective roles of clergy and laity in the church were probed with a number of questions. The first invited a straightforward judgement: do you think the clergy are more (1) a source of strength, or (2) a source of problems to the church?

	(1)	(2)	Both
Total	81	12	7
Presbyterian	82	15	3
Catholic	80	8	11

The results offer quite a strong vote of confidence in the clergy. Many interviewees commented favourably on the role of the clergy as inspirational leaders, sources of unity, and persons of theological acumen. Most would agree with the comment that:

> The clergy act as unifying figures in the church and all its members look to them as sources of strength and spiritual advice.

It may be noted that all the interviewers were lay people so there was no undue pressure on respondents to comment favourably on the clergy. Indeed the anticlerical minority were quite outspoken.

> The clergy pay little attention to church matters. They move about aimlessly doing private business.

> They pay little attention to spiritual matters. They are corrupt, immoral, partisan.

> They are corrupt. They are biased in handling cases. They are womanizers. They are too authoritarian.

The clergy, then, are not without their critics but the majority appreciate their work. This was apparent also in the responses to the question: do clergy (1) exercise power in the same way as political leaders, or (2) demonstrate a different pattern in the exercise of power?

	(1)	(2)
Total	41	51
Presbyterian	33	60
Catholic	48	43

There is evidence here of a widespread confidence that the clergy represent a different kind of power from that experienced in the political realm - "the clergy do not tell lies as politicians do." This confidence is stronger among Catholics (remarkably, 96%) than among Presbyterians (78%).

Turning to the function of clergy in the mediation of God's presence and salvation, two questions were asked. The first was: do you think God speaks (1) only through the clergy, or (2) through any godly person?

	(1)	(2)
Total	19	80
Presbyterian	18	81
Catholic	19	79
Over 30	22	78
Under 30	15	82
No education	44	56
Primary	26	72
Secondary	12	86
Tertiary	4	94

Those with the kind of sacerdotal view of Christianity which would expect God to speak only through the clergy are in a minority of 20% composed predominantly of older, less educated people. In all sections of the sample most people would expect God to speak through any godly person. Cross-tabulation reveals that this tendency is more marked among respondents with a *fellowship* ecclesiology (10/90) than among those with an *institution* ecclesiology (31/69). To push the issue a step further, the second question was asked: would you be willing to receive the sacraments (1) only from the clergy, or (2) through any godly person? The results were as follows:

	(1)	(2)
Total	68	31
Presbyterian	57	41
Catholic	78	21
No education	76	24
Primary	74	24
Secondary	65	34
Tertiary	54	46

When it comes to sacraments, the indispensability of the clergy is strongly felt, though a substantial minority are prepared to receive sacraments from lay church leaders. Even 21% of Catholics would do so! It may also be noted that the more educated a person, the more likely it is that they would be willing to receive sacraments from lay leaders. Appreciation of the clergy is combined, on the whole, with a willingness to give an extensive role to lay leadership in the life of the church.

Ecumenism and Inter-church Relations

In taking account of grassroots ecumenical experience, a basic question was: do members of your family belong to different churches?

	Yes	No
Total	37	63
Presbyterian	37	62
Catholic	37	63

Two-thirds of interviewees did not have family members who belonged to different church from themselves. This is rather surprising since earlier writers have tended to assume that, at the level of the family, Malawian Christians would be interacting directly with relatives belonging to different religious groups.[15] It may be that this familial level of grassroots ecumenism is less widespread than has been thought.

To gain an indication of views on ecumenism and inter-church relations, two questions were asked. The first was the straightforward: do you think the different churches should unite together to form one church?

---

[15] See, e.g, Patrick A. Kalilombe, "Unity from Below: Lessons from African Traditional Religion," *Occasional Paper No. 11,* Birmingham: Selly Oak Colleges, 1992.

	Yes	No
Total	30	70
Presbyterian	30	69
Catholic	29	71

Perhaps the surprising finding here is that almost one third, of both Presbyterians and Catholics, would favour the union of the churches into one organization. However, a clear majority would prefer to maintain their current distinctive ecclesiastical identity. To pitch the inter-church question at a different level was to ask: do you like your church to be (1) strongly independent of other churches, or (2) to work closely with other churches?

	Yes	**No**
Total	24	76
Presbyterian	27	72
Catholic	20	79
Over 30	26	73
Under 30	21	78
No education	48	52
Primary	30	70
Secondary	16	83
Tertiary	23	77

What is made apparent by these results is that between the 30% who favour union between the different churches and the 24% who like their church to be strongly independent of others, there are almost 50% who like their church to work closely with others while maintaining its distinct identity. In this respect the church membership in northern Malawi may be fairly well in line with trends on this issue in the church worldwide. It may be noted that there is slightly less inclination to be strongly independent among younger and more educated members.

Women and Youth

Given the sense of alienation recently expressed by some women and young people in relation to their experience of church life,[16] a pertinent area of enquiry was to identify prevailing perceptions of the role of women and young people in church life. This part of the study was particularly inviting since the churches of northern Malawi might generally be considered to be strongholds of patriarchy and gerontocracy. A very open question was asked: what do you think should be the role of women in church life? The answers fell broadly into two categories: (1) those which expressed satisfaction with the existing role of women and, on the other hand, (2) those which expressed dissatisfaction and called for women to be given a higher profile in church life.

	Yes	No
Total	34	66
Presbyterian	28	71
Catholic	39	61
Male	36	64
Female	32	68
No education	48	52
Primary	40	60
Secondary	30	69
Tertiary	12	88

---

[16] See Isabel Apawo Phiri, "Marching, Suspended and Stoned: Christian Women in Malawi 1995," in Ross ed., *God, People and Power*, pp. 63-105; of. Isabel Apawo Phiri, *Women, Presbyterianism and Patriarchy: Religious Experience of Chewa Women in Central Malawi*, Blantyre: CLAIM-Kachere, 1997; and James Tengatenga, "Young People: Participation or Alienation? An Anglican Case," in Ross ed., *God, People and Power*, pp. 107-23.

Clearly there is a groundswell of opinion in favour of reform and change in this area. Two-thirds of church members would wish to see women taking up leadership roles in church life. Often this was expressed in terms of their sharing in the responsibilities that are presently reserved only for men:

> What is the role of men in the church? The role of women should be the role of men.

> They should do all the works that are now only done by their male counterparts.

> They should preach the Word of God. They should be allowed to give sacraments. There should also be women priests.

Often mentioned was the need for women to be "involved in decision-making." It can be observed that the balance of opinion in favour of reform tends to rise according to the educational level of the interviewee. However, there is little difference, apparently, between the perspectives of women and men. Indeed it was often women who expressed themselves most strongly in favour of the existing subordination of women in church life, e.g.

> We should not be given high offices like priesthood because we are always busy with household work.

> What women are actually doing now is fine, i.e. to be sisters and helpers of men. We should not do what our male counterparts do because we are very emotional.

A feminist analysis might find here evidence of "internalized oppression" but what is striking, in the northern Malawian context, is that such an outlook appears to be a minority one. In both churches, though rather more markedly in the Presbyterian, there is a majority body of opinion that is favourable to reform which will enable women to play a full part in the church leadership. Cross-tabulation shows that those with a *fellowship* ecclesiology are more strongly in favour of reform (71/29) than those with an *institutional* understanding (58/42).

	(1)	(2)
Total	45	55
Presbyterian	47	53
Catholic	38	62
Over 30	45	55
Under 30	45	55
No education	52	48
Primary	46	54
Secondary	39	61
Tertiary	31	69

Compared with the case of women, respondents were more divided when it came to the role of young people. However, the main finding is that there is a majority view favourable to young people being given greater leadership responsibility in church life. A representative comment was:

> Christian life has no age. This brings the case that youth should participate in Christian life on the same level as elders. Apart from being choir members, they should be involved in preaching and decision-making.

It may be noted that there is a difference between Catholic and Presbyterian at this point with the Catholic respondents more favourable to a higher profile for young people. Perhaps surprisingly, there is no difference at all, statistically, on this point between those over 30 years and those under 30. It can be observed, however, that a higher level of education tends to make one more favourably disposed to increasing the leadership responsibility of the youth. We might conclude that there is a movement to give young people a higher profile in church life but it is not quite so strong as the movement to give equal status to women. Perhaps the gender gap is closing faster than the generation gap?

Current Ecclesiological Trends

In conclusion, this survey of elements of ecclesiology at the grassroots enables us to notice three areas: the first is where rapid change is occurring, the second is where the situation appears fairly static, the third is where there is division and conflict on ecclesiological issues.

(1) The evidence outlined above suggests that fairly rapid change is occurring in terms of direct church engagement with socio-political matters and in terms of the roles played in church life by laity, women and youth.

(2) It suggests that policy on church discipline commands a broad consensus, while not lacking its critics. Likewise on inter-church relations there are the eager ecumenists on one side, the fiercely independent on the other, with most people somewhere in the middle.

(3) Where there is the greatest and the sharpest division is on the issue of inculturation where opinions differ widely as to how far inculturation has gone and on how far it should go. Whether the church should be understood primarily as institution or as fellowship is a fundamental divergence affecting ecclesiological perspectives across a broad range of issues.

What is beyond doubt is that ecclesiology is a lively and contested area as northern Malawians struggle with issues of personal and communal identity. Critical readings, informed by the Malawian context, of the Bible and inherited ecclesiastical traditions are giving rise to a distinctive ecclesiological configuration as northern Malawians work out what it means for them to be the church. Some of the contours of that ecclesiology have been roughly mapped by the above sketch. While the construction of ecclesial identity is a profoundly contemporary matter, yet it invariably has deep historical roots. In the next chapter we will consider how history may be employed as a source for clarifying our understanding of what it means to be the church.

4. Crisis and Identity: Presbyterian Ecclesiology in Southern Malawi 1891-1993

Doing theology in Africa has been, for the last generation, predominantly a matter of relating Christian faith and traditional culture. The premise has been that African Christian identity will be secured only when the faith is interpreted in terms of traditional cultural categories. The task to which academic theologians have applied themselves has been, accordingly, to show how the message of Jesus Christ has resonance within the categories of a traditional African worldview. A formidable body of scholarship has been built up as theologians in different parts of the continent have sought to fulfil this task.[1] Nevertheless, efforts at theological construction have been limited in terms of their uptake at the popular level. As we noted in the first chapter, a wide gap seems to yawn between the efforts of African theologians to reconstruct our understanding of the faith, on the one hand, and popular experience of Christianity on the other. Part of the reason for this weakness might be found in the one-dimensional character of the faith-culture approach. Theology is regarded as essentially a dialogue between the biblical text and the vernacular world in Africa. On any reckoning, this is a rich and

---

[1] See, e.g, Kofi Appiah-Kubi & Sergio Torres eds., *African Theology en Route,* New York: Orbis, 1979; C.G. Baëta ed., *Christianity in Tropical Africa,* London: Oxford University Press, 1968; Eboussi Boulaga, *Christianity without Fetishes,* Maryknoll: Orbis, 1984; Benezet Bujo, *African Theology in its Social Context,* New York: Orbis, 1992; Kwesi A. Dickson & Paul Ellingworth ed., *Biblical Revelation and African Beliefs,* London: Lutterworth Press, 1969, Edward Fasholé-Luke et al ed., *Christianity in Independent Africa,* London: Rex Collings, 1978; Bolaji Idowu. *Towards an Indigenous Church,* London: Oxford University Press, 1965; J.N.K. Mugambi & Laurenti Magesa ed., *Jesus in African Christianity,* Nairobi: Initiatives Publishers, 1989; Charles Nyamiti, *Christ as our Ancestor - Christology from an African Perspective,* Gweru: Mambo, 1984; John S. Pobee, *Toward an African Theology,* Nashville: Abingdon Press, 1979.

dynamic field. However, it is one where little attention tends to be paid to the concrete historical circumstances of the believing community within which this dialogue occurs. The limitations of a 'faith and culture' approach are that it tends to posit an engagement between a static religious entity and a timeless sphere of culture. What is missed here is the fact that the community in which the meeting between Christian faith and traditional culture takes place, is a community which is moving through a particular history. All the while, on the ground, Christians have been forming a viable self-understanding as believing communities have responded to events which have occurred in their time. This offers a source for doing theology that has so far rarely been tapped: the history of the Christian communities in Africa.

Moreover, in that history there occur certain decisive and definitive events. The community comes to certain points of *kairos* where its response to a given historical situation is determinative of its understanding of the biblical gospel and of its own identity as a church. This is a reality which was given classic expression by Christians in South Africa in 1985 when they recognized that they had reached "the KAIROS, the moment of grace and opportunity, the favourable time in which God issues a challenge to decisive action. It is a dangerous time because, if this opportunity is missed, and allowed to pass by, the loss for the Church, for the Gospel and for all the people of South Africa will be immeasurable."[2] If it is true that there occur in history such moments of crisis, then, to attempt to define the self-understanding of any Christian community without taking account of its particular historical experience, it seems to me, is to be severely handicapped in the task of constructing a theology that is true to the empirical reality with which it is engaged. The process with which we are concerned was hinted at by John Mbiti at one of the earliest gatherings of the modern generation of African

---

[2] *The Kairos Document. Challenge to the 'Church: A Theological Comment on the Political Crisis in South Africa,* Braamfontein: The Kairos Theologians & London: CIIR/-BCC, 1985, p. 4.

theologians: "We cannot artificially create an 'African theology' or even plan it; it must evolve spontaneously as the Church teaches and lives her Faith and *in response to the extremely complex situation in Africa.*"³ Mbiti was pointing here to the particular history through which a church passes as the crucible within which a viable theology would be formed.

The argument of this chapter is that there are times of crisis in any such history which are especially definitive for the church's understanding of herself and her faith. As I have argued, elsewhere:

> The path of discipleship and the advance of the kingdom run through the events of history and there are 'moments of truth' when the gap between the ultimate and the penultimate narrows and a particular historical option becomes very closely identified with the kingdom of God. Without faithfulness at this penultimate level the church will not be able to be an effective sign pointing to the ultimate realities which it is charged to proclaim to the world. The integrity of the church is then at stake in the decision which it takes.⁴

Such moments of crisis and challenge are also theologically formative as a particular church develops its sense of identity and self-understanding. In this paper, a case study will be made of the Blantyre Synod of the Church of Central Africa Presbyterian (CCAP), a Presbyterian church movement begun by Scottish missionaries in 1875 and today widespread throughout the Southern Region of Malawi with membership approaching 1,000,000.⁵ We

---

³ John Mbiti in C.G. Baëta, ed., *Christianity in Tropical Africa,* London: Oxford University Press, 1968, p. 332, my italics.

⁴ Kenneth R. Ross, *Gospel Ferment in Malawi: Theological Essays,* Gweru: Mambo Press, 1995, p. 62.

⁵ For the early history see Andrew C. Ross, *Blantyre Mission and the Making of Modern Malawi,* Blantyre: CLAIM-Kachere, 1996 (Mzuzu: Luviri Press, 2018); for more recent developments see Saindi D. Chiphangwi, "Why People Join the Christian Church: Trends in Church Growth in the Blantyre Synod of the Church

shall examine four "moments of truth" which have arisen in the history of the Blantyre Synod and note ways in which the Synod's ecclesiology has been formed out of its response to such times of crisis. The argument of the paper is that this church, in the course of its history, has encountered certain decisive and definitive moments; and that its response to such kairotic moments has been of formative significance in the development of an indigenous and viable ecclesiology. After 120 years of Christian life and witness, the Blantyre Synod can draw for its self-understanding not only on the biblical text, the wider Presbyterian tradition and the communal traditions of the Yao, Mang'anja and other peoples who make up its membership, but also *on its history as a church.*

The Imposition of Colonial Rule

From 1875 to 1889 the Blantyre Mission operated in a precolonial social and political context where it made its way independently in its relations with surrounding communities. After almost collapsing in its early years under the pressures of such a situation, the Mission became well-established in the 1880s under the inspirational leadership of David Clement Scott.[6] Towards the end of the 1880s, however, the missionaries became concerned about the territorial ambitions of the Arabs and the Portuguese. A British Protectorate seemed the only satisfactory alternative to the Portuguese annexation which the missionaries believed would be injurious both to their own work and to the interests of the population at large. Accordingly, they launched a vigorous and finally successful campaign to persuade the British Government to withdraw from its initial willingness to cede the area to Portugal and to establish a formal British

---

of Central Africa Presbyterian 1960-1975," PhD, University of Aberdeen, 1978; and Silas S. Ncozana, *Sangaya,* Blantyre: CLAIM-Kachere, 1996.

[6] See Andrew C. Ross, *Blantyre Mission,* pp. 39-84.

Protectorate in 1891.[7] This portentous step resolved one crisis but immediately plunged the Mission into another. For now the missionaries would, inevitably, work in some kind of association with their compatriots in the British administration. What would this mean for the infant Christian church growing under the missionaries' care and direction? In the course of the 1890s and early 1900s three decisive steps were taken which marked out the identity of the church as it entered the colonial era.

First, Clement Scott attached paramount importance to the training and appointment of African Christian converts as church leaders. From the time of his arrival in 1881 he worked closely with Africans who had already been attracted to the Mission, notably Joseph Bismarck, Rondau Kaferanjira and Donald Malota. It was they who spearheaded many of the Mission's early advances.[8] In 1893 the training of African leadership took more formal shape with the announcement that "a deacons' class of seven but representative of many more, who will in like manner devote themselves to service, meets every morning at 7 o'clock. They take a lively interest in Biblical Criticism, Theology, Church History and Liturgics."[9] After ordination in November 1894 the seven deacons were at the heart of the work of the Mission and were entrusted with major responsibilities. When a new mission station was opened in Angoniland (Ntcheu), it was Harry Kambwiri Matecheta who was chosen to lead the work.[10] Scott's hope that the seven would be followed by many more was fulfilled to the extent that in 1916 Robert Napier could note in his diary: "For four days about one hundred native church leaders from all over the Mission have been

---

[7] See ibid, pp. 85-104; also Bridglal Pachai, *Malawi: The History of the Nation,* London: Longman, 1973, pp. 70-80.

[8] See, e.g., *Life and Work in British Central Africa,* August 1888, December 1888, July 1889, November 1890.

[9] *LWBCA, May* 1893.

[10] *LWBCA,* September 1893.

meeting in conference [at Domasi]. The debating would have done credit to the [Church of Scotland General] Assembly, and the earnestness of tone would have merited comparison with Keswick. Men faced real evils and we go home with inspiration."[11] The confidence in African leadership which characterized the Blantyre Mission from these early days would inevitably form a stark contrast to the racist attitudes of the white settlers who arrived in increasing numbers after the establishment of the British Protectorate. As Andrew Ross has argued, Scott gave his African circle a strong sense of worth just at the time when white society would begin to tell them that they were worthless.[12] They could hardly mistake the contrast between the values which guided their church life and those which prevailed in the surrounding society.

If anything, this was still more unmistakable in the Mission's appraisal of the conduct of the British administration. From the beginning the Blantyre missionaries were intensely suspicious of Sir Harry Johnston, the pioneering British Consul and an associate of Cecil Rhodes. They feared, with good reason, that Johnston was planning to allow the Protectorate to fall under the control of Rhodes' British South Africa Company. "Remember it was mainly Scott and Hetherwick," wrote Johnston to Rhodes in 1893, "who in 1890 baulked the scheme of all BCA coming under the Company's Charter. They are now up and at it again and the most serious enemies you possess."[13] On issues such as land, labour, taxation and military actions against local chiefs, time and again the missionaries sharply criticised actions of the British Administration which they judged to be harmful to the interests of the African population. No wonder Alfred Sharpe concluded that

---

[11] Alexander Hetherwick ed., *Robert Hellier Napier in Nyasaland,* Edinburgh & London: Wm Blackwood & Sons, 1925, p. 103.

[12] See Andrew C. Ross, "*Wokondedwa Wathu:* The Mzungu Who Mattered," *Religion in Malawi,* Vol. 8 (1998), pp. 3-7.

[13] Johnston to Rhodes, 7 June 1893, Salisbury Rhodesia Archives LT/1/16/4/1; cit Andrew C. Ross, *Blantyre Mission,* p. 114.

"there would be no permanent and satisfactory state of things with regard to this Mission until two missionaries, the Rev D.C. Scott and the Rev Alexander Hetherwick, were removed from the country.... The missionaries are taking a course that makes them appear in the eyes of the natives of this Protectorate as an Opposition Party to H.M. Administration."[14] In doing so, they provided the African people with an incipient critique of colonialism, one which depended not on the spear or the gun but on the power of reasoned argument.[15] This would later be exploited to devastating effect by Congress leaders in the struggle for independence but already it had marked out the identity of the church as being at odds, at least in some important respects, with the conquest to which the African people of Malawi found themselves being subjected.

Thirdly, the Mission marked out a distinct identity by launching a vigorous campaign of expansion into Portuguese territory in Mozambique. In 1910 the missionaries at Blantyre presented the following Memorial to the Foreign Mission Committee in Edinburgh: "We rejoice to know that we have practically covered the whole field available to us with our stations, only a few districts remaining to be touched, so that for future expansion we look to an advance into Portuguese East Africa that has so far been untouched."[16] This was a cause especially close to the heart of the intrepid Robert Napier who would almost certainly have led this advance had he not been killed in action in Mozambique towards the end of the First World War. Before his death, however, he had shared the vision not only with the Church of Scotland Committee but, more importantly, with the leaders and members of the churches in Nyasaland. On one occasion, he noted in his diary: "The Lomwe people will welcome us and follow us from British territory,

---

[14] Alfred Sharpe (to Kimberley, 31 October 1894. Foreign Office 2/67); cit. Andrew C. Ross, *Blantyre Mission,* pp. 114-15.

[15] See Andrew C. Ross, *'Wokondedwa Wathu."*

[16] Cit Hetherwick, *Robert Hellier Napier,* p. 50.

where they have fled for safety, back to their old homes in Lomweland - if we go. The teacher in one of our district schools made me write down his name as a volunteer whenever we go."[17] When a mission station was finally established at Mihecani in 1913, soon the Great War removed most of the white missionaries and the early development of the Lomwe mission was largely left in the hands of Lewis and Grace Bandawe, both distinguished leaders within the Blantyre Mission.[18] This demonstration of the importance of missionary expansion to the life of the church and its capacity to cross political boundaries acted to mark out the distinct character of the church at a time when it could easily have been confused with the British administration.

The Chilembwe Rising

The First World War brought a crisis for the Blantyre Mission in the form of the protest by African Christians which culminated in the Chilembwe Rising of 1915. John Chilembwe was the leader of the Providence Industrial Mission, sponsored by the National Baptist Convention Inc. in the USA, which has its headquarters at Chiradzulu. He was so outraged both, in general, by the demands which the First World War was making on the African population and, in particular, by the oppression and injustice being perpetrated by the white management of the nearby Magomero Estates, that he led an armed insurrection. This was quickly suppressed. Chilembwe himself was shot and killed, many of his followers were executed and his church was blown up by the British administration.[19] Yet the memory of the Rising remained a potent factor in the evolution of the nationalist consciousness which finally resulted in independence

---

[17] Ibid, p. 60.

[18] See Lewis Mataka Bandawe, *Memoirs of a Malawian,* ed. Bridglal Pachai, Blantyre: CLAIM, 1971, pp. 76-103.

[19] See George Shepperson & Thomas Price, *Independent African,* Edinburgh, Edinburgh University Press, 1958.

for Malawi, something which was recognized in 1995 when Chilembwe Day (16 January) was gazetted as a public holiday. The situation in 1915, however, provoked a major crisis for the Blantyre Mission and the churches emerging under its aegis. No less than 84 of the "rebels" had been found to be baptized members of the Blantyre Mission, including Chilembwe's second-in-command John Gray Kufa, one of Clement Scott's first seven deacons and a distinguished leader among the first generation of Blantyre Mission converts. This aroused strong suspicion in the British administration, and especially amongst the white settler community, that the Blantyre Mission educational policy was directly subversive. In wartime conditions, with the white settler community united in its determination to ruthlessly stamp out any seedbeds of rebellion, the identity of the church was clearly going to be tested.

A Commission of Inquiry was set up to investigate the causes of the Rising and among the prime suspects was the Blantyre Mission. In the Legislative Council, Alexander Livingstone Bruce, owner of Magomero Estates, had noted that the Rising was "a rebellion of mission trained natives" and proposed that "all schools in charge of native teachers in the Protectorate be closed at once."[20] It was therefore under intense pressure to comply with the prevailing white view that the Rising was an indication of the need to entrench the structures of colonial government and keep the native population firmly "in its place," that Alexander Hetherwick, leader of the Blantyre Mission, appeared before the Commission of Inquiry on 29 June 1915. He was examined for four and a half hours and, as his biographer remarks, "during this time not one friendly question was put to him."[21] The proceedings of the Commission reveal the wide difference in outlook between the Blantyre Mission and the British Administration. One cause for complaint was that the Mission was

---

[20] Cit. Shepperson & Price, *Independent African*, p. 365.

[21] W.P. Livingstone, *A Prince of Missionaries: Rev Alexander Hetherwick*, London: James Clarke, n.d., p. 156.

irresponsibly making Bibles available to "natives" *(sic)*. Questions and answers were as follows:

Commission: Can any native get a Bible?
Hetherwick: Yes, we will sell it to any native.
Commission: Do you think the native, educated or otherwise, is capable of understanding the Holy Scriptures?
Hetherwick: Yes, as capable as any ordinary Christian.
Commission: Do you think the Bible in Chinyanja is clear and understood?
Hetherwick : Undoubtedly.
Commission: If a teacher selects an isolated portion or verse, may he not misapply it?
Hetherwick: Yes, as a European might.
Commission: We have it on evidence that native teachers do sometimes discuss amongst themselves texts from the Bible!
Hetherwick: And why not?
Commission: Can the native interpret it correctly to others?
Hetherwick: The native is as able to interpret the Bible as you are.[22]

Not surprisingly, the gulf was equally wide when it came to questions of the degree to which "natives" could be entrusted with education and responsibility:

Commission: You say there may be 12 Europeans and 10 natives [on the Blantyre Kirk Session]. Soon the native vote may have the majority. Are you prepared for the Church of Scotland practically to be governed by a native majority?
Hetherwick: It may be.
Commission: Is there not a danger of giving the native so soon such power?
Hetherwick: We have seen nothing of danger as yet and I fear none.
Commission: Do you think the result of mission education is to lose a sense of respect for Europeans? Have you found this?

---

[22] Malawi National Archives, COM-6 2/1/1.

Hetherwick: I have had respect from every native I met.
Commission: Of course, natives get swollen heads!
Hetherwick: As Europeans do - we have met them![23]

The hostile questioning concluded with the complaint that Africans were no longer respectful because they did not remove their hats when they passed a European. Hetherwick indignantly turned the tables: "I have seen many Europeans absolutely ignore a boy's salutation. The smallest drummer boy in the British army if he salutes Lord Kitchener receives a salute in return. There will be no difficulty if the European makes acknowledgment: it indicates that two gentlemen have met and not only one."[24] This explosive affirmation of the common humanity and common dignity of black and white made it abundantly clear that the Blantyre Mission had a self-understanding which was radically at variance with the prevailing colonial mentality.

Still more significant, however, was the emergence of African church leaders who were able to respond to the crisis provoked by the Chilembwe Rising. Most remarkable was the appearance of the Blantyre church elder Joseph Bismarck before the Commission on 14 July 1915. Bismarck had come to Malawi from Quelimane with a party of Livingstonia and Blantyre missionaries in 1876, had worked for many years as a teacher/evangelist in the Blantyre Mission and early in the 20th century had acquired his own estate near Blantyre which he was running quite successfully.[25] This long experience gave Bismarck the historical perspective from which to challenge many of the assumptions of the Commissioners. To their complacent

---

[23] Ibid. When Hetherwick's younger colleague Robert Napier made reference to a "national Christian church" he was asked by the Commission: "Do you mean an African church which would be run entirely by Africans'?" He replied, "Certainly, this country is African. I am thinking ahead, more like 1960." MNA COM-6 2/1/3.

[24] MNA COM-6 2/1/1.

[25] See Joseph Bismarck, "A Brief History of Joseph Bismarck," *Occasional Papers* (Malawi Government, Ministry of Local Government, Department of Antiquities, Publication No. 7), Zomba: Government Press, 1969, pp. 49-54.

supposition that it was quite unreasonable for the "natives" to resent taxation, Bismarck responded by pointing out that "when the Europeans came into this country, they didn't say that the natives were going to be taxed.... When the treaties were made, it was only for our protection from other nations.... I think it will save trouble if you say what you intend doing."[26] On point after point, Bismarck politely but firmly demonstrated that, on issues of contention between the Europeans and the "natives," it was the Europeans who were at fault. Restrictions on native game hunting was one matter raised:

Commission:	If there were no restrictions, then all the game would be killed and there would be none.
Bismarck:	No, they did not kill all the game in the old days.
Commission:	Do you remember that in the old days there were lots of buffaloes and now there are none?
Bismarck:	But it was the European who killed them![27]

On the hot issue of the European insistence that "natives" should remove their hats whenever white people were around, the Commission pressed Bismarck with their assumption that it was wrong for natives to wish to possess and wear hats:

Commission:	Don't you think [the native] wanted to clothe himself like a white man? And when he had money he bought them. Don't you think so? He first got a coat and trouser and after that a hat?
Bismarck:	No - all the trouble lies with you. Don't you go away from that. It is your fault. If you had said at the beginning, coats and hats etc are not for you, they are for Europeans, then the natives would have understood that from the beginning. But you have tempted him to wear these things.
Commission:	What should the Government do in a matter like that?

---

[26] MNA COM-6 2/1/3.

[27] Ibid.

Bismarck: Simply put a law saying that if natives salute you and take off their hats, you must answer them and let them put on their hats and pass. We do it when you are passing and, if we get a salute, we are happy and don't find any insult, and we feel proud that you answer us. But with other Europeans, although you be polite to them, they must press a native down.[28]

Perhaps Bismarck's most audacious and telling comment, which apparently flabbergasted the Commissioners, was his challenge to their assumption that it was the "natives" who were responsible for the rising:

> Another thing I want to speak of, is this serious rising. I notice that it is called a "native rising" and it is said that it was a general rising. No. It was not; and it is not a native rising. It ought to be called John Chilembwe's rising. And also it is said, that it had been instigated by John Chilembwe. No - it ought to be said that John Chilembwe has been instigated by Mr. Booth who was his teacher and taught him at first and took him to America.... I think you as our master ought to know things, that this is not a native rising at all. You ought to call it by the name of your own countryman Mr Booth.[29]

---

[28] Ibid.

[29] Ibid. On the influence of Joseph Booth in Malawi, see Robert B. Boeder, "Reassessing Joseph Booth," *Kleio* (Pretoria), Vol. 15, (July 1983), pp. 5-24; Klaus Fiedler, "Joseph Booth and the Writing of Malawian History: An Attempt at Interpretation," *Religion in Malawi* Vol. 6 (1996), pp. 30-38; Brighton M. Kavaloh, "Joseph Booth, 1892-1919: An Evaluation of his Life, Thought and Influence on Religion and Politics with special reference to British Central Africa (Malawi) and South Africa," PhD, University of Edinburgh, 1991; Harry Langworthy, *"Africa for the African": The Life of Joseph Booth*, Blantyre: CLAIM, 1996; Harry W. Langworthy, "Joseph Booth, Prophet of Radical Change in Central and Southern Africa 1891-1915," *Journal of Religion in Africa* Vol. 16 (1986), pp. 22-43; Shepperson & Price, *Independent African*.

Similarly, in an essay submitted to the Commission of Inquiry, Harry Kambwiri Matecheta, who had been ordained to the ministry within the Blantyre Mission in 1911, clearly distanced himself from the Rising but, equally, took the opportunity to express his dissatisfaction with certain aspects of European rule.[30] After appealing to the life and work of David Livingstone, Matecheta wrote:

> We natives have this custom: never call your slave a slave when you have made him a free man. If you do so he will leave you or be against you. We know that at Magomero [where the Chilembwe Rising was centred] they were persecuted for attending Church, or for building a small grass hut for prayers. Why? We do not know; and that the case came to the hearing of the Resident at Chiradzulu, and instead of putting the matter right, one of the natives was put in prison three months with hard labour.[31]

With an African leadership which was able to bring this kind of evangelically based critique to bear on social and political affairs at a time of crisis, it is clear that the emerging church had a robust and resilient sense of identity. It was able to maintain its distinctive ground in face of powerful demands for it to fall in line with the colonialist and racist spirit of the age. The Commission of Inquiry, at a moment of crisis, allowed the church movement arising out of the Blantyre Mission to discover its identity in such a way that it was able to survive the high tide of racism and colonialism in the 1920s and 1930s and provide the womb out of which a formidable nationalist movement would be born.

---

[30] Harry Kambwiri Matecheta, "The Origin of John Chilembwe Rising," an essay submitted to the Chilembwe Rising Commission of Inquiry, MNA COM-6 2/1/3; reprinted in Kenneth R. Ross ed., *Christianity in Malawi: A Sourcebook,* Gweru: Mambo, 1996, pp. 146-51. The nature and historiographical ,merit of Matecheta's essay has been extensively discussed in George Shepperson, "The Place of John Chilembwe in Malawi Historiography," in Bridglal Pachai ed., *The Early History of Malawi,* London: Longman, 1972, pp. 405-28.

[31] Matecheta, "Origin of Chilembwe Rising," p. 151.

The Federation of Rhodesia and Nyasaland

It was when this nationalist movement had grown to maturity that history brought a third great crisis to the Presbyterian churches in southern Malawi. From its inception in 1953 the Federation of Rhodesia and Nyasaland was bitterly resented by practically the whole African population of Nyasaland. They had expressed this opposition through all available channels when the proposal was brought forward and felt betrayed that Britain had nevertheless allowed the Federation to be formed. Experience of the operation of the Federation served to confirm Malawians' fears that it was intended to entrench white supremacy throughout the region and to turn Nyasaland into a "native reserve." Hostility heightened in 1958 when the Federal Legislature introduced measures to reduce the very limited political representation which it accorded to the African population.[32] This raised again the question of identity for the church. Would a movement still controlled and directed by white missionaries prove to be inextricably bound up with white interests or would it be able to assert a distinctive identity at what was to be a turning point in the national history? The political question as to "which side" the church would be on in the struggle for independence, deepened into the theological question as to what is the identity of the church as the body of Jesus Christ? The crisis reached the point where the Blantyre Synod sensed an obligation to

---

[32] For the political history of this period see R. Blake, *A History of Rhodesia*, London: Eyre Methuen, 1977, pp. 243-344; A.E. Linden, "African Nationalism as a Factor in the Decline of the Federation of Rhodesia and Nyasaland," MA, University of Tennessee, 1967; O.R. Moyer, 'The Politics of Partnership: Central African Federation 1953-1962," MA, University of Wisconsin, 1963; Pachai, *Malawi: The History of the Nation*, pp. 256-266; C. Sanger, *Central African Emergency*, London: Heinemann, 1960. For a personal account from a CCAP point of view, see Andrew B. Doig, *It's People That Count*, Edinburgh: The Pentland Press, 1997, pp. 35-57.

issue a "Statement on the Present State of Unrest."[33] Here the Synod clearly "took sides" *with* the aggrieved African population and *against* the plans of the white settlers:

> Synod ... feels it urgently necessary to say that it is unanimously opposed to Federation as it has been seen in practice over these years.... This Synod appeals to Christians of all races in this land, and to its own members in particular, to strive by every means in their power, to help understanding between races, and to build a peaceful, righteous society.... This Synod appeals to the people of Scotland through the Church of Scotland to remember their ancient links with the people of this land, and consider their political responsibilities towards us as exercised by the United Kingdom Government.[34]

When a state of emergency was established the following year, this latter appeal bore fruit when the Church of Scotland successfully advocated the cause of self-government for Nyasaland. In his history of modern Scotland T.C. Smout has argued that this was "the last occasion on which [the Church of Scotland] swayed government policy on any matter."[35]

Within the Malawi context, the distinctiveness of the church was made very apparent since, at a time when the Federation was reducing the token African representation in its Legislature, the Blantyre Synod could speak "as a Synod whose affairs have been in mainly African hands for many years and who are now well-nigh completely independent in control of our own affairs."[36] The

---

[33] This Statement is found as Appendix I in the Report of the Committee Anent Central Africa, Church of Scotland General Assembly 1958, pp. 16-19; repr. in Ross ed., *Christianity in Malawi*, pp. 195-201.

[34] Ibid, pp. 200-201.

[35] T.C. Smout, *A Century of the Scottish People 1830-1950,* London: Collins, 1986, p. 207.

[36] Kenneth R. Ross ed., *Christianity in Malawi*, p. 200.

difference between, on the one hand, belonging to a church which had grown out of the soil of Africa and which was led by African ministers and elders of great stature and, on the other hand, being forced to belong to a political unit which aimed to entrench white supremacy, was so marked that it is unsurprising that the members of the Blantyre and Livingstonia churches were practically unanimous in their determination to end the Federation. All this came into remarkably sharp focus in the crisis provoked by the state of emergency in 1959 when hundreds of Congress leaders were summarily detained and the churches stood with them. It was in the north of Malawi, at Blantyre's sister mission at Livingstonia that the Synod Moderator Stephen Kauta Msiska perceived the importance of what was occurring and remarked: "I think this is the beginning of church history in Nyasaland."[37] It was in the heat of the crisis that the identity of the church became clear.

The Breaking of the Banda Dictatorship

The Congress movement was so much the child of the Blantyre and Livingstonia Synods, with e.g. eight out of the ten members of the first Malawi Cabinet being products of the Presbyterian Missions, that the churches were caught off guard when decisive changes in the Malawi Congress Party during the early 1960s paved the way for the dictatorship and repression of the one-party system which prevailed from independence in 1964 until the rise of the democratic movement in 1992-93. For many years the Blantyre Synod appeared to be ideologically captive to the Banda regime. Its ministers were often called upon to officiate at state occasions and its General Secretary acted as an unofficial court chaplain to the Life President and his inner circle. So far did the church appear to have compromised with the regime that many began to doubt whether it

---

[37] Rev Stephen Kauta Msiska, cit. Bill Jackson, "Breaking Down the Wall: the Diary of a Participant in the Emergency of 1959," in *Bulletin of the Scottish Institute of Missionary Studies,* New Series No. 10 (1994), p. 46; see further Bill Jackson, Send Us Friends, np, nd [1996], pp. 70-136.

was anything more than the creature of Banda and his lackeys. 1992, however, brought a new crisis which provoked a fresh assertion of the identity of the church.

The turning point of recent Malawian history came on 8 March 1992 when the Catholic bishops issued their now famous Pastoral Letter *Living our Faith* which offered the first public criticism of the excesses and injustices of the one-party system.[38] As the Banda regime attempted to repel this challenge, it sought the support of the Presbyterian Synods with which it had long been allied. The support was not forthcoming and, indeed, the regime's ideological support structure was dealt a further blow when the Church of Scotland effectively disowned Kamuzu Banda as a practising elder.[39] Still Blantyre Synod itself took no public action until, early in June, its leadership united with that of Livingstonia and a delegation from the World Alliance of Reformed Churches to meet President Banda and call for the appointment of a broadly based Commission with the mandate "to make specific proposals for structural reform towards a political system with sufficient checks and balances on the use of power, and guarantees of accountability at all levels of government; to review the judicial system in line with the rule of law; to look into the distribution of income and wealth required by the demands of social justice."[40] From that day on, the Blantyre Synod was at the centre of a movement to promote radical political reform which took concrete expression in September 1992 with the formation of the Public Affairs Committee, a church-organized body which would

---

[38] *Living our Faith*. For an account of the impact of the Letter see *Malawi: A Moment of Truth,* London: CIIR, 1993; Jonathan Newell, "A Moment of Truth? The Church and Political Change in Malawi, 1992," *The Journal of Modern African Studies,* Vol. 33/2 (1995), pp. 243-262; Kenneth R. Ross, "The Truth Shall Set You Free: Christian Social Witness in Malawi 1992-93," *Journal of Theology for Southern Africa,* No. 90 (March 1995), pp. 17-30.

[39] See chapter six of the present work.

[40] "The Nation of Malawi in Crisis: the Church's Concern," Geneva: World Alliance of Reformed Churches, 2 June 1992, p. 2.

prove to be the engine of political change in the transition from single-party to multi-party politics during the 1992-93 period.[41]

With this gradual re-opening of a critical distance between church and state, the question of identity soon came to the surface within the Blantyre Synod. When the Synod Administrators issued a "Statement on the Role of the Church in the Transformation of Malawi in the Context of Justice and Peace," they began by asking the question "What is the Church?"[42] Amongst the answers they offered were:

> The Church is people and must be concerned with the wellbeing of people.
>
> The Church is Christ together with his people - one family under God whose purpose is to unite all people in Jesus Christ.
>
> The Church is both a local Church and a universal Church and is not limited by country, continents, race or gender.
>
> The Church is a unique wonder of the presence of God in a broken world.
>
> The nature of the Church is not determined by people but is determined by God himself.

These apparently straightforward explanations of the nature of the Church, in the particular context of the political crisis engulfing Malawi at that time, had the kind of profound application to national affairs which was classically exemplified by the Barmen Declaration

---

[41] See chapter five of the present work.

[42] "A Statement on the Role of the Church in the Transformation of Malawi in the Context of Justice and Peace," produced by the Administrators' Conference, Blantyre Synod CCAP, January 22-23 1993; repr. in Ross ed., *Christianity in Malawi*, pp. 217-222.

in Germany in the 1930s.[43] Once again in a moment of crisis the identity of the church became clear and southern Malawian Presbyterians were strengthened in their self-understanding and mission as a church.

Conclusion

A succession of crises has a cumulative effect, even if experienced over a century. The Blantyre Synod has now a *history* in which it has responded to several crises and in the process discovered and affirmed its identity as a church. Reflecting on and engaging with this particular history is one of the ways in which a viable theology can be formed, one that is rooted in the local situation yet carries universal relevance. As a community the Blantyre Synod has the sense that it is a church centred on Jesus Christ, drawing its strength from prayer, rooted in African soil with growth continuously shaped and informed by engagement with the Bible, confident in the gospel it proclaims, committed to justice, holding fast both to its ultimate commitment to Christ and to its penultimate commitment to building the nation. It is a church with a clear sense of its mandate to be a harbinger of the new humanity and prepared for the occasions when fulfillment of its mission brings it into sharp conflict with the "principalities and powers" of the old order. It is a church of the people, so grounded in the life of the rural poor that it finds itself at odds with any structures which promote elitism, domination or oppression.

Yet this deeply indigenous character is balanced by the strong sense of being part of an international fellowship. Entirely local leadership is combined with an ecumenical accountability. It is a church so grounded in the gospel that at moments of crisis, even if it has temporarily forgotten itself, it is able to draw on the "dangerous

---

[43] See, e.g., Charles Villa-Vicencio, *Between Christ and Caesar: Classic and Contemporary Texts on Church and State,* Grand Rapids: Eerdmans 8, Cape Town: David Philip, 1986, pp. 89-98.

memory" of Jesus Christ to determine where it should stand. It is a missionary church, driven by the impetus that its message must reach ever wider and deeper into the life of the community. This sense of ecclesiological identity has been developed not only from the day to day interaction of Christian faith and indigenous culture but particularly by the church's response to the moments of crisis which have arisen in its history.

Lamin Sanneh and Kwame Bediako have rightly drawn attention to the importance of the vernacular expression of Christian faith as the base for African Christian self-confidence and theological endeavour.[44] As Bediako has argued: "in the African Christianity of the post-missionary era, the extent to which a church can be said to possess a viable heritage of Christian tradition in its indigenous language is the extent of that church's ability to offer an adequate interpretation of reality and a satisfying intellectual framework for African life."[45] Confidence in the vernacular is no doubt integral to a viable theology in Africa but the referent is not only the indigenous *language* and *culture* of the Christian community but also its indigenous *history*. The particular history through which it has passed, the crises it has met and the response it has offered to them, have acted to form a robust and well-defined identity. The conflicts and struggles which have marked modern times in Africa have made their demands upon the churches and it is precisely as the churches have responded to these demands that there has emerged the kind of ecclesiological sense of identity which has been exemplified by the case of the Blantyre Synod of the Church of Central Africa Presbyterian in Malawi.

Perhaps the hesitation of African theologians to draw on history as a source for theological construction stems from a sense that the churches have been formed by *someone else's* history and that therefore it is a foreign and alienating point of reference. Yet, by now, very

---

[44] See Sanneh, *Translating the Message;* Bediako, *Christianity in Africa.*
[45] Kwame Bediako, *Christianity in Africa,* p. 61.

many African church movements have *themselves* passed through a rich and challenging history which has had the cumulative effect of forming a certain ecclesiological sense of identity. This offers to the theologian material which is wholly indigenous, deeply rooted in the life of the people and calling for discernment of the work of the Spirit of God. For an African church to celebrate its centenary or other anniversary, as many are doing in southern Africa these days, is not just an opportunity to mark a milestone or indulge in some nostalgic evocation of early days. It is to mark out a source from which its own distinctive, yet nonetheless universal, ecclesiology may be elaborated. Attending to history in this way will be necessary if Africa is to drink to the full "from her own wells" in theological construction.[46] What Malawi's history may tell us about Christ, church and nation, is explored in the remaining chapters of this book, beginning with a closer look at the churches' role in the transition from dictatorship to democracy in 1992-94.

---

[46] See Tinyiko Sam Maluleke, "Black and African Theologies in the New World Order: A Time to Drink from our Own Wells," *Journal of Theology for Southern Africa,* No. 96 (November 1996), pp. 3-19.

5. The Renewal of the State by the Church: the Case of the Public Affairs Committee

Political Reform in Malawi 1992-94

Despite the winds of political change blowing through Africa at the beginning of 1992 the one-party state in Malawi appeared to be firmly entrenched. Life President Kamuzu Banda was still able to make his famous threat that any exiled political opponents who returned to Malawi would be "meat for the crocodiles!" There was absolutely no public criticism of the regime within the country and the various groups of exiles appeared to be disorganized and demoralized. Prospects for radical political reform did not look good. Yet by May 1994 Malawi was holding its first multi-party General Election since independence in 1964 with the result that Banda's Malawi Congress Party was defeated and replaced in office by the United Democratic Front, a new party only 18 months old. At the same time a provisional Constitution came into effect which secured all basic human rights, and provided for the separation of powers in a democratic political system. When this Constitution, with only minor amendments, was adopted by Parliament in May 1995, the remarkable renewal of the state in Malawi can be judged to have been completed. Given the vigour and intensity of the police state which had been developed over thirty years by the MCP, it is a matter of surprise to many that the entire apparatus of the one-party system could be dismantled in the space of two years with relatively minimal violence.

No less surprising to many observers was the role played by the Christian churches in effecting this "velvet revolution." It had been commonly assumed that the witness of the churches had been fatally compromised by their unquestioning support of the dictatorship. Very few had any confidence that the churches might be effective agents in promoting radical political reform in the country. Yet the history of the political change cannot be told without acknowledging the leading role played by the churches in the process of reform. Much attention has deservedly been given to the Lenten Pastoral Letter issued by the Roman Catholic Bishops in March 1992 - the spark which ignited the fires of protest. By contrast, however, little attention has been given to a less dramatic initiative of the churches later that year when they formed the "Public Affairs Committee" to negotiate with Government on issues of political reform. The Pastoral Letter has a unique place in modern Malawian history as a decisive "moment of truth," a *kairos* for the nation. Yet it deserves notice that the witness of the churches did not consist only in the issuing of a decisive prophetic statement. When it came to the "nuts and bolts" of dismantling the apparatus of the one-party system and building a participatory democracy, the churches took a "hands on" approach through the work of the Public Affairs Committee. It is this aspect of the churches' political engagement which this essay attempts to bring into focus.

The Background: Church and Politics in Malawi

Fundamental to an accurate understanding of church and state in Malawi is the fact that the modern state was brought into being through the presence of Christian missions. In 1889, when Britain was on the point of ceding to Portugal a large part of what is now Malawi, it was a campaign organized primarily by the Scottish Presbyterian missions which led to the establishment of a British Protectorate in 1891.[1] While the missionaries supported the colonial state they were always ready to advance criticisms of any injustices for which they judged it to be responsible and there was frequently considerable tension between the colonial administration and the Christian missions.[2] This critique of the colonial state was taken

---

[1] See Ross, *Gospel Ferment in Malawi,* pp. 118-122.

[2] See Andrew C. Ross, "The African - 'A Child or a Man': the Quarrel between the Blantyre Mission of the Church of Scotland and the British Central Africa Administration 1890-1905," in E. Stokes & R. Brown, ed., *The Zambesian Past: Studies in Central African History,* Manchester: Manchester University Press,

much further by the Christian nationalists who emerged from the early decades of the 20th century and who finally achieved independence for Malawi in 1964. The integral involvement of especially the Scottish Presbyterian missions in the struggle for independence has been well documented.[3] This close involvement with the movement which became the Malawi Congress Party made it difficult to develop any critical distance when that Party formed the first government of independent Malawi.

This was acknowledged in a statement issued by the Blantyre Synod of the Church of Central Africa Presbyterian in 1993:

> If we look at our own history as the CCAP during the time of the struggle for Independence, we will see that Blantyre Synod was very much in support of the Nyasaland African Congress (later called the MCP). Because of this very verbal stance on the side of the MCP, after Independence, the CCAP was aligned closely with the government and became so assimilated with the government's activities that the Synod was often invited to pray and participate as a Church at various government functions. However, because of this assimilation and alignment with the MCP, the Church gradually lost its ability to admonish or speak pastorally to the government. We do not want to make the same mistake at this time in order to ensure that the Church retains its prophetic voice throughout the coming years of our country's history.[4]

The fact that most of the Congress, including Banda, were products of the Presbyterian missions and that many remained active

---

1966, pp. 332-51; and Andrew C. Ross, "The Blantyre Mission and the Problems of Land and Labour 1891-1915," in R.J. Macdonald, ed., *From Nyasaland to Malawi,* Nairobi: East African Publishing House, 1975, pp. 86-107.

[3] See K.N. Mufuka, *Missions and Politics in Malawi,* Kingston, Ontario: Limestone Press, 1977, pp. 146-195.

[4] "A Statement on the Role of the Church in the Transformation of Malawi in the Context of Justice and Peace," Produced by the Administrators Conference, Blantyre Synod CCAP, 22-23 January 1994, p. 4.

members made it very difficult for the Presbyterian Church to develop an independent position. When many of its lay leaders became victims of the purge which followed the "Cabinet crisis" of 1964, the CCAP was gripped by the climate of fear which dominated the country for the next thirty years.[5] The Roman Catholic and Anglican Churches, which had been less identified with Congress in the pre-independence period, had to tread even more carefully in the intolerant atmosphere which now prevailed. Whatever private misgivings may have been entertained by church leaders and members, the public political role of the churches was practically confined to offering unquestioning legitimation of the Banda regime.

The Catholic Bishops' Pastoral Letter, March 1992

In March 1992 the Roman Catholic Bishops issued their pastoral letter, entitled *Living our Faith*. Rarely in modern times can a church document have had such an immediately explosive effect in the life of a nation. Within four days the ruling Malawi Congress Party was convened in emergency session to pass an unreserved condemnation of the bishops. Possession of the letter was declared to be an act of sedition, punishable by severe penalties. There were unrestrained calls at the party convention for the bishops to be killed.[6] When this was followed by a leader entitled "No Mercy" in the government-controlled newspaper, experienced observers

---

[5] The "Cabinet crisis" was a watershed political event which occurred only a few weeks after Malawi became independent in 1964. The ministers who favoured a more open, democratic form of government were forced to resign and flee the country. Kamuzu Banda quickly and successfully developed the structures of political violence which would sustain his dictatorship for the next thirty years. See Andrew C. Ross, "Some Reflections on the Malawi 'Cabinet Crisis' 1964-65," *Religion in Malawi* Vol. 7 (1997), pp. 3-12.

[6] Tapes of this convention were later widely circulated and transcripts published in order to discredit the MCP Government. See, e.g., *The Nation*, Vol 1 Nos. 12-21 (2 Sept.-4 Oct. 1993).

feared that the bishops were being set up for assassination.[7] Yet even as the one-party system mustered its forces to stamp out the dissent, it became evident that there had been a dramatic shift in power. Politely but bluntly the Bishops had pointed out the shortcomings of the prevailing political order and their statements had such a ring of truth that the MCP regime was suddenly exposed. It was like the moment in the fairy tale when the little boy pointed out that the Emperor had no clothes! Things could never be the same again. Practically overnight the mode of discourse in everyday conversation began to change. One moment the MCP was all-powerful; the next it was becoming a laughing stock. The sense of liberation was palpable. So decisive was this moment that, in common parlance, modern Malawian history is divided into "before the Pastoral Letter" and "after the Pastoral Letter!"[8]

To the uninformed reader, much of the content of the Pastoral Letter would seem commonplace: concern about the poverty of the people and about shortcomings in provision for health and education. Its power lay in the fact that these were concerns which no one had been allowed to raise since all were obliged to subscribe to the myth that all Malawians had prospered under the beneficent reign of Kamuzu Banda. The Pastoral Letter voiced what everyone knew but no one had ever dared to say. It thus broke the culture of deceit which had been allowed to develop. This in itself was a very powerful political action. The Bishops, however, went further to question the entire nature and structure of Malawian political life. They struck to the heart of the problem with the Banda regime when they stated that: "Accountability is a quality of any good government. People are entitled to know how their representatives fulfil their

---

[7] See *Malawi News* 14-20 March 1992.

[8] Research conducted at Ntaja, Mwanza, Dowa and Nkhata Bay in November and December 1994 revealed that recognition of the Pastoral Letter as *the* turning-point in recent Malawian political life is practically universal at the popular level. See Gerard Chigona, Research Notes on Political Transition in Malawi, November-December 1994.

duties. No disrespect is shown when citizens ask questions in matters which concern them.[9] This call for accountability to the people marked the beginning of a process of democratization which was to transform Malawian political life during the coming two years. Perhaps the most powerful part of the Letter was found in a section entitled "The Participation of all in public life." The Bishops drew on both biblical texts (Ephesians 4:7-16 and I Peter 4:10-11) and traditional African proverbs to argue that society can be strong only when it enjoys the participation of all its members.

What this meant for Malawi was explained as follows:

> Human persons are honoured - and this honour is due to them - whenever they are allowed to search freely for truth, to voice their opinions and to be heard, to engage in creative service of the community in all liberty within associations of their own choice. Nobody should ever have to suffer reprisals for honestly expressing and living up to their convictions: intellectual, religious or political. We can only regret that this is not always the case in our country.... Academic freedom is seriously restricted; exposing injustices can be considered a betrayal; revealing some evils of our society is seen as slandering the country; monopoly of the mass media and censorship prevent the expression of dissenting views; some people have paid dearly for their political opinions; access to public places like markets, hospitals, bus depots etc, is frequently denied to those who cannot produce a party card; forced donations have become a way of life.[10]

The Bishops went on to sketch the effects of all this on national life and consciousness, the dark tragedy which had overcome Malawi in the years since independence: "It creates an atmosphere of resentment among citizens. It breeds a climate of mistrust and fear. This fear of harassment and mutual suspicion generates a society in which the talents of many lie unused and in which there is little room for

---

[9] *Living our Faith,* p. 10.

[10] Ibid, p. 9.

initiative."[11] First steps towards the restoration of a climate of trust and openness were proposed and these became Malawi's political agenda for the next two years: the establishment of an independent press, open forums of discussion, free association of citizens for social and political purposes, Government accountability, the establishment of independent, accessible and impartial courts of justice.[12] What remained was to see whether a peaceful process of political reform could be developed to put into effect the vision which had been expressed in the Pastoral Letter.

The Formation of the Public Affairs Committee

Despite intense government intimidation, support for the Pastoral Letter was soon made apparent. The following Sunday students of the University of Malawi marched in support of the Bishops, an action which resulted in the closure of the main University campus for the first time in its history.[13] A month later Chakufwa Chihana, the Malawian Secretary-General of the Southern African Trade Union Coordinating Council, returned to Malawi to begin a campaign for democratic change. In the speech which he attempted to make, before being arrested on the airport tarmac, Chihana appealed to the Pastoral Letter as an indication of the need for

---

[11] Ibid, pp. 9-11.

[12] Ibid.

[13] On 15 March 1992 Catholic students issued a letter entitled "We Support our Bishops" which included the following statements: "We praise and congratulate you for your courage in bringing out the Lenten pastoral letter *Living our Faith*. Undoubtedly, this pastoral letter will go down in our history as the most soul-searching document on current realities that has ever come out.... As your daughters and sons, we have been deeply distressed by the horrible insults and open abuses against you and the whole Malawian Catholic church.... The "we support our bishops walk" held on Sunday 15th March 1992 from Chancellor College to Zomba Cathedral for Mass, followed by a visit to the bishop's house, bears testimony to our unflinching solidarity for you and what you stand for." See *Religion in Malawi*, Vol. 7 (1997), pp. 39-40.

political reform.¹⁴ Later in April an unprecedented wave of strikes swept both the public and private sectors, forcing the government to implement massive wage rises. The strikes were accompanied by rioting and looting directed particularly at properties identified with the Malawi Congress Party - it was clear that the government faced a serious crisis. However, for some months it was unclear how the initiative of the Pastoral Letter could be taken up in a positive and constructive way. The Bishops themselves found it advisable to take a low profile for a time. It fell to the Presbyterians to begin to chart a way forward. Silas Ncozana, General Secretary of the CCAP Synod of Blantyre, being closely acquainted with the MCP system, decided that the best approach was to address President Banda directly.¹⁵ However, it proved difficult to organize united and decisive action. It now proved to be of significance that the Church of Central Africa Presbyterian belonged to an international fellowship of mutual accountability, namely the World Alliance of Reformed Churches.

In early June WARC sent a delegation to meet with the leaders of the Presbyterian churches in Malawi and together they presented an open letter to the Life President entitled "The Nation of Malawi in Crisis: the Church's Concern."¹⁶ They made direct reference to the Catholic Pastoral Letter, still technically a seditious document, and insisted that the government must address the issues which it raised.¹⁷ At this stage, however, what was required was more than a Presbyterian echo of the Catholic social critique. Practical proposals were needed. The church leaders accordingly called for the

---

¹⁴ *Independent* (British newspaper), 8 April 1992.

¹⁵ Int. Very Rev Dr Silas S. Ncozana, 28 June 1995.

¹⁶ 'The Nation of Malawi in Crisis: the Church's Concern," Geneva: World Alliance of Reformed Churches, 2 June 1992. An endorsement of this letter was signed by 55 ministers of the Synod of Livingstonia who agreed to read it out in their congregations. CCAP Synod of Livingstonia, "Statement to CCAP General Synod" 9 June 1992.

¹⁷ 'The Nation of Malawi in Crisis," p. 2.

appointment of a broadly based Commission with the mandate "to make specific proposals for structural reform towards a political system with sufficient checks and balances on the use of power, and guarantees of accountability at all levels of government; to review the judicial system, in line with the rule of law; to look into the distribution of income and wealth required by the demands of social justice."[18] Meanwhile the letter called for immediate steps to be taken to remove injustices: "end the practice of detention without trial; release or bring to early and fair trial all political detainees; reform conditions of imprisonment, in accordance with human dignity; allow freedom of expression and association, so as to encourage open discussion of the nation's future."[19]

These demands were powerfully reinforced by the decision in May of the Western donor community to suspend all development aid to Malawi until there was evidence of greater respect for human rights and "good governance." A process of reform was immediately undertaken by the government. Many political detainees were released. The International Committee of the Red Cross was invited to inspect the prisons. The practice of forced donations and the harassment of people who did not possess party cards was stopped. Painfully slowly, and with many obstructions along the way, the door began to be opened to freedom of expression and freedom of association. However, it was apparent that the government was hoping to placate its critics with relatively superficial reforms while maintaining the underlying structures of repression. Though the President had given a favourable reply to the Presbyterian open letter and had invited church leaders to meet with his ministers, the government stalled and was clearly reluctant to accede to the

---

[18] Ibid.

[19] Ibid.

formation of a forum where fundamental political issues would be addressed.[20]

The resultant delay proved to be a blessing in disguise to the forces of reform. For it provided the opportunity and the constraint to work towards a more broadly representative Commission including not only church leaders but also representatives of the Muslim Association, the Malawi Law Society and the Associated Chambers of Commerce and Industry.[21] At this point it was significant that the church leaders included not only clergy but also elders with a wealth of experience in national affairs.[22] Throughout July and August the Presbyterian church leaders worked hard behind the scenes to bring together a truly national and representative Commission.[23] [23] When the Christian Council, on 26 August 1992, called upon the government to hold a referendum on the system of government their letter was signed by representatives of the Anglican Church, all three Synods of the CCAP (though one later withdrew), the African Methodist Episcopal Church, the Seventh Day Baptist Church, the Churches of Christ, the Zambezi Evangelical Church, Providence Industrial Mission, the Baptist Convention and a number of para-church organizations.[24] Two days later, when the church leaders wrote to the government again, their letter was signed by

---

[20] The Hon W.B. Deleza, Minister without Portfolio, told the church leaders on 15 July 1992 that it was no longer necessary for them to meet with government ministers since the Life President had touched on all the issues in his address to the nation on 5 July 1992. See letter of Rt Rev Dr Silas Nyirenda and Rev Misanjo E. Kansilanga to the Hon Minister of State, Mr J.Z.U. Tembo M.P., 28 August 1992, Public Affairs Committee file 1992.

[21] "It was the lack of response of the MCP government which forced us to invite other people who were interested." Int. Rev Misanjo Kansilanga, 16 November 1994.

[22] Int. T.J. Muwamba, 4 January 1995.

[23] Int. Very Rev Dr S.S. Ncozana, 28 June 1995.

[24] Christian Council of Malawi, Open Letter to the Government of Malawi, 26 August 1992.

representatives not only of the Protestant churches but also the Roman Catholic Church, the Muslim Community, the business community and the Malawi Law Society.[25]

It is worth noting that this was the first time in Malawian history that Christian and Muslim leaders had publicly united to take a strategic socio-political initiative. Despite the fact that the Muslim participants were later disowned by the more conservative leadership within their own community, the formation of the PAC was a significant event in the history of Christian-Muslim relations in Malawi.[26] The significance of this united front was not lost on the government which immediately responded by insisting that the committee should be composed of church leaders only and must exclude the business community and the Law Society.[27] In a series of exchanges the government maintained this position but the church leaders were not to be moved: "The initiative of the Church should not be interpreted in a narrow sense, as if the issues for discussion are exclusively religious. The issues which moved the Church to call for a national dialogue were and remain national issues affecting all aspects of the lives of the citizens of this country."[28]

The PAC and the National Referendum

When the "Public Affairs Committee" finally sat down with the "Presidential Committee on Dialogue" it did so as the representative

---

[25] Letter of Rt Rev Dr Silas Nyirenda and Rev Misanjo E. Kansilanga to the Hon Minister of State, Mr J.Z.U. Tembo M.P., 28 August 1992, Public Affairs Committee file 1992.

[26] Interviews conducted within the Muslim community by Dr J.C. Chakanza, February 1995.

[27] Letter of Hon J.Z.U. Tembo, Minister of State, to Rt Rev Dr Silas Nyirenda and Rev Misanjo E. Kansilanga, 7 September 1992, Public Affairs Committee file, 1992.

[28] Letter of Rev M.E. Kansilanga to Hon Bester Bisani M.P., Chairman of the Presidential Committee on Dialogue, 12 October 1992, Public Affairs Committee file, 1992.

organ of a truly national constituency. It was the first time that a non-party organization had been recognized as having a role to play in national political life. The PAC planned to press for a national referendum on the question of one-party or multi-party system of government when they met the PCD for the first time on 19 October 1992. In order to forestall this initiative the President himself, on 18 October, announced the government's intention to hold such a referendum.[29] This announcement prompted a second "pressure group," the United Democratic Front (UDF), to join Chakufwa Chihana's Alliance for Democracy (Aford) in the public arena. Chihana himself was by this time on trial for sedition. His two year sentence was reduced on appeal to six months (which, suspiciously, kept him in prison until just after the referendum campaign was completed.)

It is worth noting that his Mitigation Statement during the appeal case began with the following statement: "I come from a family which has strong Christian traditions, i.e. the fear and adoration of God, respect for human beings and the readiness to assist others in need of help. Throughout my life these Christian values have had considerable influence and have become the rockbed of my present social and political behaviour."[30] While giving attention to the institutional role of the churches, analysis of this period should not neglect the witness of lay Christians in the political arena. At the same time it must be observed that at this early stage the budding political parties worked to a considerable extent under the umbrella of the PAC which remained the engine of political reform during the referendum period. It was the Public Joint Statement indicating their resolve to "prosecute all persons who engage in incitement to

---

[29] *Daily Times,* 19 October 1992.

[30] Chakufwa Chihana, "The Bumpy Road to Freedom: Mitigation Statement on Sedition Trial 1992," undated photocopy, p. 1.

political violence and violence itself and ... to protect the fundamental right of persons to hold political views. "[31]

Despite this paper agreement the MCP government continued to use its familiar tactics of intimidation and violence in a vain attempt to stop the tidal wave of support which was gathering behind the multi-party movement. In the aftermath of the Pastoral Letter it had been immensely important that there were individuals who were prepared to defy such intimidation and to suffer for their convictions. The Bishops themselves had stood by their Letter and had defied all attempts to force an apology and retraction. Their firm stand encouraged others to speak out. Prominent among them was Rev Aaron Longwe, a Presbyterian minister in the northern town of Mzuzu, who was detained and interrogated after delivering a sermon on Micah 7:1-7 on 26 April 1992.[32] Soon the message in many pulpits included a biblically based critique of the prevailing one-party system and it was not unusual to hear of ministers being arrested.[33] Many ordinary people also suffered at this time. A woman office-worker arrested in May 1992 as a suspected multi-party sympathizer described her treatment while in detention: "They said 'You are in the hands of the government. We can do anything we like with your life.' Then they ripped the clothes off me. They left me naked. They made me lie down. One pulled my legs. One man had pliers. They forced my knees and my legs apart.

---

[31] Joint Statement by the President's Committee on Dialogue and the Public Affairs Committee, Kwacha Conference Centre, Blantyre, 13 November 1992.

[32] On his release he was told not to preach again from the book of Micah! See J.L. Wilkie, "The First Detention (in Mzuzu, Malawi) of the Rev Aaron Longwe and Mr Chenda Mkandawire 27-30 April 1992, Confidential Church of Scotland Report, 7 May 1992.

[33] E.g. when the Church, Peace, Justice and Politics Committee of Livingstonia Synod met on 1 September 1992 its business included the arrest and detention of three of its ministers. Committee Minutes, Livingstonia Synod office.

They started putting the pliers into my anus. I was crying at the top of my voice."[34]

Even after the PAC-PCD dialogue had begun the intimidation continued. A series of assassination attempts on the Acting PAC Chairman Rev Emmanuel Chinkwita has been documented by Amnesty International: "The most recent incident occurred on 4 January 1993, when Reverend Chinkwita was at a bus stop on the outskirts of Lilongwe late at night. A car drove at high speed directly at him and he was only saved by a friend who pulled him out of its path. Eye-witnesses believed that the car had deliberately aimed to hit him. On two separate earlier occasions, in November and December 1992, it appeared that he had been the victim of an attempt to poison him by impregnating his clothes with organo-phosphate poisons, which function by interfering with the transmission of nerve impulses, leading to impairment of basic body functions and, in some cases, to irreversible damage and death."[35]

Another target was the PAC Secretary, Rev Misanjo Kansilanga, who on one occasion was denounced as a dissident at a public meeting by an MCP district chairman who remarked to the Life President: *"Bwana kuli chiswe chanu ku MCP Headquarters ... ndipo tithana nawo anthu oterewa"* which was taken to mean that the President had death squads at the MCP Headquarters who would deal with such people.[36] Kansilanga himself has described his experience during this period: "MCP top brass went to our home areas and informed our relatives that we were not good people. We had become rebels. They were inciting people in our home areas to bash our cars, to burn our property and all sorts of things. I lost a whole granary in my home

---

[34] *Malawi: Presenting the One-Party State - Human Rights Violations and the Referendum,* London: Amnesty International, 18 May 1993, p. 2.

[35] Ibid, p. 10.

[36] See Letter from the CCAP Synod of Blantyre to the Hon J.Z.U. Tembo, Minister of State, on "Public Denunciation of the Rev Misanjo E. Kansilanga," 6 November 1992.

area and my two houses were burnt down during the referendum campaign period.... My car was stoned and I was followed on several occasions - a car following me wherever I went. So we knew that we were in danger."[37] The fact that there were people willing to defy such intimidation meant that the long-established system of political control by means of violence was now breaking down. When relatives and friends of Misanjo Kansilanga advised him to withdraw from his involvement with PAC he told them: "I am not doing my own thing. I did not choose this. But I believe that this is God's work. If it is God's work then it is God himself who has life in his hands, so if I am killed praises will go to God and you shouldn't cry."[38] The fact that there were individuals who were moved by this level of faith and commitment was a highly significant factor in introducing accountability to Malawian political life.

As the national referendum of 16 June 1993 approached, it became ever more apparent that the government was fighting a losing battle. Huge crowds flocked to the multi-party rallies while MCP campaign meetings in much of the country were subject to a virtual boycott. Only in its heartlands in the Central Region were traditional MCP tactics successful in retaining substantial support.[39] It was no surprise when the electorate voted for a multi-party system by a two-thirds majority. Significant for the future was the fact that the one third which supported the maintenance of the one-party system was concentrated very largely in the Central Region. In the conscientization process necessary to the achievement of such a result, the churches were prominent. The PAC set up an organization called PACREM - Public Affairs Committee Referen-

---

[37] Int. Rev Misanjo E. Kansilanga, 16 November 1994.

[38] Ibid.

[39] These tactics included the use of poison to eliminate opponents, intimidation by Nyau dancers and the threat that all multi-party supporters would be exterminated after the MCP had won the referendum. Gerard Chigona, Research Notes on interviews conducted at Madisi, 29-30 November 1994.

dum Monitoring - which quickly drew attention to any abuses and gave people the confidence that they could vote freely.[40] When interviewed many people have indicated that it was at church that they learned of the possibility of political reform and began to give their support to the multi-party cause.[41]

Particularly influential was a further Pastoral Letter from the Roman Catholic Bishops entitled "Choosing our Future." The Bishops' assessment was that "what people are seeking is genuine democracy in which the leaders are servants of the people who elected them and not their masters, in which leaders are answerable and accountable for their actions to those they lead, a true government of the people: not a government by or for the privileged few."[42] The Letter aimed to be educational, explaining the issue to be decided by the referendum and listing the advantages and disadvantages of both single-party and multi-party systems. While genuinely attempting to be balanced, the Letter was read as a stinging indictment of the injustices of the one-party system. This point was not lost on the government whose newspaper carried this response: "The contents of this letter are clearly advocating a multi-party system of government without considering the dangers that this system can bring to this country.... The Church is instilling FEAR and HATRED in the people. This is done every time people congregate at various churches."[43] With such statements the government itself testified to the telling effect which the churches' witness had in mobilizing public opinion and bringing the regime to account. The Catholic Press at Balaka was particularly effective as a publisher of

---

[40] See document entitled "PAC Referendum/Election Monitoring Unit," Public Affairs Committee file, 1992.

[41] See Gerard Chigona, Research Notes on Political Transition in Malawi, conducted at Ntaja, Mwanza, Dowa and Nkhata Bay, November-December 1994.

[42] "Choosing our Future: Pastoral Letter to the Catholic Faithful on the occasion of the National Referendum 1993," Episcopal Conference of Malawi, 2 February 1993.

[43] *Malawi News,* 6-12 March 1993.

material suitable for education in democracy. It was able to produce small pamphlets which sold for 10 tambala (US$ 0.025) and were therefore affordable by ordinary people. These were often composed of short extracts from papal encyclicals or UN declarations but also included some locally written statements.[44] Officially, the churches restricted themselves to spelling out the principles which should guide people in voting. The gap between Christian principles and MCP rule was so obvious, however, that the church was clearly perceived to be on the side of political reform. With few exceptions the "mainstream churches" had effectively "taken sides" with the multi-party movement.[45]

---

[44] Amongst the pamphlets are the Universal Declaration of Human Rights, the Human and People's Rights Adopted by the Organization of African Unity, extracts from *Centesimus Annus,* quotations from Jon Sobrino on "Political Holiness," a Pastoral Letter by the Diocese of Lilongwe, and anonymous statements on such topics as "What is Democracy," Balaka: Montfort Press, 1992.

[45] For studies of the 1992-93 period see [Kenneth R. Ross], *Kirche und Gesellschaft in Malawi: Die Krise von 1992 in historischer Perspektive,* Hamburg: EMW Informationen No. 98, February 1993; *Malawi: A Moment of Truth,* London: CIIR, July 1993; Trevor Cullen, *Malawi: A Turning Point,* Edinburgh: The Pentland Press, 1994; Nzunda & Ross ed., *Church, Law and Political Transition;* Jonathan Newell, "A Moment of Truth?' The Church and Political Change in Malawi in 1992," *The Journal of Modern African Studies,* Vol. 33/2 (1995), pp. 243-62; Jonathan Newell, "A Difficult Year for us in Many Respects': Pressure for Change and Government Reaction in Malawi in 1992: An Exercise in Contemporary African History," in J. Hyslop ed., *Democratic Movements in Africa.* forthcoming; Kenneth R. Ross, "Not Catalyst But Ferment: The Distinctive Contribution of the Churches to Political Reform in Malawi 1992-93," in Paul Gifford ed., *The Churches and Africa's Democratization,* Leiden: Brill, 1995, pp. 98-107; Jan Kees van Donge, "Kamuzu's Legacy: the Democratization of Malawi," *African Affairs,* Vol. 94 (1995), pp. 227-57.

The Church as Power-Broker

The victory of the multi-party advocates in the National Referendum of June 1993 led to the legalizing of opposition political parties and the promise of a General Election which was finally held on 17 May 1994. In the struggle for legitimacy between government and opposition during this period the churches played an important role as power brokers. By virtue of the fact that they were not seeking political office for themselves church leaders came to exercise a distinctive influence on the unfolding political drama. The MCP government had long been aware of the ideological power of religion in the political realm. Systematically and successfully over many years it had pressed the churches into service to supply it with religious legitimation. It was a major blow, in the aftermath of the Pastoral Letter, when the Church of Scotland made it clear it no longer regarded Banda as an active elder.[46] The extent to which the government was stung into serious over-reaction at that time is a measure of how much it depended on the unquestioning support of the church. This was further indicated, after almost all churches had rallied behind the work of PAC, by the importance which the government attached to the continuing support of the Nkhoma Synod - the Central Region section of the CCAP which had strong historical links with the MCP leadership.[47]

As it struggled to retain an air of legitimacy it turned to ministers of the Nkhoma Synod to officiate at government functions and to generally show solidarity with the MCP. This they were willing to do especially during the early referendum period.[48] Belatedly the Nkhoma Synod did seek to draw back from its unqualified support of the MCP government with a statement in April 1993 that "the

---

[46] See chapter six of the present work.

[47] For the history of the Nkhoma Synod see C. Martin Pauw, "Mission and Church in Malawi: The History of the Nkhoma Synod of the Church of Central Africa Presbyterian 1889-1962," DTh., University of Stellenbosch, 1980.

[48] See, e.g., *Daily Times*, 6 November 1992.

Synod believes that genuine Christians can support either side of the referendum question without violating the genuine ideals and principles of Christianity."[49] This attempt at "neutrality" did not convince the other churches which saw it simply as an evasion of the demands of the gospel. It did, however, leave the government even more bereft of the church endorsement on which it had depended in the past. In desperation, the MCP attempted to supply its own religious legitimation. When it launched its campaign newspaper, the *Guardian Today*, it was striking to note how many articles were devoted to portraying the MCP as having a divine mandate. This was epitomized by a cartoon series on the theme "MCP Points to God! Multi-Party - Horns of the Devil!"[50] Such desperate propaganda revealed how much the MCP government had depended on the legitimation which it had received from the churches in the preceding years. Once the churches had broken out of that ideological captivity, the MCP government faced a crisis of legitimacy which it was unable to surmount.

On the other hand, the emergent opposition was able constantly to appeal to the prophetic critique of the churches as justification for its political initiative. Indeed, the manifesto of the United Democratic Front, the first to be issued by an opposition party after the referendum, began with a quotation from the Pastoral Letter and stated that the movement for political reform had been initiated in response to the call from the Catholic Bishops.[51] Occasions such as the Requiem Mass held in May 1993 for four politicians who were widely believed to have been assassinated by government agents ten years earlier, were highly charged politically and very damaging to the credibility of the government.[52] It was no surprise that, when UDF

---

[49] *Daily Times*, 30 April 1993.

[50] See, e.g., *Guardian Today*, Vol 1 No 7, 19-25 May 1993.

[51] *UDF Manifesto*, July 1993, p. 1.

[52] See *The Monitor*, Vol 2 No 13, 18 May 1993. One of the fist actions of the newly elected UDF government in June 1994 was to appoint a Commission to investigate

leader Bakili Muluzi made his victory speech after the National Referendum, he went out of his way to thank the churches: "In particular, I would like to single out the seven Catholic Bishops and the [Presbyterian] Blantyre Synod."[53] In a country where the Christian faith is highly esteemed by a large proportion of the population, the legitimacy which the churches bestowed on the opposition movement, in face of government attempts to brand its leaders "dissidents" and "confusionists," was a considerable factor in enabling the forces of change to succeed.

At the popular level, a significant factor was that many church songs were adapted to give expression to the movement for political liberation. Church choirs are very popular among young people and they took their church music as a medium for expressing a particular political message. So *Ndiri ndi Bwenzi Langa Yesu* (I have my beloved friend Jesus) became *Ndiri ndi Bwenzi Langa Muluzi* (I have my beloved friend Muluzi - the leader of the UDF).[54] In this way there occurred at the popular level a conflation of Christian belief with the call for political reform. Particularly influential were the songs of Paul Banda and the Alleluya Band. In a powerful song like *Tiyamike Chiuta* (Let us praise God) they played on the symbols of the opposing sides in the referendum - the hurricane lamp of the multi-party side and the black cock of the one-party side - to suggest an identification of multi-party with the light of Jesus Christ and of one-party with the darkness of Satan.[55] A notable feature of the ideological struggle was that the opposition began to argue that Rev John Chilembwe, a Baptist pastor, not *Ngwazi* Kamuzu Banda. was

---

the "Mwanza accident." The release of its report, which confirmed suspicions of foul play, in January 1995 led to the immediate arrest of former President Kamuzu Banda and his right hand man John Tembo, who were later acquitted of charges of conspiracy to murder.

[53] *UDF News,* Vol 1 No 21, 17-24 June 1993.

[54] Gerard Chigona, Research conducted at Ntaja, 23 November 1994.

[55] Paul Banda, *Chikondi,* (cassette tape), Andiamo Productions 1993.

the father of Malawian politics.⁵⁶ There were good historical grounds for doing so since Chilembwe led an armed rising against British colonial rule in 1915.⁵⁷ A popular song during the campaign period, entitled *Kuno Kwathu ku Malawi*, suggested that just as Chilembwe fought against the oppression of the colonialists so he would fight against the oppression of Dr Banda and the MCP.⁵⁸ It was notable that when the new government announced the public holidays for the 1995 calendar, Kamuzu Day was missing and Chilembwe Day had been introduced!⁵⁹

For the churches there was a struggle involved in adapting to the new role as power-broker. On the one hand, some church leaders became so involved in the political arena that they eventually left the church ministry in order to devote themselves to politics. From Blantyre Synod Rev Peter Kaleso became Aford Vice-President before later joining the UDF and becoming Ambassador to South Africa.⁶⁰ From Livingstonia Synod Aaron Longwe embarked on full-time human rights work with the newly established Foundation for Justice, Peace and the Integrity of Creation.⁶¹ From the Baptist Convention, Emmanuel Chinkwita became first a shadow cabinet minister and parliamentary candidate then later ambassador to Mozambique.⁶² In each case it had to be made clear that they were acting as politicians in their own right and no longer as representatives of their churches. On the other hand, there were

---

[56] See, e.g., *The Monitor*, Vol 1 No 9, 28 April to 4 May 1993.

[57] A full account of the rising is found in Shepperson & Price, *Independent African*, Edinburgh: University Press, 1958.

[58] Gerard Chigona, Research conducted at Ntaja, 24 November 1994.

[59] For discussion of the political importance of the "Chilembwe myth" see Klaus Fiedler, "Joseph Booth and the Writing of Malawian History: An Attempt at Interpretation," *Religion in Malawi*, Vol. 6 (1996), p. 38.

[60] See, e.g., *The New Voice*, 15 March 1994.

[61] See, e.g., *The Democrat*, 29 November-2 December 1993.

[62] See, e.g., *Daily Times*, 19 November 1993.

those who believed that the churches became too detached from the political process, especially in the post-referendum period. When legislation was being passed in Parliament to establish the National Consultative Council and the National Executive Committee as the bodies which would oversee the transition to a multi-party political system, the Public Affairs Committee declined to be represented and thus left the process of reform entirely in the hands of the political parties.[63] This allowed the government later to claim that PAC was a body which had a role only in the pre-referendum period and which was now obsolete.[64]

However, the Christian Council responded by affirming very clearly that "PAC is a relevant body and there is need for its continuity now and after the General Elections. The Church being the Conscience of Society shall continue to play this noble and prophetic role.... The formation of NCC and NEC does not mean the non-existence of PAC. PAC is here to stay forever in Malawi."[65] In the run-up to the General Election PAC was particularly active in working to avoid the "Kenyan scenario" of a divided opposition allowing the old regime to remain in power.[66] In civic education and election monitoring the churches remained by far the most effective organization and contributed significantly to the General Election being a very peaceful and highly efficient exercise.[67] The Public Affairs Committee made the church a significant force as a power broker. Integral to this development was the unity of the various groupings which allowed the PAC Secretary to sign himself in communications

---

[63] Int. T.J. Muwamba, 4 January 1995.

[64] *Daily Times,* 9 November 1993.

[65] Christian Council of Malawi, Press Release, 12 November 1993.

[66] See PAC meetings with Leaders of Different Political Parties, 14 December 1993 and 6 January 1994, Public Affairs Committee files, 1993, 1994.

[67] PACREM was replaced by PACGEM - Public Affairs Committee General Election Monitoring. See Public Affairs Committee file, November 1993.

with government: "On behalf of the country's Religious Communities I beg to remain, Yours very sincerely, Misanjo E. Kansilanga."

The Future of the Public Affairs Committee

It has come to be widely recognized that the churches acted to a significant extent as the midwives of the new political dispensation in Malawi. The Public Affairs Committee was a key instrument in this process. Having reviewed the role which it played, the outstanding question concerns the future of PAC. Was it simply an ad hoc Committee addressing a particular set of needs at a particular time? Or does it have a permanent place at the interface between religion and politics in Malawi? It is too early to answer this question with any certainty. However, it is notable that in mid-1995, when a number of the new human rights organizations had already lost their credibility, the voice of PAC still carried considerable weight. In May 1995, e.g., PAC was able to bring together leading politicians from all the main parties for a "Round-table" aimed at promoting tolerance and reconciliation. The new PAC Chairman, Bishop Tarsisius Ziyaye, warned the political leaders: "Nobody will come from outside to find solutions to our problems.... Collectively we should endeavour to find solutions instead of pointing fingers at each other."[68] In August PAC sent an open letter to the President criticizing the government for being accountable to international institutions rather than its own people and, in particular, for resisting World Bank recommendations to trim the cabinet while agreeing to remove the subsidies on fertilizers.[69]

It is worth noticing the attention which this letter was given in an editorial of the Nation, the country's most respected daily newspaper: "We find this statement significant not only because of its contents but more because of its source. This is the same body

---

[68] *Nation*, 19 *May* 1995.

[69] *Nation*, 24 August 1995.

under which the two coalition partners [UDF and AFORD] fought with the MCP to get rid of the one-party dictatorship. This is a body composed of clergy who played a very effective role to transform the country's political system, and whose influence surpasses any other in this country. The statement is reminiscent of the historic Pastoral Letter through which the Catholic bishops unleashed their might behind the suffering of the people of Malawi and helped transform society. We are very hopeful that, coming from the clergy as it does, the concern will be taken seriously by government and that appropriate action will be taken."[70] Such a response to a PAC open letter in the second year of the new political dispensation suggests that it may well continue to play an important role in national affairs. Perhaps the real test of its effectiveness, however, will be how far it is able to galvanize participatory democracy at the grassroots level. The current challenge of democratization in Malawi is to undergird the multi-party system with a vibrant civil society.[71] No network is better placed than that of the churches to promote active local participation in the political process and the Public Affairs Committee could have a major role to play in the realization of that massive potential.

---

[70] *Nation,* 25 August 1995.

[71] See Kings M. Phiri & Kenneth R. Ross ed., *Democratization in Malawi: A Stocktaking,* Gweru: Mambo Press, 1998; especially chapters by J.R. Minnis, "Prospects and Problems for Civil Society in Malawi," pp. 127-145; and Peter von Doepp, "The Kingdom Beyond *Zasintha:* Churches and Political Life in Malawi's Post-authoritarian Era," pp. 102-126.

6. Partnership in Mission and Postcolonial Politics: the Case of the Church of Scotland and the CCAP

If the churches have socio-political significance because of their strength on the ground in Malawi, it is equally true that their relationships at the international level can prove to be of strategic importance. Of all such relationships, the longest standing is that between the Church of Central Africa Presbyterian and the Church of Scotland. Something of the political importance of the Scottish Missions in Malawian pre-colonial and colonial history has already been indicated in chapter four. Here we turn our attention to the post-colonial period. Already, well before political independence, the Blantyre and Livingstonia Missions had "handed over" full responsibility for the church to local leadership. Now they would relate as "church to church" rather than "church to mission." It was also expected that direct Church of Scotland engagement with Malawian socio-political issues would not continue. That would be the business of the local church. This position was maintained for thirty years, even in face of the development of a highly oppressive political system which brought deep injustice and much suffering to the people of Malawi. As World Mission General Secretary Chris Wigglesworth explained:

> The feeling was that people on the spot had to get on with things. For a long time, while providing economic assistance and skilled personnel that was clearly needed (and still is), the Church of Scotland leaned over backwards to respect the self-government rights of our sister church in Malawi wanting to make up its own mind on various things. This approach was partly the result of a corrective mechanism to counter the colonial mentality which assumed that direction should come from the outside. So, if the Malawi church leadership felt that the best thing was not to say too much then we had to be

guided by that rather than appearing to interfere. But as everybody knows, the situation towards the end of 1991 was clearly deteriorating.[1]

In fact, the situation in 1991, in terms of human rights abuse, was much better than at earlier periods when the Church of Scotland had felt justified in remaining silent. In reality, it was not the internal situation in Malawi which had changed so much as the international context. The collapse of Communism in eastern Europe, the end of the Cold War and the new-found concern of Western nations about good governance and human rights in Africa had given rise to what Larry Diamond has called "a global democratic 'zeitgeist' of unprecedented scope and intensity."[2] It was within this new international situation that there opened up new possibilities for church engagement with the Malawian political order. This chapter, through an examination of recent history, will question whether it was realistic for the Church of Scotland to expect to be able to withdraw from direct political responsibility in Malawi. The main focus will be on the part played by the Church of Scotland in the rapid political change of 1992-94 but to put this in context it is necessary to review certain aspects of earlier post-independence history.

---

[1] Chris Wigglesworth in Joanna Lewis, Peggy Owens & Louise Pirouet eds., *Human Rights and the Making of Constitutions: Malawi, Kenya, Uganda,* African Studies Centre, University of Cambridge, 1995, pp. 101-102.

[2] Larry Diamond, "The Globalization of Democracy: Trends, Types, Causes and Prospects" in R. Slater et al. eds., *Global Transformation and the Third World,* Boulder: Lynne Rienner, 1992, p. 37; cf. Samuel P. Huntington, *The Third Wave: Democratization in the Late Twentieth Century,* Norman: University of Oklahoma Press, 1992.

Legitimation of a Dictator: Kamuzu Banda as Kirk Elder

As the post-independence period unfolded it became clear that the Church of Scotland would not have any choice as to whether it should play a part in the political ideology of independent Malawi. Kamuzu Banda, the Life President (Dictator) who ruled Malawi from 1964 to 1992, had been ordained an elder of the Church of Scotland while he was a medical student in Edinburgh in 1941.[3] When he came to power in Malawi, Banda was shrewd enough to recognize that he ruled over a religious, predominantly Christian and notably Presbyterian population. Religious, Christian and, if possible, Presbyterian legitimation of his authority would form an important part of the ideological apparatus which would be required to keep him in power. Hence it became a familiar part of his rhetoric that he was an "elder of the Church of Scotland." Given the high esteem in which the Church of Scotland was generally held, this status acted to bolster his authority.

Curiously, he never became a member of the Church of Central Africa Presbyterian and appeared at worship only on national occasions. In the business of religious-political power play, it seems that he preferred to appeal "over the head" of the local church to his status as kirk elder. This was consonant with the quasi-European persona which he developed, e.g., by always wearing an immaculate three-piece suit, raincoat and Homburg hat and by refusing to speak any language other than English. It meant that, whether it liked it or not, the Church of Scotland was a potent factor in the legitimation of the dictatorship. As Lupenga Mphande explains:

> Upon [Banda's] arrival in Malawi, he publicly declared that while in Scotland he had become an Elder of the Church of

---

[3] "It was in 1941 in Guthrie Memorial Church in Easter Road my father and the Kirk Session of that congregation ordained Hastings Banda as an Elder." Rev. Dr Fergus Macpherson, Verbatim Record of the Proceedings of the General Assembly of the Church of Scotland, 1992, p. 648.

Scotland. With that announcement his mission and that of the Livingstonian missionaries in the country were enjoined: during the more than thirty years of his atrocious reign of terror never once did the Scottish-oriented Church in Malawi raise a voice of protest.[4]

The importance of the Church of Scotland connection was particularly apparent when the Banda regime began to come under pressure following the end of the Cold War in 1989.

As the government struggled to sustain its legitimacy there was a renewed emphasis on Banda's status as kirk elder. Indeed he travelled to Edinburgh in 1991 in order to receive a scroll honouring him for being an Elder of the Church of Scotland for fifty years. This was presented to him by the Moderator, Rt Rev. W.B.R. Macmillan, on 29 October 1991 at a special luncheon at Edinburgh Castle hosted by Rev. Charles Robertson of Canongate Kirk. This was not an event organized by the Board of World Mission and Unity and was regarded by its officials as a private occasion arranged by a few friends of Dr Banda.[5] It did not feature in the British press. Very different was the interpretation advanced by the Malawi Government. When Parliament opened in December members were instructed that they must congratulate the President on his achievements as an elder and make reference to the Edinburgh Castle ceremony. Many speakers in the House dwelt on the fact that the President had been recognized not only as a great statesman but also as a great churchman![6] When the government-controlled *Daily Times* reviewed the year 1991, its front page carried a colour photograph of Banda receiving the scroll from the Moderator, with

---

[4] Lupenga Mphande, "Dr Hastings Kamuzu Banda and the Malawi Writers Group: The (un)Making of a Cultural Tradition," *Research in African Literatures*, Vol. 27/1 (Spring 1996), pp. 80-101 [86].

[5] Rev. Jim Wilkie, interview, Edinburgh, 31 October 1996.

[6] *Hansard,* December 1991 *passim.*

Robertson and "Official Hostess" Mama Kadzamira looking on.[7] This is described as a "TRIUMPHANT MOMENT." As the dictatorship approached a time of testing, the Church of Scotland was playing a prominent role in providing it with the religious legitimation without which no government in Malawi would be secure.

To people in Malawi it was perplexing that the Church of Scotland should appear to be unhesitatingly supporting the dictatorship under which thousands upon thousands of Malawians were harassed, beaten, maimed, raped, imprisoned, exiled and murdered. The number of those subjected to torture during the Banda era was recently estimated at between 250,000 and 500,000.[8] The tip of this iceberg of suffering was made known internationally by such human rights organizations as Amnesty International and Africa Watch.[9] Still the Church of Scotland was silent and allowed itself to be manipulated by the propaganda of the dictatorship so as to function as an ideological prop to the Banda regime. The bafflement of the Malawi people was not restricted to those who suffered physical torture. As broadcaster Joyce Ng'oma vividly put it: "I think we all felt detained, though we didn't go into detention."[10] In this context the Church of Scotland's identification with the repressive "Big Brother" was difficult for people to understand. The rationale for remaining silent was that the Church of Scotland had "handed over"

---

[7] *Daily Times* 30 December 1991.

[8] Mr Y.A. Lambat, UDF MP for Blantyre Rural-East, speaking in the Malawi Parliament during the debate on the National Compensation Tribunal. *Hansard,* Tuesday 19 March 1996, p. 500.

[9] See, e.g., *Malawi: Human Rights Violations 25 Years After Independence,* London: Amnesty International, 1989; *Where Silence Rules: The Suppression of Dissent in Malawi,* Washington and London: Africa Watch, 1990; and *Malawi: Prison Conditions, Cruel Punishment and Detention Without Trial,* London: Amnesty International, 1992.

[10] Mrs Joyce Ng'oma, interview by Dr Isabel Apawo Phiri, Blantyre, 9 January 1995.

to the "local church" and it would not be legitimate to "interfere" in the church-state relations in independent Malawi. Indeed, in the post-independence period there was a sense of allowing time for Malawians to address social and political problems on their own initiative. As Stanley Hood, writing as Convener of the Sub-Saharan Africa Committee in 1992, explained: "For many years the Church of Scotland remained silent on the denial of human rights in Malawi. We were much criticised for our silence. But we recognized that Malawi was a young country, and hoped that, in due time, the situation would improve."[11]

Furthermore, those holding office in Edinburgh were deeply conscious that any move they made that was unfavourably received by the Banda regime could have very serious repercussions for the church and its leaders on the ground in Malawi.[12] As they explained, when breaking their silence in 1992: "We in Scotland have been reluctant so far to comment publicly on these matters out of a concern not to place members of our sister church in Malawi in danger."[13] It was also considered advisable to keep Church of Scotland personnel on the ground in Malawi while hoping for a better day. For these reasons they felt justified, even if uncomfortable, to keep quiet and allow the Church of Scotland to be part of the ideological support structure of the Banda regime. David Lyon, General Secretary of the Overseas Council (later Board of World Mission and Unity) from 1974 to 1987 has recalled the "anger, disappointment and frustration" with which he regarded the Banda dictatorship and has stated that, "my conscience is not clear."[14] The Kirk's position is viewed today with equal regret by many Malawians. As the present Blantyre Synod General Secretary, Misanjo

---

[11] Rev. Stanley Hood to Hon. Dr Hetherwick Ntaba, 18 June 1992.

[12] Rev. David Lyon, interview, Edinburgh, 31 October 1996.

[13] Statement by Department of World Mission and Unity, Church of Scotland Press Office News Release, 16 March 1992.

[14] Rev. David Lyon, interview, Edinburgh, 31 October 1996.

Kansilanga, commented: "The silence of the Church of Scotland gave the impression that everything was okay in Malawi. We *could* not speak. How we wished *you* would speak for us!"[15]

Finally, the time did come for the Church of Scotland to speak. On 8 March 1992 the Roman Catholic bishops issued their Pastoral Letter *Living our Faith*. This was the first public criticism of the Banda regime to be made within Malawi and it proved to be the catalyst of profound political change in the two years which followed, as we indicated in chapter five. At the time, Banda reacted angrily to the Letter and, perhaps in an attempt to divide the churches at this critical point, appealed to his Scottish Presbyterian credentials. As the *Daily Times* reported: "Referring to the Irish Catholic bishop in Mzuzu, who is reported to have drafted the pastoral letter, the Ngwazi said as an Elder of the Church of Scotland he was not surprised since the Catholics in Dublin, Ireland, did not like the Presbyterians in Scotland."[16] In what was by now clearly a *kairos* for Malawi, the decision was taken within the Church of Scotland's Board of World Mission and Unity to express solidarity with the Catholic bishops and to distance itself from the Banda regime. For Africa Secretary Jim Wilkie and General Secretary Chris Wigglesworth, the Edinburgh Castle affair had been "the last straw" and they had awaited an opportunity to set the record straight.[17] Within a few months, that opportunity had come.

On the evening of 13 March 1992, the BBC World Service broadcast into Malawi an interview with Chris Wigglesworth in which he made it clear that he could not regard Banda as a serving elder of the Church of Scotland.[18] The effect was dramatic! As it

---

[15] Rev. Misanjo Kansilanga, interview, Blantyre, 1 July 1996.

[16] *Daily Times*, 13 March 1992.

[17] Rev. Jim Wilkie, interview, Edinburgh, 31 October 1996.

[18] After consultation with the Principal Clerk of the General Assembly the technical position was made clear in the following terms: 'We ... wish to make it a matter of public record that Dr Banda is not an elder of the Church of

dawned on the Malawian public that there was something bogus about Banda's claims, the dictator began to suffer a loss of legitimacy from which he never recovered. As one of John Lwanda's youthful informants indicated: "It was then that we knew that the 'force' was not really with this guy."[19] Banda's loss of face continued when the Church of Scotland General Assembly of 1992 agreed to "place on record that it is erroneous to describe Dr Hastings K. Banda as an 'elder of the Church of Scotland'."[20] This statement, issued in a context where the "mainline" churches in Malawi were distancing themselves from the government, helped to provoke a crisis of legitimacy which the Banda regime proved unable to surmount. The subsequent two years witnessed a desperate struggle by the Malawi Congress Party propagandists to identify alternative sources of religious legitimation.[21] These were taken ever less seriously and the fact that Banda could now no longer claim to be a kirk elder was interpreted as a massive loss of face for the once invincible *Ngwazi*.

Awaiting the Kairos: the Nurture of an Alternative Vision

At an official level the Church of Scotland was, until the *kairos* of 1992, mostly silent concerning the human rights abuses and oppressive policies of the Banda government. Yet, within the wider

---

Scotland in any meaningful sense. While technically, ordination to the eldership is for life, a person with that status is not properly regarded as an elder unless they are a member of a kirk session (local Church committee). Dr Banda has not been such a member for nearly fifty years." Statement by Department of World Mission and Unity, Church of Scotland Press Office News Release, 16 March 1992.

[19] John L.C. Lwanda, *Promises, Power, Politics and Poverty: Democratic Transition in Malawi (1961-1999)*, Glasgow: Dudu Nsomba, 1996, p. 108.

[20] Minutes of the General Assembly of the Church of Scotland, 1992, p. 61.

[21] See Ross, Not Catalyst but Ferment" pp. 103-104.

web of the links which unite Scottish and Malawian Christians there were forces at work to prepare for the day when the Banda regime would be challenged and a new dawn would break for Malawi. From the beginning of the one-party era there were Church of Scotland missionaries, such as Hamish and Anne Hepburn and Andrew and Joyce Ross, who identified with Malawian opposition to Banda. Their stand encouraged those who opposed Banda on grounds of Christian conviction even when this meant going into exile and/or risking their lives. Amongst those who would play a leading role in marshalling the opposition to Banda which finally led to his defeat in the Presidential Election of May 1994, were people with long family connections with the Church of Scotland missions. The leader of the United Front for Multi-Party Democracy, a movement of exiles based in Lusaka, was Harry Bwanausi who was born in 1925 at Blantyre Mission where his family had lived since his grandfather was employed to carry goods from the River-Shire at Chikwawa during the earliest days of the Mission."[22] The church elder who was most prominent in organizing the Public Affairs Committee, the church-based body which proved to be the engine of political change in the 1992-93 period, was Jake Muwamba, the grandson of the first theological student to be trained by the Livingstonia Mission.[23] Edda Chitalo, the first woman to occupy a prominent position in the multi-party movement, was born and raised on the Blantyre Mission.[24] These were people of strong character and deep Christian faith who were able to weather the storm of the Banda era and contribute to political renewal when the time came. Families with a long association with the Church of Scotland missions proved to be

---

[22] Dr H.W. Bwanausi, interview, Zomba. 8 December 1994.

[23] Mr T.J. Muwamba, interview, Blantyre, 4 January 1995. McCracken, *Politics and Christianity in Malawi*, pp. 144, 149.

[24] Mrs Edda Chitalo, interview by Dr Isabel Apawo Phiri, Blantyre, 15 May 1995.

among those who nurtured an alternative vision and sustained it even through the darkest days of repression.[25]

Notable amongst such families were Orton and Vera Chirwa, exiled after the "cabinet crisis" of 1964, leaders of the opposition in Tanzania and Zambia, who were abducted from a border area of the latter country and sentenced to death by a "traditional court" in 1982. It was this incident which provoked the only public intervention by the Church of Scotland in Malawi's internal affairs during the Banda era. At the 1983 General Assembly it was agreed to "respectfully request the Life President of Malawi, himself ordained as an elder in the Church of Scotland, to exercise the Presidential Prerogative of Mercy."[26] The Very Rev. Dr Andrew Doig was sent as a special envoy to plead for clemency for the Chirwas. Though Dr Banda responded angrily and refused to see his old friend Dr Doig, the death sentence was commuted to life imprisonment. They remained in prison under very harsh conditions until Orton died in 1992 shortly before all political prisoners were released. Vera survived to emerge as an inspirational figure in the social and political reconstruction undertaken from 1993. Banda's very clearly expressed resentment at the Church of Scotland initiative made it clear that he would maintain his kirk elder status on his own terms and would not take kindly to any pastoral admonition from the church. The President's anger at Dr Doig served as a warning to local church leaders who became even more careful to avoid any possible confrontation.[27] Nevertheless the Church of Scotland's intervention was not

---

[25] Terence Ranger has recently drawn attention to the role of Christian families in African politics with his case study of the Methodist Christian faith and nationalist political involvement of the Samkange family in Zimbabwe. Malawi offers interesting Presbyterian parallels. See Terence Ranger, *Are We Not Also Men? The Samkange Family and African Politics in Zimbabwe 1920-64*, London: James Currey, 1995.

[26] Minutes of the General Assembly of the Church of Scotland, 1983, p. 71.

[27] Very Rev. Dr Silas Ncozana, interview, Blantyre. 28 June 1995.

forgotten and gave a signal that the Banda regime could not count on unquestioning Presbyterian legitimation.

One young CCAP minister who picked up this message very clearly was Rev. Peter Kaleso. His case provides an example of another way in which the Church of Scotland played a role in nurturing an alternative vision for Malawi. It was during a year of study at New College in Edinburgh under Church of Scotland sponsorship, that Kaleso began to be deeply troubled about the political situation prevailing in his country.[28] On his return he began preaching sermons which fairly directly challenged the excesses of the one-party system. Following the "Mwanza accident" in which four senior politicians were brutally murdered on government orders,[29] Kaleso's was the lone voice in the church which publicly condemned the action. After he fled on foot into Mozambique and finally found refuge in Swaziland. it was the Church of Scotland which came to his rescue and provided the means for him to take another period of study in Edinburgh. After his return to Malawi he remained an uncompromising critic of the Banda regime and emerged as a fiery orator in the campaign for political reform in 1992-93. Kaleso himself makes it very clear that the Church of Scotland's role in his formation was very important in enabling him to understand the application of the biblical gospel to the social and political situation prevailing in Malawi.[30]

The long history of Church of Scotland involvement in Malawi created another, rather unusual, form of political influence during the one-party era. When Banda returned to Malawi to lead the independence movement in 1958 he had been out of the country for more than forty years. Hence he had no close friends among

---

[28] Rev. Peter Kaleso, interview. Blantyre, 10 April 1995.

[29] See [Mtegha] Commission of Inquiry, Mwanza Road Accident Report (Malawi Government), 4 January 1995.

[30] Rev. Peter Kaleso, interview, Blantyre. 10 April 1995. See further chapter seven below.

Malawians and preferred to maintain an air of austere detachment.[31] Combined with other quirks of his personality and the politics of dictatorship, this ensured that he became an isolated figure to whom no one spoke on equal terms. One of the very few exceptions to this, was a Church of Scotland minister, the Rev. Dr Fergus Macpherson. Banda had been ordained to the eldership in 1941 by Macpherson's father and had been a frequent visitor to the Manse. Later, Banda had taught Chinyanja to the young Macpherson who was preparing to go to Central Africa as a missionary. The two therefore enjoyed a longstanding intimacy and Macpherson could always be sure of access to the Life President.[32] On occasion he made use of this privilege to plead for clemency for particular victims of repression who were known to him and to probe for opportunities to discuss with Banda the nature of his presidency. Banda's responses were suggestive of a deeply disturbed personality as he switched between affectionate familiarity one moment and hysterical paroxysms of rage the next. This was particularly evident when Banda invited Macpherson to Gleneagles Hotel during the Commonwealth Heads of Government meeting in 1977. Macpherson's request for the release of a political detainee named Mrs Serenje provoked fits of apparently uncontrollable rage before Banda finally acceded to the request.[33] There is no evidence that anything was achieved by Macpherson's visits beyond the release of individual detainees. Yet it is of some significance to notice that if there was any hope of Banda being alerted to the excesses and injustices of his regime, it probably lay with a minister of the Church of Scotland.

---

[31] Prior to his return to Malawi Banda wrote to Fergus Macpherson, then Principal of Livingstonia, requesting his confidential opinion of the Congress leadership since "I know none of them." Macpherson wisely declined. Rev. Dr Fergus Macpherson, interview, Edinburgh, 20 November 1996.

[32] Rev. Dr Fergus Macpherson, interview, Edinburgh, 18 August 1994.

[33] Rev. Dr Fergus Macpherson, interview, Edinburgh, 20 November 1996.

"We Want Change": Solidarity with Rebels and Confusionists

We have already alluded to the impact felt in Malawi when the Church of Scotland signalled its support for the Catholic bishops epochal Pastoral Letter of 8 March 1992, first through the BBC broadcast of World Mission General Secretary Chris Wigglesworth on 13 March and later by the General Assembly in May. It is necessary to appreciate that all public media in Malawi at this time were dominated by the government propaganda which provided massive ideological support for the dictatorship. Hence at a time of political crisis all ears (of the educated) were tuned to the BBC "Focus on Africa" programme. Wigglesworth's disowning of Banda as an elder therefore had an electric effect in the country. Next morning people talked of nothing else! The broadcast of the General Assembly debate on 19 May had, if anything, a still more powerful effect. When I returned to Malawi in September of that year, people were still talking about that momentous evening. It is doubtful if any General Assembly debate of modern times has had such a nationally stirring effect even in Scotland itself! The Assembly called "upon the Government of Malawi to provide 'tangible and irreversible evidence of a basic transformation' in its observance of the fundamental human rights of all Malawi's citizens" and "regretfully endorse[d] the action of Malawi's major donors in withholding development aid for a limited period."[34] The importance of this deliverance was indicated immediately in a faxed message[35] from the leader of the United Front for Multi-Party Democracy, Dr Harry Bwanausi, to Church of Scotland Africa Secretary Jim Wilkie:

---

[34] Minutes of the General Assembly of the Church of Scotland, 1992, p. 61.

[35] For the importance of the "fax revolution" to political change in Malawi in 1992-93 see R.M. Nkhalambayausi Chirwa, "Information Technologies in Malawi's Political Transition" in Nzunda & Ross eds., *Church, Law and Political Transition*, pp. 111-120.

Please convey the exiles' grateful thanks to Fergus Macpherson, Dr Ross and to your dearself and to the General Assembly of the Church of Scotland for the support on the Malawi issue. The Moral Authority of the KIRK [sic] will emancipate us for the second time, the first being when its resolution dismantled the Federation of Rhodesia and Nyasaland in 1960.[36]

Not without some hyperbole, Bwanausi thus indicated the importance of the General Assembly's deliverances for those working for progressive political change in Malawi. Meanwhile the Church of Scotland was becoming involved in the movement for political change in other ways besides making use of the airwaves.

One important way in which the relationship between the Church of Scotland and the Presbyterian Synods in Malawi has developed in recent times is that they have come to relate not only on a one-to-one basis but also through their common membership of the World Alliance of Reformed Churches. As the World Mission and Unity Department waited for an initiative to come from the CCAP within Malawi, it became clear that one opportunity for decisive action to be taken lay with WARC. Meeting in Lusaka early in May, leaders of the WARC Southern Africa region issued a strong letter supporting the Catholic bishops and calling the CCAP "to be prophetic."[37] Operating within the WARC framework, the Church of Scotland could use its knowledge of the Malawi situation to influence policy, yet without adopting the domineering patron-client relationship which, since the 1950s, it had been seeking to outgrow. The value of this new framework became clear early in June when a WARC delegation visited Malawi. Chris Wigglesworth was on the team which also included church elders from Lesotho and the

---

[36] Faxed letter from Dr H.W. Bwanausi to Rev. James Wilkie, 20 May 1992.

[37] "Statement on the Current Situation in Malawi," issued by The Southern Africa Alliance of Reformed Churches, meeting in Lusaka, 29 April to 5 May 1992.

Netherlands and a minister from the USA.[38] In a situation where, according to Misanjo Kansilanga, the CCAP "knew what it wanted to say, but not how to do it"[39] and where all the machinery of the police state was being mobilized to keep them quiet, the presence of the WARC delegation provided the opportunity for decisive action.

The letter addressed to President Banda was signed by representatives of Blantyre and Livingstonia Synods and of the General Synod, as well as by the four members of the WARC delegation. It endorsed the Catholic bishops' Pastoral Letter and went further to call for the appointment of a broadly based Commission with the mandate "to make specific proposals for structural reform towards a political system with sufficient checks and balances on the use of power, and guarantees of accountability at all levels of government; to review the judicial system, in line with the rule of law; to look into the distribution of income and wealth required by the demands of social justice."[40] This was the origin of the influential Public Affairs Committee, as outlined above in chapter five. The visit of the WARC delegation therefore proved to be vitally important to the achievement of peaceful political change in Malawi. While the Catholic bishops were responsible for the prophetic inspiration which sparked off the whole process, the WARC-CCAP initiative in taking on the tough task of engaging directly with the government and constructing the machinery for the achievement of radical political reconstruction was no less important. Working within the WARC framework the Church of Scotland was able to exercise influence in Malawi at a time of profound political crisis, while still fully respecting the integrity of the local church.

Another ecclesiastical organization within which the Church of Scotland could work to influence the Malawi situation was the

---

[38] See "The Nation of Malawi in Crisis: the Churches' Concern," World Alliance of Reformed Churches, Geneva, 2 June 1992.

[39] Rev. M.E. Kansilanga, interview, Lilongwe, 16 November 1994.

[40] "The Nation of Malawi in Crisis," p. 2.

Council of Churches for Britain and Ireland. Early in 1993 the Church of Scotland had been instrumental in the formation of a Malawi Sub-Group of the CCBI Africa Forum. The key players in this group were Fr Bill Turnbull of the White Fathers, the Rev. Christopher Race. representing Bishop Mark Santer of the Anglican Diocese of Birmingham, the Rev. Donald Arden, formerly Anglican Archbishop of Central Africa, and later the Rev. Pat Davies, representing the English Catholic Bishops Conference.[41] Shortly after the visit of the WARC delegation, the CCBI decided to send a further high-level team in the persons of Rt Rev. Mark Santer, Anglican bishop of Birmingham, Rt Rev. James O'Brien, Roman Catholic bishop in Hertfordshire, and Very Rev. Robert Davidson, Moderator of the Church of Scotland General Assembly 1990.[42] The administration of the CCBI visit was conducted at the Church of Scotland offices where Africa Secretary Jim Wilkie acted as its "Ecumenical Coordinator." This set a pattern for CCBI action which was followed during the following two years of rapid political change in Malawi (as will be illustrated below in respect of the 1993. Referendum and the 1994 General Election). To the WARC and CCBI initiatives, the Church of Scotland sought to add the influence of the Conference of European Churches which met in Prague in September 1992. A Kirk delegation was successful in persuading the CEC Assembly "to press the Government of Malawi for the release of Christian detainees and an immediate top-level conference on constitutional reform."[43] Through these ecumenical networks the Church of Scotland found a new way, at a strategic time, to influence events in Malawi.

A more traditional method was to make representations to the British Government. Baroness Chalker of Wallasey, the Minister in

---

[41] Letter from Rev. J.L. Wilkie, 15 November 1996.

[42] See Statement by Representatives of the Council of Churches for Britain and Ireland, 26 July 1992.

[43] Church of Scotland Press Office News Release, 9 September 1992.

the Foreign Office with direct responsibility for Britain's relations with Malawi, recognized that "the Church of Scotland's influence in Malawi and with Banda personally has been a powerful force for progress."[44] The officials of the Board of World Mission and Unity could also provide information to MPs concerned to raise questions about Malawi in the House of Commons, notably Sir David Steel. The importance of the Church of Scotland's role was recognized early in January 1993 when Robin Christopher of the Foreign Office visited the church offices to meet with the Moderator and officials of the Board of World Mission and Unity and the Committee on Church and Nation. The democratization process in Malawi was at a particularly delicate stage and the British Government wished to ensure that Dr Banda would not take too reactionary a line. The request of the Foreign Office (at the urging of Kenneth Kaunda of Zambia) was that the Church of Scotland might send a special envoy to see Banda in person.[45] This led to the Moderator writing directly to Banda requesting that Fergus Macpherson might have a "personal meeting" with the President.[46] At a time when almost no one outside the ruling clique could speak directly with Banda, Macpherson was eventually granted a private audience and spoke with the President of the urgent need for democratization in Malawi.[47] The direct effect of this conversation is impossible to calculate but Banda did take a more conciliatory line towards the opposition in the run-up to the Referendum and in his acceptance of the results. What the incident

---

[44] Baroness Chalker of Wallasey to Sir David Steel, quoted by Jill Clements (secretary to Sir David) to Dr Chris Wigglesworth, 25 March 1993.

[45] J.L. Wilkie, "A Peaceful Transition to Democracy in Malawi: Some Reflections about how to achieve it," Confidential World Mission and Unity Briefing Document, 20 February 1993.

[46] Rt Rev. Hugh R. Wyllie, Moderator of the General Assembly to His Excellency the Life President of the Republic of Malawi Ngwazi Dr H. Kamuzu Banda, 21 January 1993.

[47] Fergus Macpherson, "Personal Record of a Special Visit to Malawi, 31 January to 7 February 1993."

does clearly indicate is that the Church of Scotland had a voice which was respected in the formation of British Government policy and, on occasion, could even play a part in British diplomacy.

Another critical contribution of the Church of Scotland to the movement for political change was to offer solidarity and support to those Malawi church leaders who exposed themselves to the wrath of the totalitarian system by speaking and acting in favour of political change. The most prominent and outspoken minister in the weeks following the Pastoral Letter was the minister of St Andrew's Mzuzu, within the Livingstonia Synod, Rev. Aaron Longwe. So strong was his biblically based condemnation of the one-party system that it was no surprise when he was repeatedly detained and his life was perceived to be in danger. In this situation Longwe testifies: "It was the backing of the church worldwide that saved me."[48] At the centre of this worldwide support was the Church of Scotland, whose Africa Secretary Jim Wilkie visited Longwe and wrote a confidential report on his experiences of harassment and detention.[49] The fact that Longwe was married to a former Church of Scotland missionary heightened public interest in Scotland. The experiences of the couple were featured in the Scottish press and an interview with Longwe at the height of his persecution was broadcast on Radio Scotland.[50] In this way the Church of Scotland provided for Longwe the lifeline of international publicity. "If it were not for the Church of Scotland," he later declared, "some of us would have been dead by now."[51]

Later in the year when Silas Ncozana, General Secretary of the Synod of Blantyre, became the key figure in the organization of PAC, he

---

[48] Rev. Aaron Longwe, interview by Dr Klaus Fiedler, 3 December 1994.

[49] J.L. Wilkie, "The First Detention (in Mzuzu, Malawi) of the Rev. Aaron Longwe and Mr Chenda Mkandawire 27-30 April 1992," Confidential Report, Church of Scotland Board of World Mission and Unity, 7 May 1992.

[50] Interview with Rev. Aaron Longwe, Mzuzu, Malawi, Radio Scotland, 12 May 1992.

[51] *Scotsman,* 23 February 1993.

was extremely grateful to be able to count on Church of Scotland support in a situation where he had his fax line cut, received a series of death-threatening telephone calls, heard frequent reports that he had been targeted by MCP hit squads, had to travel incognito every time he went on the road for fear of assassination, and was generally left in no doubt that he was out of favour with the government and that his life was therefore at risk.[52] As Malawi church leaders such as Ncozana and Senior Clerk to the General Synod, Misanjo Kansilanga, manoeuvred to secure peaceful and progressive political change, they were significantly strengthened by the kind of support expressed in an Open Letter from the Moderator of the General Assembly of the Church of Scotland: "Until there is real progress on freedom of speech, freedom of association, freedom of worship, and respect for the rule of law, Malawi will remain on a rapid downhill course which can only increase the suffering of her people. We pray that God will give wisdom to the Government, Church and people of Malawi as you discharge your urgent and historic responsibilities."[53] Such solidarity served to steel the nerve of those who were branded "rebels and confusionists" by the official media as they sought radical political change in Malawi.

The Church of Scotland and the Making of the Second Republic

As it became clear early in 1993 that the one-party system was crumbling and that there was need for radical political reconstruction, church leaders and others were struggling to find

---

[52] Very Rev. Dr Silas Ncozana, interview, 28 June 1995. Ncozana had given to the Church of Scotland a code which would be used to signal his arrest: "PAUL AND SILAS REPEAT'. Very Rev. Dr Silas Ncozana to Rev. Jim Wilkie, 8 May 1992.

[53] Open Letter to the General Secretary, the Christian Council of Malawi, and to the Senior Clerk of the General Synod, and the General Secretaries of the Synods of Blantyre, Livingstonia and Nkhoma, the Church of Central Africa Presbyterian, from the Rt Rev. Hugh R. Wyllie, Moderator of the General Assembly of the Church of Scotland, 1 September 1992.

the way forward. The event which gave them the necessary orientation was the Swanwick Conference of February 1993 which was hosted by the Council of Churches for Britain and Ireland but with the Church of Scotland playing the central role in the organization. The significance of this meeting has been highlighted by Rev. Emmanuel Chimkwita, who was then Acting Chairman of the Public Affairs Committee:

> The meeting of the Public Affairs Committee with the Council of Churches in Britain and Ireland (CCBI) in February 1993 was a very important meeting in the history of Malawi. The Pastoral Letter was really a catalyst but the pivotal event in the process of change was the Swanwick meeting where the strategy was formed which guided the PAC in the National Referendum and the General Election.[54]

The MCP government seems to have recognized the importance of this meeting at the time since it sent two (uninvited) ministers to present its case and suffered considerable loss of face when the ministerial delegation was turned away from the conference which condemned the resistance of the Malawi Government to democratic change.[55] The conference also put in place the mechanisms by which support would be channelled to the emergent democratic movement in Malawi.

Immediately after the conference Jim Wilkie, as Chair of the CCBI Africa Forum, appealed for support for the Public Affairs Committee Referendum Monitoring Programme (PACREM) and the Education for Participatory Democracy Programme.[56] Peter With of DanChurchAid had attended the Swanwick Conference and was able to secure the granting of substantial sums to enable the churches in

---

[54] Rev. Emmanuel Chimkwita, interview by Dr Klaus Fiedler, 4 December 1994.

[55] See *Daily Times*, 4 March 1993.

[56] Circular letter from Rev. Jim Wilkie. Chair, CCBI Africa Forum, 22 February 1993.

Malawi to prepare people for the Referendum. Funds from the Westminster Foundation for Democracy were channeled through the Church of Scotland office. Without this support it is doubtful whether there would have been sufficient civil society activity to sustain the democratization process. The one-party government sought to capitalize on its immense advantages in organization, transport, finance and the media to snuff out the pro-democracy movement.[57] The support for the Public Affairs Committee orchestrated by the Church of Scotland facilitated a certain levelling of the playing field.

Further solidarity was offered a few weeks before the Referendum by the visit of another CCBI delegation which encouraged work for democratic freedom and protested against harassment, intimidation and violence on the part of the Government.[58] The 1993 General Assembly agreed to "deplore the continuing efforts of the present Government of Malawi to frustrate a free and fair expression of the wishes of the people of Malawi through harassment, intimidation and violence."[59] When the Referendum finally took place on 14 June 1993 its conduct was witnessed by a team of "ecumenical observers" from the CCBI coordinated by Peggy Owens, a volunteer from the PC(USA) working with the Church of Scotland Board of World Mission in Edinburgh.[60] What remained, following the 63% vote in favour of multi-party democracy, was the campaign leading up to the General Election of 17 May 1994. The Church of Scotland remained in close touch with the Public Affairs Committee in Malawi and was

---

[57] See *The Referendum in Malawi: Free Expression Denied*, Article 19 Issue 22 (April 1993).

[58] Statement by Representatives of the Council of Churches for Britain and Ireland Visiting Malawi 27 April to 2 May 1993, signed by Rev. Patrick Davies, Assistant General Secretary, Catholic Bishops Conference of England and Wales, Rev. Stanley Hood, Convener, Church of Scotland Africa Committee. Rt Rev. Humphrey Taylor, Anglican bishop of Selby.

[59] Minutes of the General Assembly of the Church of Scotland, 1993. p. 62.

[60] Statement of the United Kingdom Ecumenical Observers, 16 June 1993.

again responsible for coordinating an ecumenical delegation of observers to monitor the conduct of the General Election.[61] By involving itself, usually on an ecumenical basis, at strategic points in the democratization process, the Church of Scotland was able to play a constructive role in the making of the Second Republic in Malawi.

Conclusion

In the mission history of the Church of Scotland, Malawi is a unique case since the Scottish missions were integral to the emergence of the nation. Recent events have shown that, while the relationship of the Church of Scotland to its "daughter" churches in Malawi was transformed by the "hand-over" to local leadership in the late 1950s, still the Church of Scotland retained a powerful influence in Malawian national life - for good or ill. It was an influence on which Kamuzu Banda capitalized in order to secure powerful religious legitimation for his despotic rule. In the end, however, this tactic rebounded on him when the "moment of truth" came for Malawi and his claims to eldership were dramatically disowned by the Church of Scotland. This leaves the outstanding question: should this not have been done much earlier? Were the churches wrongfooted by the Banda dictatorship when the President was able to appeal "over the head" of the CCAP to the Church of Scotland for religious legitimation and neither of the "partners in mission" was able to make any sustained protest? The silencing of church social witness in post-independence Malawi raises questions about the missiology of partnership as it took effect at that time, particularly when, as Malawian novelist Paul Tiyambe Zeleza has pointedly observed: "To be silent is to promote tyranny."[62]

---

[61] See Joint Supplementary Report on Malawi by the Board of World Mission and the Church and Nation Committee to the General Assembly of the Church of Scotland, May 1994. *Reports,* p. 693.

[62] Professor Paul Tiyambe Zeleza, Guest Lecture, Chancellor College, University of Malawi, 22 July 1996.

Meanwhile however, the Kirk, through a variety of channels, had been working to nurture an alternative vision. These efforts bore fruit when the *kairos* came and among the key players were some who had been nurtured in important ways by the influence of the Church of Scotland. When Malawian church leaders were very exposed and vulnerable as they took the lead in confronting the totalitarian regime during 1992, the solidarity of the Church of Scotland was a powerful factor in strengthening their resolve. Moreover, the fact that the Church of Scotland could orchestrate international support for the struggle of the Malawi churches, through, e.g., the World Alliance of Reformed Churches and the Council of Churches in Britain and Ireland, acted powerfully to turn the tide in favour of the pro-democracy movement initiated by the churches' witness. This much more ecumenical approach reflects the fact that, compared with earlier years, the Presbyterian axis is only one connection in a complex network of international political, economic and ecclesiastical relations. It is a sign of the times that it was the Roman Catholic bishops whose witness first drew attention to the need for radical political reform. Nevertheless, as has been shown, Malawi's success in peacefully dismantling the one-party system and introducing democratic government owed not a little to the Church of Scotland engagement with the process of political reform. The long historical connection did prove to be a valuable resource at a time of social and national crisis. This study suggests that church links which transcend national boundaries *can*, in the post-colonial post-Cold-War world, be of strategic political significance. However, it must be noted that a missiology of "hands-off" partnership proved inadequate to address the evils of the Banda dictatorship. What, however, was the CCAP itself doing during this period to expose the prevailing injustice and oppression? Was it completely silent? To these questions we now turn by taking again the Synod of Blantyre as a case study.

7. Where were the Prophets and Martyrs in Banda's Malawi? Four Presbyterian Ministers

Introduction: The Church's Guilty Silence

The advent of multi-party politics in Malawi in 1992-93 quickly led to the exposure of the political oppression, economic injustice and gross human rights abuse which characterized the one-party system under Kamuzu Banda from 1964 to 1993.[1] The Christian churches, notably through the Catholic Bishops' Pastoral Letter of 1992 and the formation of the Public Affairs Committee, played a leading role in this exposure and in the transition to democratic politics. The plethora of ecclesiastical letters and statements addressing the political situation was welcomed by those concerned for social justice and political reform but it also served to highlight how silent the churches had been during the preceding thirty years. Indeed, not only had the churches been silent about the abuses of the Banda regime but they had actively echoed the propaganda of the ruling Congress Party. Year after year church leaders had solemnly given thanks to God for the "dynamic, far-sighted and God-fearing leadership" of the "Ngwazi" and had prayed for him to have long life.

In a Joint Message on the 10th Anniversary of Independence, e.g., the Catholic and Presbyterian Churches stated that:

> What has been achieved during this period in all fields is so unbelievable that it confounds even the most optimistic

---

[1] Early studies include John L. Lwanda, *Kamuzu Banda of Malawi: A Study in Promise, Power and Paralysis*, Glasgow: Dudu Nsomba, 1993; and *Malawi: A Moment of Truth*, London: CIIR, 1993.

expectations of most of us and there is no doubt that all of this achievement is due to the untiring efforts, dedicated, selfless and responsible leadership of His Excellency, the Life President Ngwazi Dr H. Kamuzu Banda. If this country has grown from the ranks of the poor nations into a nation with a viable booming economy, with a healthy educated people, it is due to His Excellency's own dynamic leadership and the stable and peaceful conditions that leadership has created.[2]

Given the Pastoral Letter's dramatic exposure of the emptiness of such rhetoric and its demonstration of the wide gulf between the MCP rule and the values of the Gospel, it becomes a sharp question for the church to explain how it could justifiably have "gone along with" a political system which brought suffering, fear and demoralization to the people of Malawi. Did not the church let the people down by failing to speak forthrightly on their behalf concerning the evils of the dictatorship?

Undoubtedly, the church's first response to this question must be one of contrition and repentance. It is necessary to acknowledge, as the new Blantyre Synod General Secretary Misanjo Kansilanga has stated, that "the silence of the church was costly to thousands of Malawians who lost their lives and spent their time in prison."[3] It is to the credit of the Blantyre Synod of the Church of Central Africa Presbyterian that it sounded this note early in the transitional period:

> If we look at our own history as the CCAP during the time of the struggle for Independence, we will see that Blantyre Synod was very much in support of the Nyasaland African Congress (later called the MCP). Because of this very verbal

---

[2] *Joint Message from the Churches of Malawi on 10th Anniversary of Independence,* 6 July 1974, signed by Most Reverend James Chiona, Archbishop of Blantyre, and Very Reverend J.D. Sangaya, General Secretary, CCAP Synod of Blantyre, p. 2.

[3] Rev Misanjo E. Kansilanga, address on "Church and Politics in Malawi Today," at CCAP General Synod Human Rights Training Workshop, Chongoni, 8 November 1995.

stance on the side of the MCP, after Independence, the CCAP was aligned closely with the government and became so assimilated with the government's activities that the Synod was often invited to pray and participate as a Church at various government functions. However, because of this assimilation and alignment with the MCP, the Church gradually lost its ability to admonish or speak pastorally to the government. We do not want to make the same mistake at this time in order to ensure that the Church retains its prophetic voice throughout the coming years of our country's history.[4]

There are understandable reasons why the CCAP should have fallen into this trap. The fact that most of the Congress leadership, including Banda, were products of the Presbyterian missions and that many remained active members,[5] made it very difficult for the Presbyterian Church to develop an independent position. Church and State shared a sense of solidarity in the struggle to throw off the shackles of colonialism and to build the nation. Furthermore, after many of its lay leaders became victims of the purge which followed the "Cabinet crisis" of 1964, the CCAP was gripped by the climate of fear which dominated the country for the next thirty years.[6]

Like all other national institutions, the churches were co-opted to support the Banda dictatorship and, to the casual observer, they appeared to be offering unquestioning legitimation to the one-party system. The particular problem this raises in respect of the church is that it has a mandate to speak for truth and justice even when such

---

[4] "A Statement on the Role of the Church in the Transformation of Malawi in the Context of Justice and Peace," Produced by the Administrators Conference, Blantyre Synod CCAP, 22-23 January 1994, p. 4.

[5] See K.N. Mufuka, *Missions and Politics in Malawi,* Kingston, Ontario: The Limestone Press, 1977, pp. 146-95.

[6] See Andrew C. Ross. "Forty-five Years of Turmoil: Malawi Christian Churches, 1949-1994," *International Bulletin of Missionary Research,* Vol. 18/2 (1994), pp. 53-56, 58-60.

witness is very costly. The church is heir to a martyr tradition and there is a legitimate expectation that it is Christians who will be first to place themselves at risk when there is need to confront some great evil in society. Where, then, were the Christian prophets and martyrs of the Banda regime? Many observers have reached the conclusion suggested, e.g., by John de Gruchy in his *Christianity and Democracy*, that "in Malawi ... political protest on the part of the dominant Protestant churches was virtually unknown after independence in 1964."[7] Such an assessment of the churches' social witness during the one-party period is becoming the conventional wisdom but does it do justice to a complex issue which has so far received little systematic study? This chapter examines the leadership of the Church of Central Africa Presbyterian Synod of Blantyre, a section of the church which, historically, was particularly close to the Blantyre-based government. Consideration is given to the three successive General Secretaries of the Synod during the Banda era and also to one other minister who did not figure in the ecclesiastical hierarchy hut was highly influential at the popular level. Examination of their ministries will reveal that the Synod was not quite so silent and compromised as might first appear but also that there were serious limitations to its capacity to address the gospel message to the contemporary political situation. The study is offered as a contribution to the formation of a more critical and more carefully nuanced understanding of Christian witness during the one-party era in Malawi.

Jonathan Sangaya

The first Malawian General Secretary of the Blantyre Synod is a clear example of the close relationship of church and state which impeded the prophetic witness of the church leadership. Jonathan Sangaya had been closely involved in a pastoral capacity in the struggle of the

---

[7] John W. de Gruchy, *Christianity and Democracy*, Cambridge: Cambridge University Press, 1995, p. 184.

Nyasaland African Congress (later Malawi Congress Party) to break the Federation of Rhodesia and Nyasaland. He had courageously protected students and members of staff in the Blantyre schools when they were threatened by Federation troops. During the State of Emergency in 1959 he frequently visited the detainees and came to know them well.[8] It was largely from among these detainees that the first government of independent Malawi was formed so it is not surprising that they continued to regard Rev Sangaya as a "chaplain" and often invited him to pray on national occasions. He was also able to form a close relationship with the Prime Minister (later Life President) Kamuzu Banda and was one of the few Malawians who could relate to the Head of State on reasonably equal terms. Besides his stature as a church leader of national importance, Sangaya was able to capitalize on his being fairly close in age to Banda, an advantage which his successors certainly missed.[9] This allowed him to speak frankly to the President about evils which were prevailing in the country. It is widely believed, though difficult to confirm, that on one occasion he confronted Banda about his relationship with his companion Miss Kadzamira which many felt was inappropriate for a professing church elder.[10] The outcome is said to be that Banda was extremely angry and ordered that Sangaya should be beaten. It is this incident which gave rise to a martyr image being ascribed to Jonathan Sangaya, particularly among the exile community. It was believed that Sangaya's death was brought about, either directly or indirectly, by an MCP "hit-squad."[11] However, the most authoritative source casts

---

[8] Int. Mrs Christian Sangaya and Mrs Eleanor Kanyuka (widow and daughter of Very Rev Jonathan Sangaya), Namaka, 20 February 1995.

[9] Int. Very Rev Dr Silas S. Ncozana, 28 June 1995.

[10] Mrs Eleanor Kanyuka believes that this story is true and was informed by people from Sanjika Palace that they had seen her father being beaten as a result of this interview. Int. Sangaya and Kanyuka.

[11] This belief was so strongly held that a cousin of Sangaya's who returned from exile in 1993 wanted to open a murder case against Dr Banda. However, the family decided that it was by then too late for such action. Int. Sangaya and Kanyuka.

serious doubt on the truth of this story. Silas Ncozana, who was Deputy General Secretary at the time of Sangaya's death, ascertained to his own satisfaction that Sangaya, who by this time was certainly aged and in poor health, had died of natural causes.[12] It is highly improbable, therefore, that Sangaya was actually killed on account of his witness.

The truth of the martyr stories, however, lies in the well-attested ill-treatment which he did suffer. The family remember several occasions when he was detained and tortured. Ncozana, in his biography of Sangaya, makes reference to the following episode:

> In 1978, Sangaya went to attend an All Africa Council of Churches meeting in Zambia. While he was there, he met with Willie Chokani, Harry Bwanausi and others who were Dr. Banda's political opponents, and had run away from Malawi in 1964 for fear of their lives. When Sangaya returned to Malawi after the one week conference in Lusaka, he was interrogated by the Malawi Police. When he admitted that he had indeed met the dissidents in Zambia, Sangaya was driven to Zomba, where he was kept by the police for three days. Asked why he had met in Zambia the men who had rebelled against the "Ngwazi," Sangaya replied, "I am not a politician but a religious leader. As a religious leader, I minister to both bad and good, to both high and low." Here Sangaya communicated his unbreakable leadership and total obedience to his Lord. He was not prepared to compromise his faith and leadership for cheap popularity.[13]

It is significant that Sangaya never talked about the ill-treatment he received during his brief periods of detention. Among his family his only reference to these episodes was to joke about them. Despite

---

[12] Int. Ncozana.

[13] Silas S. Ncozana, *Sangaya*, Blantyre: CLAIM-Kachere, 1996, pp. 21-22. The main disappointment in this excellent biography is that it concentrates so heavily on Sangaya's ecclesiastical concerns that it touches social and political issues only in passing - but perhaps this emphasis is characteristic of the subject himself.

enjoying a very close working relationship with his Deputy, Silas Ncozana, he never disclosed the details of his confrontations with Banda and the resultant ill-treatment. An ex-soldier and a formidably powerful personality, Sangaya seems to have felt that he should carry alone the burden of confronting a leader and a political system in need of correction. He made no effort to mobilize the church as a body to make a prophetic witness concerning the excesses of the dictatorship which must have greatly concerned him. Having seen many people suffer under the repressive system it may be that he did not want to expose anyone else to risk and preferred to "lay down his life for his friends." The search for motives can only be a matter of conjecture.

What is beyond doubt is that Sangaya's ministry did not include any significant "conscientization" of the church at large to promote a critical social witness. In his preaching it was noted that he confined himself to personal and spiritual issues and never addressed contemporary social evils or the conduct of government.[14] Hence the silence of the church whose leader's dealings with the state were kept so quiet that not even his family and friends knew any details! It is also significant that Sangaya, unlike many of his contemporaries, was always released from detention after a few days. Was he too hot to handle? Was Banda afraid of alienating the church by holding someone of Sangaya's stature? Or did his respect for his friend cause the President to relent and order his release? These are questions which suggest that the church may have had the capacity to challenge the abuses of power that occurred in the early one-party period much more effectively than it did.

Its failure to do so under Sangaya's leadership owes something to the closeness of the Blantyre Synod to the MCP government. Another factor to be considered is that, ecclesiastically, this was the period when the Synod was completing its transformation from mission to church. The Scottish missionaries had "handed over" power in 1959,

---

[14] Int. Sangaya and Kanyuka.

well before political independence. Sangaya was the first Malawian General Secretary. In this historical context his major concern was the integrity and continuing growth of the church.[15] It is understandable if he judged it best to take a low profile so far as the political arena was concerned. Finally, it must be noted that the church and its leadership could not be expected to be immune from the climate of fear which had prevailed in the country since the Cabinet crisis of 1964. The Blantyre Synod had lost the cream of its lay leadership at that time and suffered a certain demoralization. In the ensuing years church leaders and members were all too aware of the grisly fate which awaited those like the Jehovah's Witnesses who actively dissented from the one-party system on religious grounds.[16]

This fear undoubtedly had a paralyzing effect on the life of the church and Sangaya's response to it shows both his greatness and his weakness as a church leader. His greatness is that he was able to break through this fear in his own personal witness and was not intimidated when the powers of the state were deployed against him. His own stand can be known not only from the incidents mentioned above but also from the fact that he lived his life under the suspicion that he was a dissident. His whole family shared in this unpopularity with those in power which was so strong that "you could feel it."[17] This was not a case of a church leader giving his blessing to a repressive state. He took his stand and it was well known that he was regarded by the regime as a troublesome critic. This introduced a small but significant distancing of church and state. The weakness of his leadership was that he took up this stance *alone*. The church as a

---

[15] See Ncozana, *Sangaya*, pp. 22-32.

[16] See Klaus Fiedler, "Power at the Receiving End: the Jehovah's Witnesses Experience in One-Party Malawi," in Kenneth R. Ross ed., *God, People and Power in Malawi: Democratization in Theological Perspective*, Blantyre: CLAIM-Kachere, 1996, pp. 149-76.

[17] Int. Sangaya and Kanyuka.

body appeared to acquiesce in the prevailing political system and did not raise any critical voice.

Saindi Chiphangwi

Jonathan Sangaya died in 1979. Three years earlier, in 1976, the Blantyre Synod had celebrated its centenary, an event which was treated as a major national occasion. One of the Synod's most promising younger ministers, Saindi Chiphangwi, was chosen to deliver the sermon at the centenary service in St Michael and All Angels which was attended by Dr Banda, his cabinet and all senior civic leaders. Chiphangwi called the congregation to look to the future, pointing out that a great danger engulfing Malawi was that of a "personality cult" and that there was need to be clear about "whom we serve." This was interpreted by all present as a direct attack upon Banda since there was certainly no one else in the country who might be developing a personality cult! There was an almost universal feeling that Chiphangwi had overstepped the boundary and that he would immediately be arrested. The atmosphere at the end of the service was therefore very highly charged until Banda himself shook the preacher's hand and declared: "I know what you are trying to say. If anyone failed to get the point, he should go to the Mental Hospital!" Chiphangwi believes that this comment saved his life and that, had he preached the same sermon in Banda's absence, he would have been killed.[18] This was only one of a series of quite critical sermons preached by Chiphangwi at national occasions and it is part of the Banda enigma that the dictator regularly accepted these statements with comments such as, "I know what you are getting at. We need to hear that." Chiphangwi was even told that Banda listened to his sermons on tape![19]

Significantly, when Sangaya died it was Chiphangwi who was elected to succeed him. As a much younger and more junior figure

---

[18] Int. Rev Dr Saindi D. Chiphangwi, Gaborone, 18 December 1995.

[19] Ibid.

Chiphangwi did not enjoy the *tete-a-tete* contact with Banda within which Sangaya had sought to exercise a corrective influence. However, he continued to use the pulpit, especially on national occasions, to address himself to abuses in social and political life. While there was a certain guardedness to his language, within the carefully nuanced discourse of the one-party state there was no mistaking the sharply critical note which he was sounding. Since the sermons were broadcast on national radio, a thrill could run through the whole country when he spoke such words as:

> Our choices and decisions either as private individuals or as public figures matter *immensely*. If we choose aright we help to build Malawi into "the warm heart of Africa," but if we decide wrongly we make hell for ourselves and for future generations. For this matter, let us not let things drift. Do not leave the future shape and image of Malawi to chance. Assume responsibility now for we are all answerable to God for the future character and image of Malawi.... Being at peace with God includes among other things according God his rightful and undisputed place in our personal and public life. Choices and decisions made without this divine factor in mind can only go so far and not the whole way in ensuring a peaceful nation of Malawi.... Being at peace with neighbour includes among others according to them due respect as children of God made in his own image, to be treated as full human beings and not as nonentities.... [In conclusion] If we love our country as I'm sure we do, we will choose to do *right* and not *wrong;* to do *good* and not *evil.* If we love our country, as I'm sure we do, we will choose *truth* and not *untruth*.[20]

Chiphangwi reports that many expected him to "disappear" after uttering such words.

Sometimes prominent figures such as the chief of police and the army commander would send him messages of disappointment over

---

[20] Rev Dr S.D. Chiphangwi, Sermon at Martyr's Day Service, St Michael and All Angels Church, 3 March 1985.

texts he had chosen and sermons he had delivered in church. In the context of the time this was highly intimidating and no one should underestimate the stress under which Chiphangwi sought to exercise a prophetic ministry. On the other hand, there were many appreciative letters giving thanks that the authentic voice of the church was at last being heard. There is no doubt that Chiphangwi's sermons had a major impact in the country.[21] Jack Mapanje, the poet who was one of Malawi's most famous political detainees in the late 1980s, reported that the prisoners used to recall Chiphangwi's sermons and take courage from the knowledge that the church was on their side![22] So, in his own way, the new General Secretary maintained the critical distance between church and state which had been opened up by the witness of Jonathan Sangaya. He retired from office in 1985 physically unscathed but having so exposed himself to the risk of a grisly death that the language of martyrdom is not far-fetched. The church, again, had a leader who did not hesitate to put himself at risk in order to address the evils which threatened the nation.

Again, however, it had a leader who took a lonely stand. It was alone in the pulpit that Chiphangwi discharged his prophetic calling. In the administration of Synod affairs and in the meetings of its Boards and Committees no attempt was made to initiate any action which might promote needed political reform. He found himself in an intensely lonely position. Many other church leaders regarded him as a problem and there was no one in whom he could unreservedly confide.[23] The pressure of operating under the vigilance of the one-party system eventually began to tell. It has been said that you could

---

[21] When President Muluzi visited Malawians in Gaborone after his election victory in 1994, he recalled Chiphangwi's sermons of the early 1980s, a time when Muluzi was serving as Secretary-General of the MCP. Int. Chiphangwi.

[22] Int. Chiphangwi.

[23] Ibid.

smell the fear in the General Secretary's office![24] This will not be a matter of surprise to anyone who is familiar with the way in which the MCP system of terror dominated Malawian society from the highest government office to the humblest village hut. It is a mark of the integrity of the church that Chiphangwi was able to break through the system to sound out the words of truth which acted as a sign of hope for many Malawians at that time. Yet still he acted as an isolated individual and the church as a body was unable to develop a critical social witness.

Peter Kaleso

During Chiphangwi's time in office there occurred one of the greatest outrages of the entire one-party period. In 1983 four senior politicians, who had offended the inner circle of the MCP regime, were summarily arrested and brutally murdered on government orders.[25] The official media reported that the four had died in a car accident at Mwanza while trying to flee the country. The party leadership made it clear that they had died as rebels and that no mourning should be observed in connection with their funerals. The truth of what had happened soon spread by word of mouth. People were shocked and outraged but feared that any word of protest would swiftly result in a similar fate to that suffered by the murdered four. However, there was one young minister in the Synod of Blantyre who found that he could not remain silent. Peter Kaleso had studied in Scotland from 1979 to 1981 and had returned home determined that the church should firmly challenge the political

---

[24] Unattributable interview.

[25] See [Mtegha] Commission of Inquiry, Mwanza Road Accident Report, 4 January 1995, esp. pp. 81-85. The Commission found that "The killing of the four gentlemen was by members of the Police Force. It was premeditated, brutal and diabolic." (p. 82, #12.07) Further, "Messrs Gadama, Matenje and Chiwanga were killed by the Police on Dr Banda's orders, because Dr Banda perceived that they were aspiring for his position and that they had rebelled against him." (p. 84 #12.17)

oppression and social injustice which he identified in Malawi.[26] He noted with deep concern how closely the Synod leadership appeared to be identified with the government and was troubled that the CCAP raised no voice of protest about the abuses of power which were by then very evident. He made a study of the Old Testament prophets and came to identify himself especially with the prophet Amos.[27] On one occasion, e.g., he preached a sermon in which he addressed to Malawi's political leaders the words of Amos:

> You trample on the poor and force him to give you corn. Therefore, though you have built stone mansions, you will not live in them; though you have planted lush vineyards, you will not drink their wine. For I know how many are your offences and how great your sins.[28]

Naturally, concerned friends and church members warned Kaleso that he was exposing himself to serious danger by preaching such fiery sermons. However, he had made up his mind that the church must speak the truth for the people and that if he suffered as a result this was "part of the whole process of carrying the cross" to which a Christian is called.[29] St Columba's, the large congregation in the Soche area of Blantyre where Kaleso was minister, became known as a place where injustices and abuses of power were being confronted.

No wonder that people turned to Kaleso when the four politicians were murdered in 1983, coming to his house night after night pleading for the church to speak. Kaleso responded by preaching a series of very strong sermons, all directed at the abuse of power which had been so brutally exemplified in the Mwanza "accident." On one occasion his theme was that, when people covet the power

---

[26] Int. Rev Peter Kaleso, Ryall's Hotel, Blantyre, 10 April 1995.
[27] ibid.
[28] Amos 5:11-12.
[29] Int. Kaleso.

or possessions of others, this will always result in killing.[30] On another, he contrasted the peace of Jesus with the peace of the world in terms which made it very clear that he identified the MCP system with the latter. On another, he preached on poverty and challenged Kamuzu Banda's three slogans: that people have enough to eat, good houses that do not leak when it rains, and beautiful clothes to wear.[31] In the political context of the time, such a direct challenge to the Life President was regarded as revolutionary and it was not surprising that Kaleso began to receive tip-offs that the police were planning some action against him. Finally, matters came to a head when the Synod leadership, under orders from the police, required Kaleso to leave Blantyre immediately and return to his home village.[32] Even as he went, he was warned that the police were planning to assassinate him so he fled, on foot, to Mozambique where he was held under house arrest for six months until finally he went to Swaziland and thence to Scotland for further studies.[33]

Kaleso's case holds the significance that there was at least one leading minister in the Synod of Blantyre who was prepared to risk everything in order to address the Word of God prophetically to the

---

[30] It IS interesting to compare with the closing words of the Mtegha Commission Report, a quotation from Nicolo Machiavelli: "It cannot be called prowess to kill fellow citizens, to betray friends, to be treacherous, pitiless.... These ways can win a prince power but not glory." [Mtegha Commission Report, p. 85, #12.23.

[31] Int. Kaleso.

[32] Rijk A. van Dijk has argued that Kaleso's departure from St Columba's was occasioned by his promotion of "revival" activities which were unpopular with the Synod leadership. It is worth noting that there was indeed tension at St Columba's over "revivalism" and this may have influenced some sections of the congregation to seek an opportunity to get rid of Kaleso. However, van Dyck's interpretation is inadequate because he fails to take account of the Mwanza accident and Kaleso's response to it which was the major factor in precipitating the crisis which led to his abrupt departure. See Rijk A. van Dijk, "Young Malawian Puritans: Young Puritan Preachers in a Present-day African Urban Environment, PhD, University of Utrecht, 1992, pp. 138-40.

[33] Int. Kaleso.

social injustices and flagrant abuse of power which had become prevalent in Malawi. It would not speak well for the integrity of the church's social witness if such a grim and disgraceful event as the Mwanza "accident" could occur without the slightest murmur of protest being heard from the church. It is significant, therefore, that there was at least one "voice crying in the wilderness." While Kaleso was obliged to flee the country, it remained important for the future that he had registered his concern. It was marginal and fragmentary but he had spoken as the conscience of the nation. Mwanza was not forgotten and resurfaced as one of the first words to be spoken when the time came in 1992 for the people of Malawi to take account of the Banda regime. Kaleso's credibility and popularity as one of the outstanding orators of the campaign for political reform in 1992-93 owed not a little to the stand which he took as a minister of the Word in 1983. Again, however, the loneliness of his position indicates how ill-equipped was the church to act as a body even in face of an event so obviously scandalous as the Mwanza accident.

Silas Ncozana

The third Blantyre Synod General Secretary to be elected during the Banda era was Silas Ncozana who entered the office in 1985 and remained until he retired in 1995, following the advent of a new political dispensation in which he was one of those who played the role of "midwife." Temperamentally, Ncozana was less inclined than his predecessors to the lonely heroic stand but was more of a "fixer." This was the very quality which would most be needed in the social and political crisis into which Malawi was to be plunged by mid-1992. However, to the casual observer in the mid to late 1980s there was little to indicate that Ncozana might be an active figure in a movement for political change. On the contrary, he seemed to be a central figure in the MCP system, the "chaplain" who would often open the Life President's meetings with prayer and the confidante of the inner circle of the one-party system. He was one of very few people, besides the party hierarchy, who had direct access to the

President. There were hopes that he might use this access, as Sangaya had done, to counsel and, if necessary, to confront Dr Banda.

However, Ncozana points out that the situation had changed since Sangaya's time.[34] Banda had grown older and even more intolerant of any questioning or objection to his decisions. Ncozana had noted that when Banda's old friend Andrew Doig had been sent by the Church of Scotland to plead for the lives of Orton and Vera Chirwa in 1983, the President had not only refused to see the distinguished visitor but had immediately broken off their longstanding friendship. If this was how Banda responded to counsel from an old friend and contemporary, Ncozana reasoned, how would he react to a young Malawian minister who questioned any of his more draconian decisions?[35] Discretion seemed the better part of valour and Ncozana, who was deeply troubled personally by the national situation, waited for the day when there would he opportunity for critical and constructive engagement on the part of a church leader. He has confessed the profound sense of powerlessness which he felt, e.g., when a Jehovah's Witness came to plead with him that the church might take a stand for religious freedom and he had to decline to take any action or speak a single word.[36] As Chiphangwi had done before him, however, Ncozana found himself in a lonely position. He could not confide in his colleagues any such concerns for fear that the slightest hint of disloyalty to the MCP government would swiftly lead to his "disappearance."

It is important to notice that none of the Presbyterian Synods was able to break through this vicious circle of fear and mutual suspicion. It was broken, as is well known, by the Roman Catholic Bishops with their historic Pastoral Letter of Lent 1992. Not the least remarkable

---

[34] Int. Ncozana.

[35] Ibid.

[36] Very Rev Dr Silas Ncozana at the Ku Chawe Consultation of the Theology of Life Project organized by the University of Malawi Department of Theology and Religious Studies, 3-5 August 1995.

feature of this devastating critique of the one-party system was the way that the Bishops were able not only to maintain mutual confidence during its composition but even to distribute it to every parish in the land without anything being leaked to the party. The Pastoral Letter dramatically broke through the circle of fear and the web of deceit within which Malawi had been trapped. It also created a highly unstable social and political situation. It was clear that there was a groundswell of response to the Bishops' message from a wide spectrum of Malawian society. It was not clear how this nascent reform movement could be channelled in a constructive direction. When Chakufwa Chihana returned to the country, having pledged to launch a pro-democracy movement, he was arrested on the airport tarmac. When workers in Blantyre went on strike and began to riot, there was shooting in the streets and it became clear that the government was ready to use its familiar tactics of violence and intimidation to stamp out the emerging challenge to the one-party system.

It was in this situation that Silas Ncozana began to exercise a decisive role. With his knowledge of the political system he was convinced that the only possible way to achieve some rapprochement with the government was for the churches to form a united front and go direct to the President himself.[37] It was not easy to organize such an initiative but Ncozana's strategy was successfully adopted when a delegation from the World Alliance of Reformed Churches visited the country in early June and, together with local Presbyterian leaders, was received by the President.[38] The strategic goal seemed to have been achieved when Banda invited the church leaders to meet with his cabinet ministers to discuss the issues they had raised. However, the government stalled at this point and was clearly

---

[37] Int. Ncozana.

[38] See chapter five above.

reluctant to accede to the formation of a forum where fundamental political issues would be addressed.[39]

It was during this period of delay that Silas Ncozana came to occupy a central position in the struggle for constructive and peaceful political reform. During July and August he worked "behind the scenes" to bring together the broadly representative Commission which had been envisaged in the CCAP/WARC initiative.[40] When the Christian Council, on 26 August 1992, called upon the government to hold a referendum on the system of government, their letter was signed by representatives of the Anglican Church, all three Synods of the CCAP (though one later withdrew), the African Methodist Episcopal Church, the Seventh Day Baptist Church, the Churches of Christ, the Zambezi Evangelical Church, Providence Industrial Mission, the Baptist Church and a number of para-church organizations.[41] Two days later, when the church leaders wrote to the government again, their letter was signed by representatives not only of the Protestant churches but also the Roman Catholic Church, the Muslim Community, the Business Community and the Malawi Law Society.[42] This was the origin of the Public Affairs Committee which

---

[39] The Hon W.B. Deleza, Minister without Portfolio, told the church leaders on 15 July 1992 that it was no longer necessary for them to meet with government ministers since the Life President had touched on all the issues in his address to the nation on 5 July 1992. See letter of Rt Rev Dr Silas Nyirenda and Rev Misanjo E. Kansilanga to the Hon Minister of State, Mr J.Z.U. Tembo M.P., 28 August 1992, Public Affairs Committee file 1992.

[40] Int. Silas Ncozana.

[41] Christian Council of Malawi, Open Letter to the Government of Malawi, 26 August 1992.

[42] Letter of Rt Rev Dr Silas Nyirenda and Rev Misanjo E. Kansilanga to the Hon Minister of State, Mr J.Z.U. Tembo M.P., 28 August 1992, Public Affairs Committee file 1992.

became the central engine of political transition in the 1992-93 period.[43]

It was here that Ncozana was able to exploit to the fullest his talents as a "fixer" to bring together a Commission which was universally recognized as the representative organ of a truly national constituency. It was the first time that a non-party organization had been recognized by the government as having a role to play in national political life. This was the achievement of Ncozana, more than any other single individual.[44] For our present purposes it is necessary especially to note the personal risk and suffering to which Ncozana was exposed as he manoeuvred to organize the PAC. Although an era of greater openness was dawning, in mid-1992 all the structures of repression and terror which had sustained the one-party regime were still in place. When a delegation of British lawyers visited in September, they reported that "the emotion we encountered, among citizens at every level, from villages to Government officials, was fear."[45] It was in this climate that Ncozana had his fax line cut, received a series of death-threatening telephone calls, heard frequent reports that he had been targeted by MCP hit squads, had to travel incognito every time he went on the road for fear of assassination, and was generally left in no doubt that he was out of favour with the government and that his life was therefore at risk.[46]

Ironically, at the time this experience was at its height, Ncozana was still not fully trusted by his colleagues in the PAC who knew of his former closeness to the regime and feared that he might have been

---

[43] See chapter five above.

[44] It should be acknowledged, however, that from the beginning he worked hand-in-hand with the Senior Clerk to the General Synod, Rev Misanjo Kansilanga, who became the PAC Secretary. See chapter five.

[45] "Human Rights in Malawi," Report of a Joint Delegation of the Scottish Faculty of Advocates, the Law Society of England and Wales and the General Council of the Bar to Malawi, September 17-27, 1992, p. 8.

[46] Int. Ncozana.

planted as an informer in the emerging opposition movement.[47] Ncozana therefore found himself for a while in a very lonely and exposed position and it was only later that he came to be recognized as one of the architects of the new political dispensation in Malawi. In the crucial months between the issue of the Catholic Bishops' Pastoral Letter on 8 March 1992 and the first meeting of the PAC with the Presidential Committee on Dialogue on 19 October, Ncozana acted, at considerable personal cost, to begin the process of dismantling the one-party system and building "the new Malawi." When the *kairos* came, the Synod of Blantyre was not lacking either the critical distance or the courageous leadership to witness powerfully to the demands for truth and justice which the Gospel of Christ made upon Malawian society.

Conclusion

Can we use the language of martyrdom and prophecy in relation to the witness of the Blantyre Synod leadership during the one-party era? The resistance to, and criticism of, the injustices of the regime and the sufferings endured as a result cannot he compared to those of Yatuta Chisiza, Attati Mpakati, Vera and Orton Chirwa and the thousands of unnamed, unremembered Jehovah's Witnesses, Chipembere supporters and others who were tortured, maimed and killed by the MCP regime. Nor would it be fair to cast the Synod leadership in the Oscar Romero mould, as having offered an outright public condemnation of social injustices in the name of Christ and having defied the regime to act directly against the church. With only rare exceptions, criticism of the regime was carefully measured and nuanced so that it did not cause any head-on confrontation of church and state. More seriously, the church was never able to act *as a church* to address a gospel-based agenda to Malawian politics.

Nevertheless, it would be incorrect to assume that the Blantyre Synod was so close to the regime that it lacked all critical distance

---

[47] Ibid.

and was unreservedly guilty of complicity in its repression. The face-to-face confrontations of Sangaya with Banda, the sharply critical sermons of Chiphangwi, the prophetic fire of Kaleso and, finally, the marshalling of opposition on the part of Ncozana, all worked together to signal that the excesses of the one-party system were not being condoned by the church. In a totalitarian system where no whisper of dissent was being tolerated, this witness helped to keep people sane and to implant the hope that truth and justice would one day be restored. The Synod retained a latent prophetic quality which broke into the open sufficiently often to allow people to keep faith with the church as they looked for a better day. The fact that this prophetic critique was so limited was largely owing to the success of the one-party system in isolating the church leaders and so neutralizing the potentially powerful witness of the church *as a body*.

The four ministers we have considered were all highly capable leaders, men of great integrity, each in their own way taking the strain of leading the church in an extremely oppressive political climate - but each one very lonely and not able to organize the church so as to achieve united action in social witness. Their loneliness indicates a failure on the part of the church and perhaps an important challenge for the future is to build up the mutual trust and confidence which will facilitate decisive united action when evils arise in society which call for a clear witness from the church. The Blantyre Synod leadership was not without its share of suffering as it sought to be faithful to Christ in the context of political oppression. Yet the church as a whole was not rallied to counter the gross injustices of the one-party period and, if necessary, to suffer in the process. A renewed sense of the identity, purpose and unity of the church will hopefully equip the Synod in future to take decisive, corporate action when a prophetic social critique is required.

8. Christian Faith and National Identity

The emergence of the Public Affairs Committee and the central role of the churches in Malawi's political transition highlighted afresh the national importance of Christianity. As powerful divisive forces were unleashed, the integrity of the nation came under pressure. What is the role of Christianity in such a situation? It may at first sight seem unlikely that the Christian faith should be a potent factor in the moulding of national identity. After all is not the central drive of Christianity to direct our attention to "another country"? Does the Gospel not tell us that our true place of belonging is not in any earthly institution but only in the kingdom of Christ? May we not therefore conclude that national identity is a secular concern, a matter of indifference so far as Christian faith is concerned?

In the case of Malawi, Christian faith and national identity have grown up together over the past 120 years. At a time when the unity of the nation appears to be under some strain, there may be value in considering that history. Equally, such a time provokes a search for an authentically Christian theology of the nation which might guide Christian thinking and action. The context in which this paper is being written is one where Malawian national identity is under question. Leroy Vail and Landeg White, in an important article published in 1989, have argued that tribal rather than national identity has been the more powerful force shaping Malawian history.[1] This argument appears to have been vindicated by the outcome of independent Malawi's first multi-party General Election, held on 17 May 1994. Though the three main contestants all purported to be parties with a national following, the results made it clear that each of the three regions gave overwhelming support to the party with which each identified - AFORD in the Northern

---

[1] Leroy Vail and Landeg White, "Tribalism in the Political History of Malawi," in Leroy Vail ed., *The Creation of Tribalism in Southern Africa,* London: James Currey & Berkeley and Los Angeles: University of California Press, 1989, pp. 151-192.

Region, the Malawi Congress Party (MCP) in the Central Region and the United Democratic Front (UDF) in the Southern Region.[2] National unity now emerged as an urgent political question.[3] This chapter seeks to address the issue from the perspective of the Christian presence within the national life. It is not possible here to consider the problem of the alien imposition of the nation by the colonial state nor the question of how far various sections of the population share the sense of national identity. For a working definition of the nation the pragmatic approach of Hugh Seton-Watson will suffice:

> A nation exists when a significant number of people in a community consider themselves to form a nation, or behave as if they formed one. It is not necessary that the whole of the population should so feel or so behave, and it is not possible to lay down dogmatically a minimum percentage of a population which must be so affected. When a significant group holds this belief, it possesses 'national consciousness.'[4]

On that basis we may be confident that a nation exists in Malawi. The task set in this paper is to examine its history in relation to the growth of Christianity in the country; and to ask what theological resources the Christian faith might have to offer in relation to national identity at this time.

Christianity and National Identity in Malawian History

The Missionary Vision

An important consideration in this history is the fact that the coming of Christianity predates the emergence of Nyasaland/Malawi as an

---

[2] *Daily Times*, 20 May 1994.

[3] *Daily Times*, 19 May 1994; *The Enquirer*, 21-24 May 1994.

[4] Hugh Seton-Watson, *Nations and States: An Enquiry into the Origins of Nations and the Politics of Nationalism,* London: Methuen, 1977, p. 5.

identifiable political unit. The Scottish Presbyterian missions of Livingstonia and Blantyre began their work in 1875 whereas it was not until the 1890s that the British Protectorate was established and the borders of what is now known as Malawi were laid down.[5] Moreover, not only did the Christian missions play a key role in attracting British interest to the area but it was their lobbying of the British government during the "scramble for Africa" which resulted in the borders of Malawi taking their present shape. The British were on the verge of accepting the Portuguese proposal that the Shire river should be the dividing line between their respective spheres of influence. When rumours of this proposed arrangement reached the Blantyre Mission the response was immediate and direct:

> This is disastrous if it is true: it is indeed 'keeping the shell and giving Portugal the kernel'. We must hold fast to this stronghold and gateway of African civilization whatever comes, and in face of what Lord Salisbury and home authorities know of the Shire Highlands, we feel persuaded enough to say of the possibility of its becoming eventually Portuguese, that we don't believe it![6]

The Scottish missionaries regarded the Shire Highlands as the appointed territory for the implementation of the distinctive vision of "Christianity and commerce" which had been imparted by David Livingstone and had led to the founding of the missions. Accordingly they launched a vigorous and finally successful campaign to persuade the British government to withdraw from its initial willingness to cede the area to Portugal, and to establish a formal British Protectorate over the territory now known as Malawi.[7] If we take Benedict Anderson's seminal definition of a nation as "an

---

[5] Bridglal Pachai, *Malawi: The History of the Nation,* London: Longman, 1973, pp. 81-94; also K. John McCracken, *Politics and Christianity in Malawi 1875-1940,* Cambridge: Cambridge University Press, 1977, pp. 17-109, 157-183; and Andrew C. Ross, *Blantyre Mission and the Making of Modern Malawi.*

[6] *Life and Work in British Central Africa,* June 1889.

[7] See Pachai, *Malawi: The History of the Nation,* pp. 70-80.

imagined community"[8] then it is clear that Malawi began as a product of the missionary imagination! Though few of the indigenous population would have identified with it at that time, the Scottish missionaries had a vision of an African Christian civilization the fulfilment of which required that the territorial integrity of Nyasaland/Malawi be secured. To this extent the modern nation grew out of the Christian presence. David Clement Scott, the leader of the Blantyre Mission, clearly stated his conviction that it would be a "land where church and state must be in closest connection."[9]

This same vision also sustained the struggle, after the establishment of the British Protectorate, to defend the emerging nation from the influence of Cecil Rhodes' British South Africa Company.[10] National identity often owes a good deal to what it is *against*. In the case of the missionary vision of Nyasaland it is clear that what it was against was the "Cape colonization" of the country, i.e. its being incorporated within Rhodes's sphere of influence. This suspicion of Rhodesian intentions remained evident in the discussions of Scottish missionaries during World War I when they continued to be guided by a determination that any attempts to draw the country closer to Southern Rhodesia must be resisted at all costs.[11] The territorial integrity of what would become Malawi was sustained at that stage to

---

[8] Benedict Anderson, *Imagined Communities,* rev. ed., London: Verso, 1991 [1983]; cit Ian Linden, "Religion and Nationalism Today," *The Month,* January 1994, p. 26.

[9] *Life and Work in British Central Africa,* October 1890; see the discussion of John McCracken, "Church and State in Malawi: The Role of the Scottish Presbyterian Missions, 1875-1964," in Isabel A. Phiri, Kenneth R. Ross & James L. Cox ed., *The Role of Christianity in Development, Peace and Reconstruction: Southern Perspectives,* Nairobi: All Africa Conference of Churches (African Challenge Series No. 8), 1996, pp. 48-73.

[10] See Ross, *Gospel Ferment in Malawi,* pp. 107-25.

[11] See George A. Shepperson, "External Factors in the Development of African Nationalism, with Particular Reference to British Central Africa," *Phylon,* Vol. XXII, No. 3 (Fall 1961), p. 214.

an important degree by the vision that, as opposed to being incorporated in a racist political union, it must be defended as a place where an African civilization would be developed.[12]

The (Christian) Nationalist Movement

This struggle finally reached its climax in the successful campaign of an African nationalist movement to effect the secession of what soon became Malawi from the Federation of Rhodesia and Nyasaland in 1963.[13] By that time the distinctive identity of Malawi was no longer a matter of missionary imagination but an established political reality among the people of the land. The connection between the missionary work and the eventual achievement of national independence has been attested by Donald Siwale, one of the pioneer Zambian nationalists: "Without the Livingstonia missionaries we could not have articulated our demand for independence."[14] This remark can be understood at different levels. There is the well-documented educational provision offered by the missionaries which broadened the horizons of the people and enabled them to see beyond the immediate and the local. By 1912 this broader vision was being given effect politically in the Native Associations from which the nationalist movement developed.[15] Furthermore, many of those who received a mission education were employed in government service and came to be concentrated in Zomba and Blantyre. Their very context disposed them to think in national rather than ethnic or

---

[12] The classic expression of this was David Clement Scott's declaration that "'Africa for the Africans' has been our policy from the first, and we believe that God has given this country into our hands that we may train its peoples how to develop its marvellous resources for themselves." *Life and Work in British Central Africa*, January 1895.

[13] See Pachai, *Malawi: The History of the Nation*, 241-43, 265-66.

[14] Fergus MacPherson, personal communication, Edinburgh, 25 August 1994.

[15] See Roger K. Tangri, The Rise of Nationalism in Colonial Africa: The Case of Colonial Malawi," in B. Pachai, G.W. Smith and R.K. Tangri ed., *Malawi Past and Present,* Zomba: University of Malawi, 1968, pp. 101-2.

regional terms and it was this group which organized the Nyasaland African Congress (later Malawi Congress Party) in the 1940s. A close and sympathetic observer of the nationalist movement, Guy Clutton-Brock, made the following observation in 1959:

> Arising from its land and its people, Nyasaland has a spiritual and economic asset of high potential in its growing nationalism. In this lovely land of widely differing terrain, climate, peoples, customs and languages, the population is increasingly integrated by the common feature of the people's love of their own country, Nyasaland.... This patriotism is more marked in Nyasaland than it is in any other part of Central Africa."[16]

At the same time the missionary educational enterprise had another, and quite unintended, social effect. Since the local economy could not offer the employment opportunities which their education led them to seek, large numbers of men travelled beyond Nyasaland to become migrant workers in the industrial centres to the south. Paradoxically, the experience of migrant labour was a further formative factor in the formation of national consciousness. Andrew Ross commented that:

> Livingstonia and Blantyre men took the lead in those (migrant) communities, and soon it was usual for the migrants, from whatever tribe in Malawi, to enter "Nyasa" where the official form required them to name their tribe. There is no such tribe! The men from Nyasaland were simply asserting their oneness. This response to the experience of migrant employment was one of the roots of nationalism in Malawi.[17]

---

[16] Guy Clutton-Brock, *Dawn in Nyasaland,* London: Hodder & Stoughton, 1959, p. 20.

[17] Andrew C. Ross, "Forty-five Years of Turmoil," p. 54: Mike Kamwendo has written similarly of the "collective nationality" of the *Nyasa* community in Harare "There were Tumbukas, Chewas, Yaos, Lomwes as well as Senas and Tongas, but all collectively known as *Nyasas." Daily Times,* 23 December 1994.

In addition to its direct social impact, missionary education also promoted a confidence in local African history and culture without which it would have been difficult for a viable national identity to be developed. The publications of a missionary like Thomas Cullen Young[18] gave people a pride in their history and culture which, though in the first instance tribal in expression, was later developed in a nationalist direction.[19] These are all factors in the development of national identity which have been well recognized.

Less attention has been given to the impact which receiving the Christian Gospel may have had in opening up new possibilities at the level of identity. Can the case be made that the experience of a new sense of belonging in Jesus Christ opened the hearts and minds of the converts to a broader community identity? The hymns which some of them composed to give expression to their new faith are suggestive of this. The Ngoni composer Mawelera Tembo wrote:

> Jesus, Jesus is among us
> He's calling *everybody*
> O hear him for yourself.
>
> Jesus, Jesus is our Saviour
> Who saves *the whole creation*
> O hear him for yourself
>
> Welcome, welcome *everybody*
> To life in all its fullness
> O hear him for yourself.[20]

---

[18] See T. Cullen Young, *Notes on the Speech and History of the Tumbuka-Henga Peoples,* Livingstonia: Mission Press, 1923; Saulos Nyirenda, "History of the Tumbuka-Henga People," trans. and ed. T. Cullen Young, *Bantu Studies,* 5 (1931), 1-75; T. Cullen Young, *Notes on the History of the Tumbuka-Kamanga Peoples in the Northern Province of Nyasaland,* London: Religious Tract Society, 1932.

[19] See Peter G. Forster, *T. Cullen Young: Missionary and Anthropologist,* Hull: Hull University Press, 1989, 156ff.

[20] Fergus Macpherson, *"Sumu za Chifipa:* Christian Songs in Malawi," *Bulletin of the Scottish Institute of Missionary Studies,* 6-7 (1990-91), p. 50, my italics.

Another Ngoni, Peter Thole, remembered as *ng'ombwa ya zingtombwa*[21] wrote exultantly:

> Leap up my soul; leap up and sing
> Take heart again; here comes your king.
> Redemption done by God's right hand
> Is breaking forth *through all the land.*
>
> Dance, dance my heart; rejoice and sing
> This is the morning of the king.
> Break forth in praise, let men declare
> The dawn is breaking *everywhere.*[22]

The practical implications of being part of this new Gospel reality are brought out in the simple words of an anonymous hymn dating from the same period:

> We're one blood with one Creator, one Saviour
> So let's help one another.
>
> Know that you are here to help
> That's why you are created. Don't forget.[23]

It was the impact of Christian conversion which brought this broader perspective. It broke through geographical distances and historical differences to give people a sense of belonging together, united by the momentous event of the coming of the Gospel of Christ. Their common belonging as Christians relativized their tribal identities and so prepared the way for the emergence of a nation. It was not only their education but also their experience of faith which enabled mission "graduates" such as Levi Mumba, Charles Chinula, Lewis Bandawe, Orton Chirwa and Henry Chipembere to emerge as nationalist leaders. It has been well established that a shared negative

---

[21] "King of minstrels."

[22] Macpherson, *"Sumu za Chifipa,"* p. 52, my italics.

[23] Ibid, p. 40, my italics.

response to the experience of colonialism was basic to the development of a national self-consciousness.²⁴ However, such a negative interpretation requires to be balanced by an appreciation of the positive impulse which the experience of Christian faith brought to the formation of a national identity.

The Attempted Chewa Hegemony

There is nothing like a common enemy to foster national unity. So it was that the struggle against the Federation of Rhodesia and Nyasaland, the existence of which was understood to be a threat to the national integrity of Malawi, caused the people in the late 1950 and early 1960s to be united - as never before or since - in the common purpose of achieving independence. Men and women from every part of the country stood shoulder to shoulder in the struggle; ethnic, social or political differences being regarded as inconsequential in light of the common objective of securing the integrity of the nation. Within weeks of independence, however, this unity was shattered by the "Cabinet Crisis" in which the earlier leaders of the Congress movement, such as Henry Chipembere, Orton Chirwa and Kanyama Chiume, were forced to resign and go into exile and the Prime Minister Kamuzu Banda laid the foundations of the dictatorship which was to hold Malawi in thrall for the next thirty years.²⁵ While there were profound political differences between the two sides in the Cabinet crisis,²⁶ it could not escape notice that the

---

²⁴ Tangri, "The Rise of Nationalism in Colonial Africa," p. 98.

²⁵ See Andrew C. Ross, "Some Reflections on the Malawi 'Cabinet Crisis,' 1964-65.

²⁶ "[The ministers] believed in government based on collective responsibility; Banda favoured a presidential style of government where all authority would be concentrated in his office. In foreign policy the 'rebel' ministers were pan-Africanist and advocated links with China and the development of close relations with Zambia and Tanzania; Banda preferred to improve links with the Portuguese colonial government in Mozambique and other white-ruled countries to the south. Similarly, the younger ministers supported Africanization

ousted ministers came either from the north like Chirwa and Chiume or from the south like the Yao Chipembere. Furthermore, it must be noted that "the repression which followed the break-up of the cabinet was clearly directed by region. Chiefs from both the Northern and Southern Regions were dismissed, but none from the Central Region. Likewise a majority of regional councils in both the Northern and Sothern Regions were dissolved - but again none from the Central Region."[27]

With his own authority under threat Banda had opted to play the tribal-regional card and to attempt to maintain his highly authoritarian rule by means of a hegemony of his own Chewa-speaking people of the Central Region.[28] This divide-and-rule policy has been well-described by Vail and White:

> the language in which the politics of this period (1964-75) were discussed increasingly drew upon a store of ethnic symbols and stereotypes. The restructuring of relationships of power that occurred was seen explicitly as a campaign against the Yao-speaking peoples of the southern part of the country and all the peoples of the Northern Region. These attacks were coupled with an affirmation of the special authenticity of the culture of the country's Chewa-speaking people. These events, accompanied by repeated purges of the Party's leadership and a steadily declining real income for Malawi's workers and peasants, were responsible for the

of the civil service; Banda wanted expatriate whites to continue to run it." *Malawi: A Moment of Truth,* London: CIIR, 1993, p. 12.

[27] *Where Silence Rules: The Suppression of Dissent in Malawi,* New York, Washington and London: An Africa Watch Report, 1990, p. 57.

[28] The case of Banda provides a good illustration of Ibbo Mandaza's thesis that *"Ethnic politics* are almost always played in the *state* field, in the pursuit of social, political or economic advantage." Ibbo Mandaza, "The National Question, Ethnicity and the State: Towards a Conceptual and Research Framework," Paper presented at the Annual Colloquium of the Southern African Regional Institute for Policy Studies, Harare, 25-30 September 1994, 13.

destruction of sentiments of national unity which the campaign against the Federation of Rhodesia and Nyasaland had inspired during the late 1950s and early 1960s and encouraged the fragmentation of the country along ethnically defined fault lines.[29]

Banda himself undertook the task of providing an ideological justification for the Chewa hegemony. He liked to claim that over 50% of the Malawi population were Chewa, though many of them had not realized this![30] Moreover, he "equated 'Malawian-ness' with Chewa-ness, and he has depicted the Chewa as the very soul of the country."[31]

It was on this ideological basis that Tumbuka was abolished as an official language in 1968. From then on Chichewa was the sole national language. No other African language could be used in the press or on the radio and Chichewa became mandatory in all schools.[32] This imposition of a national language could be presented as conducive to national unity but, in fact, it alienated the north and the country became ever more divided on regional lines. This reality was, however, disguised by Banda's propaganda which was so successful that as late as 1988 an American State Department Report maintained that "Malawi enjoys a large degree of ethnolinguistic uniformity" and that "the economic and social needs of ethnic Africans are generally met on a non-discriminatory basis."[33] The true nature of Banda rule became apparent, however, in what John

---

[29] Vail and White, 'Tribalism in the Political History of Malawi," 151.

[30] Ibid, 180. A reliable breakdown of the 1966 population suggests that, in fact, there were 28.3% Chewa, 15.3% Nyanja, 11.8% Lomwe, 11.2% Yao, 9.0% Ngoni, 7.4% Tumbuka, 2.8% Sena 2.0% Tonga and 12.2% others. See F. Pryor, *The Political Economy of Poverty, Equity and Growth: A World Bank Comparative Study of Malawi and Madagascar,* Oxford: OUP, 1990, 25.

[31] Ibid, 182.

[32] Ibid, 183.

[33] Cit. *Where Silence Rules,* 55.

Lwanda has called "the 1989 regional 'ethnic cleansing' of teachers."[34] The President's banishment of all teachers of northern origin to their own region was such a blatant act of regionalism that it brought this aspect of his rule out into the open and raised the question of whether the regime contained the seeds of its own destruction. Had it introduced so much alienation into Malawian society that its own legitimacy was threatened? A concomitant question was whether the years of Chewa hegemony had irreparably fragmented the national unity with which Malawi had begun its independent history in the early 1960s?

The Survival of National Identity?

The political fragmentation of the country was clearly manifest in the results of the 1994 General Election, as outlined above. No less significant, however, was the dismay with which this aspect of the election results was received. Now that regionalism was out in the open it was universally regarded as a danger. So much so that AFORD and the MCP, sworn enemies hitherto, could justify their sudden alliance on the grounds of the need to secure national unity.[35] The fact that appeal could be made to the security of the nation as a moral and political necessity is indicative of how deeply held the national identity remains. Where Vail and White's thesis is open to challenge is at the point where they go so far as to say that the Chewa hegemony has led to "the *destruction* of sentiments of national unity."[36] It has to be acknowledged that grave damage has been done to the sense of national identity. The capture of the state apparatus and the national symbols by the Banda dictatorship have done much to discredit them. His manipulation of the earlier nationalist ideology so as to turn it into a personality cult has turned its symbols into forces for alienation rather than for unity. This was

---

[34] Lwanda, *Kamuzu Banda of Malawi*, p. 259.

[35] See, e.g., *The Monitor,* 29 June 1994; *The New Express,* 30 June 1994.

[36] Vail and White, 'Tribalism in the Political History of Malawi," p. 151.

seen in the aftermath of the UDF victory in the General Election in, e.g., the ambivalence over the use of the national flag on state occasions since it had become for many the symbol not of the nation but of MCP/Chewa rule.[37] Likewise the new government found it impossible to celebrate the national independence day on 6 July 1994 since it had been made a symbol not of the nation but of the dictator who had now been rejected. The propaganda had ceaselessly proclaimed Banda to be the "Father and Founder" of the nation. Loyalty to the nation was construed as personal loyalty to the *Ngwazi*. Now that this loyalty was repudiated what was left of national identity?

All national institutions had been, to a greater or lesser extent, infiltrated and corrupted by the propaganda of the dictatorship. The only institutions which were able to exist on a national scale with relatively little interference in their internal affairs were the churches. This opened up the possibility that the churches could be the custodians of the national identity which traced its origins, *inter alia*, both to the vision of the early Scottish missionaries and to the nationalist movement of the later Malawian Christians. As a matter of fact, it was from one of the churches that a critique of the excesses of the dictatorship finally came: the Roman Catholic Bishops' *Pastoral Letter* of Lent 1992. Clearly the Bishops spoke on behalf of their church and took their guidance explicitly from Gospel teaching. Yet there were important points at which they spoke also on behalf of the nation:

> *Mutu umodzi susenza denga.*[38] No one person can claim to have a monopoly of truth and wisdom. No individual - or group

---

[37] This problem was strikingly illustrated in December 1994 when the cockerel which formed the centrepiece of the Independence Arch in Blantyre was removed. During the nationalist struggle the cockerel (tambala) had symbolized the breaking of the dawn (kwacha) of independence. In the succeeding years, however, it was so subverted by the MCP for use as a party emblem that it could no longer be accepted as a national symbol.

[38] Lit "One head cannot lift a roof," i.e. you cannot do anything on your own.

of individuals - can pretend to have all the resources needed to guarantee *the progress of the nation.*³⁹

The tremendous nationwide response which the *Pastoral Letter* evoked was an indication of how effective the Bishops had been in speaking not only for their own constituency but for the nation as a whole. The ruling regime sought to isolate and disgrace the authors of the letter but events soon proved that the country was with Bishops and that it was the MCP which was out on a limb!⁴⁰

The role of the churches as custodians of national identity over against Banda's attempted Chewa hegemony was further demonstrated in their ability to bring together a representative and truly national body to negotiate with government on the transition to multi-party politics. The Public Affairs Committee was composed primarily of church and Muslim leaders but also included representatives of the Malawi Chamber of Commerce and the Malawi Law Society. This body acted as the central engine of political reform in the critical period between the Pastoral Letter of March 1992 and the national referendum on the multi-party issue held in June 1993.⁴¹ This action revealed that the churches had not been immune from the fragmentation of the Banda years. The predominantly Chewa Nkhoma Synod refused to play any part in the PAC and closed ranks with the outgoing MCP government.⁴² Nevertheless, while the churches faced their own struggle for unity, they proved to be a clear focal point for a national regrouping and a recovery of national identity. Recent history gives grounds for suggesting that the churches did maintain a Christian vision of the nation which outlasted the years of attempted Chewa hegemony and

---

[39] *Living our Faith*, p. 8, my italics.

[40] See *Malawi: A Moment of Truth*, 2-5.

[41] See chapter five above.

[42] See Ross, "Not Catalyst but Ferment, " p. 104.

proved to be an important source of national renewal when the Banda regime finally collapsed.

It is therefore necessary to challenge Vail and White's argument that the Banda era brought about the destruction of the sense of nationhood which had been evident at the time of the struggle against Federation. Nevertheless, at a time when Malawians are struggling to reassert their national identity Vail's judgement is a salutary one: "Nationalism ... in Malawi ... had been basically a negative force, directed against colonialism, with little positive vision about the nature of the new society after colonialism's demise."[43] Basil Davidson has gone further to speak in terms of the "curse of the nation-state" in Africa.[44] Given the history of the churches in relation to the nation in Malawi, it seems to be time to unfold something of the positive theology of the nation which the Christian faith is able to offer.

A Theology of the Nation for Malawi Today

The Nation in Biblical Perspective

The Christian faith has both a "no" and a "yes" to address to those communities which have come to take on the identity of nations. It says "no" to every tendency to regard nationhood as part of the natural and necessary order of human existence. It is ready to denounce as idolatry any nationalist ideology which ascribes ultimacy to any of the symbols of national life, such as the motherland, the state, the race or the president. This is because the Bible introduces the nations not as part of God's original creation. Rather, in the story of the Tower of Babel, the diversity of the nations is seen as indicative of God's judgement on humanity for its

---

[43] Leroy Vail, Preface to *The Creation of Tribalism in Southern Africa,* p. ix.

[44] Basil Davidson, *The Black Man's Burden: Africa and the Curse of the Nation-State,* London: James Currey, 1992.

presumption![45] Authentic Christianity will therefore always have the effect on the nation of "cutting it down to size" - as was evident in Malawi in 1992 when the churches began to challenge the pretensions of the one-party state.[46] When the church is true to itself it will always have a "no" to address to the state. There is also, however, a "yes." In Genesis 10 we find recognition being given to the integrity of the nations as diverse communities developing after the judgement of the great flood. Very soon the biblical narrative comes to be concentrated on the history of God's chosen nation, Israel. Yet this divine election is not aimed at the exclusion of the other nations. On the contrary, Abraham was called to be a blessing to all peoples on earth.[47] It is made clear in Israel's prophetic literature that the "gentile" nations also are accountable to the God of Israel and have a place in the divine destiny.[48] The calling of the nations is finally made plain in John's vision of the new Jerusalem recorded in Revelation 21:

> The city does not need the sun or the moon to shine on it, for the glory of God gives it light, and the Lamb is its lamp. *The nations will walk by its light,* and the kings of the earth will bring their splendour into it. On no day will its gates ever be shut, for there will be no night there. *The glory and honour of the nations will be brought into it.*[49]

The focus in the New Testament is on the church as the community in which God's redemptive purposes in Christ are brought to

---

[45] Genesis 11:1-9.

[46] See Ross, "Not Catalyst But Ferment," pp. 102-3.

[47] Genesis 12:3.

[48] See, e.g., Amos 1:1-2:5 for the prophet's remarkable proclamation of divine judgement on Israel's neighbours - Damascus, Gaza, Tyre, Edom, Ammon and Moab. Isaiah 19 indicates clearly the place which Egypt and Assyria have in God's redemptive plan, concluding with v. 25: 'The Lord Almighty will bless them, saying, 'Blessed be Egypt my people, Assyria my handiwork, and Israel my inheritance."

[49] Revelation 21:23-26, my italics.

fruition. The Lamb with his blood has "purchased men for God *from* every tribe and language and people and nation."[50] Yet the calling of the nations to respond to the divine initiative is not lost to view. Indeed the identity of both church and nation is secured in Jesus Christ.

This has sometimes been portrayed on the model of concentric circles with the church as the inner circle and the nation as the outer, both with their centre in the Lordship of Jesus Christ. A better model, however, may be that offered by William Storrar in a recent study of nationhood within the Scottish context: "The biblical model of nationhood may be thought of as an ecological one in which the three communities of Church, Nation and Kingdom exist as three living systems within the divine economy revealed in Scripture."[51] God's kingdom, in which all that is wrong in human life is put right, is established through the church and among the nations. The church is the prototype and corporate sign of coming rule of God on earth, and will give way to that everlasting kingdom in the new heaven and the new earth. The nations have no such calling or ultimate reference. Yet the life of each nation is addressed by the Word of God which calls God's kingdom into being and the distinctive genius of each nation is given a place in that kingdom. Thus church, nation and kingdom are set in the relationship of mutual interaction which constitutes God's "yes" to the identity of the nation. Providential and provisional communities they are, yet nations are called to sanctify and transform their identity according to the promise and command of God in the gospel of the kingdom. The nation must not be confused with either the church or the kingdom of God: hence God's "no." Yet the Word of God must be released into the national life so that the latter can fulfil its God-given

---

[50] Revelation 5:9, my italics.

[51] William Storrar, *Scottish Identity: A Christian Vision,* Edinburgh: Handsel Press, 1990, p. 128.

destiny in relation to the church and the kingdom: hence God's "yes."[52]

The Kingdom of Christ and the Nation of Malawi

To be a disciple of Christ is to refuse to offer ultimate loyalty to anything other than the Lord himself. Paradoxically, it is within that commitment that the nation finds its true identity. The Christian resists all tendencies to idolize the nation but gives glad recognition to what the nation really is - a community called into being by the providence of God and invited to bring its distinctive riches into God's everlasting kingdom. The nation is then upheld not by the blind love of patriotism but by the critical solidarity that arises from a knowledge of Christ crucified. By faith Christians are able to identify with their country for Christ's sake and embrace their nation with the kind of unconditional love which sent Christ to the cross. What Malawi needs, in the aftermath of a period which has provoked much shame and distress, is what Storrar, addressing the life of another nation, describes as

> not the idolatrous love of a patriotism that [is] blind to the nation's mortality and failings, but the unconditional love of Christian charity, *agape*, which alone [has] the power to contemplate the beloved country in all its shame, and yet still love it with an undiminished clarity and compassion... This is what is meant by a Christian identification or affirmation of the nation and its national identity. Such an identification is possible because the nation is seen with the love of God revealed in the death of his Son, Jesus Christ. But it is obvious also from this definition that identification is inseparable from the Christian calling to separate from and oppose in a

---

[52] See ibid, pp. 124-131.

nation's life all that denies the image and purpose of God for humanity as revealed in Christ crucified.[53]

It is by offering this unique form of critical solidarity that Christian people can contribute to the nation's becoming all that it is called to be.

Such a Christological understanding of national identity is a demanding one in terms of discipleship. For it calls believers to walk the way of Jesus in the midst of the national life. When the doctrine of the Lordship of Christ has been applied to national affairs it has often been in a triumphalist fashion with ill-disguised theocratic pretensions on the part of the church. Talk of a "Christian nation" even today often reflects a domination model in the understanding of the relation of church and society. The Lordship of Christ can easily be used as a cipher for intolerance and exclusion. However, Jesus did not come to dominate but, rather, to serve and to give his life. He was the "man for others," remarkable for his humility and openness to others. It is therefore as servants, humbly walking the way of Jesus in the midst of the nation's life, that believers bear witness to the crucified and risen Lord. Not through their own domination but, on the contrary, by their reaching out and lifting up the poor, the weak and the despised will Christian people become a sign to the nation of its true destiny. For the nation too is called "to act justly and to love mercy and to walk humbly with its God."[54] National identity is so often understood in terms of pride, not humility. Yet here again, Christ turns things upside down as he opens for us the way of life.

---

[53] *Ibid*, p. 168. I am indebted at this point in the discussion to William Storrar's attempt to elaborate a Christian understanding of the identity of Scotland - that other small nation which has so many historical links with Malawi.

[54] Micah 6:8.

The Triune God and the Life of the Nation

A fully Christian understanding of the identity of the nation will not only refer the national life to the life, death and resurrection of Christ but will do so within the framework of a trinitarian understanding of God. The life of God, as John Zizioulas has stated with remarkable clarity, is a matter of "being as communion."[55] It is not the case that there is an inner substance of God which can be considered prior to the interpersonal relations of the Trinity. Rather, it is precisely in the mutual relationality within the triune life of God, and nowhere else, that the being of God consists![56] This profound reality came to be described in Christian thought as *perichoresis* - the mutual indwelling and interpenetration of Father, Son and Holy Spirit in the glorious triune life of God. This dynamism of mutual constitutiveness, furthermore, is not only characteristic of God but also of the world which God has made! God's creating and redeeming love gives to the world what Colin Gunton has described as "a perichoretic reality which in different ways reflects within the structures of the temporal and spatial the perichoresis which is God in eternity."[57] This means in practical terms that everything in the world "contributes to the being of everything else, enabling everything to be what it distinctively is."[58] This is something well understood in African thought, uncorrupted by Western individualism, where it is held that true humanity can be found only in community. *Muntu wakuchemeka muntu chifukwa cha wanyake*.[59] being as communion! One of the

---

[55] John D. Zizioulas, *Being as Communion*, London: Darton, Longman & Todd, 1985.

[56] See ibid. pp. 29-54 for a detailed elaboration of how the Christian Fathers came to give priority to *hypostasis* (personal being) in their understanding of God.

[57] Colin E. Gunton, *The One, the Three and the Many: God, Creation and the Culture of* Modernity, Cambridge: Cambridge University Press, 1993, p. 179.

[58] Ibid, p. 166.

[59] "It is only in relation to the others that I am enabled to be myself."

temporal and spatial structures which is called to such *perichoresis* is the nation. It means that the identity of the nation is secured not by the hegemony of a unitary centre of control. Rather, it is found within the *perichoresis* which enables each constituent part to be what it truly is. The fact that the nation contains those who are different from "us" is not a threat to be countered. On the contrary it is a call to find our being in reciprocal relatedness with our neighbour.

Gunton's study of the Holy Spirit concludes that the aim of the Spirit's work in human life is not homogenization but rather "relation in otherness, relation which does not subvert but establishes the other in its true reality."[60] It is from this perspective that the thesis of Vail and White may be open to question. For it is fallacious to suppose that tribal and ethnic identity is necessarily antithetical to national identity.[61] The very awareness of diversity has the potential to become the sense of reciprocal relatedness in which true humanity is to be found. Of course, it *can be* developed in another direction which *is* subversive of national identity - as was well-illustrated by Dr Banda's attempts from 1964 to 1992 to manipulate nationalist ideology so as to entrench structures of domination favourable to the Chewa at the expense of others. The fact that a viable sense of nationhood survived that experience is indicative of the fact that there remains hope of something better. At the dawn of a new era, perhaps that may be found in an understanding that ethnic and regional identities are not subversive of but rather *constitutive of* the identity of the nation. From the perspective of Christian faith we are able to hold forth a vision of an enabling nationhood where each constituent part becomes what it distinctively is through its reciprocal relatedness to the others. Diverse identities within the national life are not then a threat to be crushed by the sledgehammer of homogenization. Rather they are the means through which the

---

[60] Gunton, *The One, the Three and the Many*, p. 182.

[61] The possibility of "multiple choices of identity" in the Malawian context has been discussed in Wiseman C. Chirwa, "Regionalism, Ethnicity and the National Question in Malawi," unpublished paper 1994, p. 4.

nation may bring to fruition the fullness of the multicultural riches which it is called to bring into the new Jerusalem. On the basis of a thankful, humble and repentant sense of nationhood, Malawi can move forward in its unity and in its diversity towards the *eschaton* in which it is called to have a place.

9. After Freedom: Christ's Kingdom and Malawi's Second Republic

This book began with Peter Thole's exultant words: "Leap up, my soul; leap and sing; Take heart again, here comes your king." Evidence has been gathered to suggest that, indeed, the king is coming. Though always provisional and ambiguous in its historical manifestation, the kingdom of Christ has "broken forth through all the land." This is particularly evident at those "moments of truth" when the gap between the ultimate and penultimate narrows and a particular historical option becomes very closely identified with the kingdom of God. Such a moment came for Malawi in 1992-93 when the First Republic began to disintegrate and the foundations were laid for the Second. The celebrated Pastoral Letter of the Catholic Bishops bore witness to the kingdom dimensions of the political crisis. It stands, as John Lwanda has written, as: "an as yet unsurpassed high point in its demands for economic, political and moral welfare for Malawians."[1]

Now that the Second Republic has taken shape and its contours and structure are clearly visible, it is necessary to look at it in the light of the dawning kingdom of Christ. Are there indications that the Malawian social and political order is being significantly shaped by the coming kingdom, or are the two in contradiction? It is with this question that we consider Malawi's Second Republic as it has taken effect in the mid-1990s. In approaching such a study it is well to bear in mind the aphorism coined by Jan Kees van Donge, that in discussion of Malawian politics, those who *know* do not talk; while those who *talk* do not know![2] Humility and restraint must be

---

[1] John L.C. Lwanda, *Promises, Power, Politics and Poverty: Democratic Transition in Malawi (1961-1999)*, Glasgow: Dudu Nsomba, 1996, p. 104.

[2] Jan Kees van Donge (political scientist at the University of Malawi), personal communication, June 1997.

exercised in the attempt to construct a theological (or any other) discernment of the currents which move the polis in Malawi. Yet the theologian, concerned with what Paul Lehmann called the "permanent revolution"[3] set in train by the lure of the coming kingdom of God, cannot allow such humility and restraint to reach the point of silence. Rosa Luxembourg is reported to have said: "The most revolutionary deed is and always will remain to say out loud what is the case."[4] Hence we must make as plain as possible the outstanding features of the Second Republic, using the light shed on them by the dawning kingdom of Christ.

Reshuffling the Cards or Starting a New Game?

Zygmunt Bauman has astutely observed the irony that in the struggle for justice, the forces for change often remain chained to the dominant order - even when they succeed in toppling it! They "demand the reshuffling of the cards, not another game. They do not blame the game, only the stronger hand of the adversary."[5] Notwithstanding the indisputable gains at the level of personal freedoms, most Malawians would agree that little has changed in terms of the social, political and economic order which governs their lives. The shuffling of the pack has redistributed some of the trump cards but the game is still played by the small, dominant political class which fell heir to the colonial state. As John Minnis has observed: "the party tends to be seen by the masses as *the* site of politics, the source of political truth and wisdom. On the other hand, the people

---

[3] Paul Lehmann, cit. Charles Villa-Vicencio, *Civil Disobedience and Beyond: Law, Resistance and Religion in South Africa,* Cape Town: David Philip & Grand Rapids: Eerdmans, 1990, p. 132.

[4] Rosa Luxembourg, cit. Miroslav Volf, *Exclusion and Embrace: A Theological Exploration of Identity, Otherness, and Reconciliation,* Nashville: Abingdon Press, 1996, p. 235. I gladly acknowledge the stimulus and inspiration which I derived from this book in the preparation of this chapter.

[5] Zygmunt Bauman, *Postmodern Ethics,* Oxford: Blackwell, 1993, p. 216; cit Volf, *Exclusion and Embrace,* p. 116.

believe that politicians view them as being politically immature, and in need of strong leadership."[6] In the language of Mahmood Mamdani, the people at large remain "subjects" and only a tiny elite can truly be said to be "citizens."[7] This is glaringly illustrated in the requirement that debates in the National Assembly be conducted in English and that only those competent in English are eligible to be elected as members of Parliament. At a stroke, this excludes the majority of the population from participation in the political decision-making and law-making process.[8] Active citizenship is restricted to the small circle of the dominant elite; the others remain subjects, alienated from the centres of power and with no choice but to resign themselves to their fate.

Further evidence of reluctance to "start a new game" is found in the delay in holding Local Government elections. Despite protests from the Public Affairs Committee and others, four years into the new political dispensation the promised directly elected Local Government has yet to materialize.[9] It is apparent that the dead weight of a highly centralized political system holds back any movement to give people in local areas power to manage their own affairs. The manifest reluctance of government to relinquish its monopoly on broadcasting is also indicative of a determination to maintain power at the centre.[10] Indeed, the trend in the balance of power since the General Election

---

[6] J.R. Minnis, "Prospects and Problems for Civil Society in Malawi," in Kings M. Phiri & Kenneth R. Ross ed., *Democratization in Malawi: A Stocktaking*, Blantyre: CLAIM-Kachere, 1998, pp. 127-145 [143].

[7] See Mahmood Mamdani, *Citizen and Subject: Contemporary Africa and the Legacy of Late Colonialism*, Princeton: Princeton University Press, 1996.

[8] See F.E. Kanyongolo, "The Limits of Liberal Democratic Constitutionalism," in Phiri & Ross ed., *Democratization in Malawi*, pp. 353-375 [366].

[9] *The Lamp*, No. 10 (October-December 1997), pp. 4-7.

[10] The Malawi Chapter of the Media Institute of Southern Africa (Misa) is attempting to achieve liberalization of broadcasting in face of government intransigence. See, e.g, *The Star*, 20 December 1997.

of 1994 has been towards a renewed concentration of authority in the office of the President. It is striking to notice that the 50 resolutions passed at the National Constitutional Conference held in Lilongwe from 20 to 24 February 1995 were mostly concerned to limit the powers of the President and to strengthen the Legislature. Yet this popular concern was brushed aside in Parliament which took no heed of the Conference's rejection of the office of 2nd Vice President and its call for a Senate or Upper House of Parliament to be established.[11] Looking back on the discussions of 1993-94 Jande Banda observes that "by far the most vexatious aspect of the constitutional change debate concerned the amount of power to be vested in the Presidency."[12] The centralizing tendency of the political system has acted, however, to stifle such debate and to revert to a situation where everything revolves around the authority of the President. The problem with a strongly Presidential system, in a context where politicians are accustomed to ruling by means of patronage, is that it is likely to consolidate power at the centre rather than promoting democratic participation on the part of the people at large.[13]

The most common complaint against the Muluzi government has been that its members use the resources of the state to enrich themselves and to entrench their own position by means of patronage. This reached the stage, at the end of 1997, where Britain, the European Union and the World Bank decided to suspend development aid unless action was taken to curb government overspending/corruption.[14] John Lwanda has observed that the

---

[11] See Jande Banda, "The Constitutional Change Debate of 1993-95," in Phiri & Ross ed., *Democratization in Malawi*, pp. 316-333 [329-333].

[12] Ibid, p. 323.

[13] For the instructive comparison of the Zambian situation see C.J.J. Mphaisha, "Retreat from Democracy in Post One-Party State Zambia," *The Journal of Commonwealth and Comparative Politics*, Vol. XXXIV/2 (July 1996), pp. 65-84.

[14] *The New Vision*, 12 December 1997; *The Weekend Nation*, 20-21 December 1997.

concentration of economic power in the office of the President "enables the leader to establish a core group of the elite, whose responsibility in turn is to establish secondary patronage groups, all owing loyalty to the centre. In this scheme of things the rural and urban poor ... are at the bottom of the heap."[15] Democratization has evidently done little to challenge the "gravy train" mentality inherited from the colonial and one-party periods in which access to resources was centrally controlled and political involvement a matter of bettering oneself through the patronage of the powerful. As Lewis Dzimbiri has observed: "The problem with the leadership that has emerged in Malawi since the beginning of the democratic transition is that it has been committed to democracy in rhetoric only. In practice it has mystified the masses by being unprincipled, unpredictable, and as obsessed with personal material gain as that of the previous, autocratic era."[16]

A serious question for the democratization movement is why it has failed to dislodge or even challenge this anti-democratic system of political control. In the light of the kingdom of the God, who has "filled the hungry with good things but has sent the rich away empty,"[17] are not the cards too heavily stacked in favour of those already holding power? Is it not time to start a new game? The kingdom promises a dramatic transformation, one where "you are no longer a slave, but a son; and since you are a son, God has made you also an heir;"[18] one where "once you were not a people, but now you are the people of God; once you had not received mercy, but now you have received mercy."[19] Such a discovery of identity, dignity and participation is at the heart of the coming of God's kingdom. It involves subjects

---

[15] Lwanda, *Promises, Power,* p. 71.

[16] Lewis B. Dzimbiri, "Competitive Politics and Chameleon-Like Leaders," in Phiri & Ross ed., *Democratization in Malawi,* pp. 87-101 [88].

[17] Luke 1:53.

[18] Galatians 4:7.

[19] I Peter 2:10.

becoming citizens, slaves becoming sons and "not-a-people" becoming "the people." Insofar as this may find some provisional expression in the life of the Second Republic, the new game promised in the kingdom will begin to be played.

The Republic, the Kingdom and the Poor

It was the prospect of a "new game" which made the events of mid-1992 such a moment of truth for Malawi. The Pastoral Letter began its call for political renewal by focusing on prevailing economic conditions:

> In our society we are aware of a gap between the rich and the poor with regard to expectations, living standards and development. Many people still live in circumstances which are hardly compatible with their dignity as sons and daughters of God. Their life is a struggle for survival. At the same time a minority enjoys the fruits of development and can afford to live in luxury and wealth. We appeal for a more just and equal distribution of the nation's wealth. Though many basic goods and materials are available, they are beyond the means of many of our people. One of the reasons for this is the deplorable wage structure which exists. For many, the wages they receive are grossly inadequate ... and this leads to anger, frustration and hopelessness. Another example of glaring injustice is the price paid to producers, especially subsistence farmers, for some of their crops. We wish to state that every person has a right to a just reward for work done, a wage which will ensure a dignified living for his or her family.[20]

At the next stage in the process of political change, when the WARC/CCAP delegation called for the appointment of a "broadly based Commission," it was to have the mandate, inter alia, "to look into the distribution of income and wealth required by the demands of social justice.[21] In the event, the work of the Public Affairs

---

[20] *Living our Faith*, p. 2.

[21] 'The Nation of Malawi in Crisis: the Church's Concern," Geneva: World Alliance of Reformed Churches, 2 June 1992, p. 2.

Committee came to be very much focused on the reform of the political system and it was the economic dimension of the prophetic critique which was most neglected. Indeed, the new constitution was marked by the conspicuous absence of any provisions which might allow for affirmative action in favour of those who were dispossessed by the colonialism and neo-colonialism of the past. As Edge Kanyongolo has argued: "The constitution does not articulate any principles to guide the solution of major social and economic problems of inequalities resulting from culture and tradition, internal government policies and the adverse positioning of Malawi in the international political economy. The significance of the constitution is therefore diminished in the eyes of a society which finds that it does not clearly address their concerns on matters such as equitable distribution of wealth, the transformation of the relationship between labor and capital, and the balance of power among the various cultures."[22] The conservatism of the constitution of the Second Republic ensured that, in effect, it "took sides" with the rich and against the poor.

No wonder that people are wondering whether their sense of political empowerment is delusory as they see the benefits continuing to flow to the wealthy elite while they remain in deepening poverty. The PAC General Assembly of 1997 voiced this concern when it stated: "Democracy is supposed to benefit the people, but as we look back at two and a half years of democracy in our country, we believe that too often the people's voice and their needs are sidelined, as only the rich and powerful seem to benefit."[23] Viewing this trend of the Second Republic in the light of the kingdom, we might recall the emphatic statement of Karl Barth that: "in the relations and events in the life of people, God always takes

---

[22] F.F. Kanyongolo, "State and Constitutionalism in Malawi," paper presented at Social Change in Malawi Seminar, University of Malawi, 30 June 1996, p. 12, author's italics.
[23] Statement of the Public Affairs Committee General Assembly, 16 January 1997.

his stand unconditionally and passionately on this side and on this side alone: against the lofty and on behalf of the lowly; against those who already enjoy right and privilege and on behalf of those who are denied and deprived of it."[24] Until the gross economic inequalities are addressed and there is a genuine empowerment of the rural population, the social structure of the Republic is going to be skewed in the opposite direction to the reality of the kingdom of God. The churches, with their "preferential option for the poor," should be in a position to pursue this question with vigour unless their own leadership is too enmeshed in the existing exploitative structures. Furthermore, it is the churches which may be best placed to take up this issue at the global level. For the impoverishment of the majority in Malawi has to be understood in relation to the world economic order and the point has to be made that, ultimately, there will be no authentic democratization without a serious endeavour to address the gap between rich and poor at a global level. The church, with its ecumenical vision, may have to take responsibility for developing a world-wide engagement with this issue.

Identity, Otherness and National Life

Well before the rise of the democratization movement, it had been established that, despite the nationalistic rhetoric, part of the legacy of the Banda years was the regional fragmentation brought about by Kamuzu's attempts to establish a hegemony of his own Chewa people of the Central Region.[25] Hence it was no surprise that the democratic transition took on a markedly regionalistic character. While the two powerful opposition parties sought to be national movements it soon became apparent that Aford was predominantly a northern party while the UDF was predominantly southern. The

---

[24] Karl Barth, *Church Dogmatics*, Vol. 11/1, Edinburgh: T. & T. Clark, 1957, p. 386.

[25] See Leroy Vail & Landeg White, 'Tribalism in the Political History of Malawi," in Leroy Vail ed., *The Creation of Tribalism in Southern Africa*, London: James Currey & Los Angeles: University of California Press, 1989, pp. 151-192; cf. pp. 156-58 above.

strength of Banda's MCP, meanwhile, became concentrated in its heartlands in the Central Region. This was borne out in the results of the 1994 General Election when each of the three regions gave overwhelming support to the party with which it identified.[26] The problem of national unity now came into the open as an urgent political issue.[27] So much so that Aford and the MCP, sworn enemies hitherto, were able to justify their sudden and short-lived alliance on the grounds of the need to secure national unity.[28] It was the same concern which convinced President Muluzi that he must have a Vice-President from each of the other regions and led to the controversial creation of the office of 2nd Vice President for Chakufwa Chihana. National political life in the post-election period often appeared to be no more than a contest between competing regional power blocks.[29]

As the defining reality of the effective political order in the Second Republic, ethnicity/regionalism has a number of pronounced effects. First, it places identity-focus on what divides rather than what unites. The political arena becomes a battlefield in the struggle to acquire scarce resources, rather than a forum in which common problems can be addressed and collaborative solutions found. Hence there is a marked lack of debate on such urgent national issues as environmental degradation, economic regeneration, population growth, health services or educational provision. Rather than the

---

[26] In the presidential election, Chakufwa Chihana of Aford took 85% of votes in the Northern Region against his 8% in the Centre and 7% in the South; Kamuzu Banda of the MCP took nearly 70% of the votes in the Central Region against his 16% in the South and 9% in the North; Bakili Muluzi of UDF took 75% of votes in the Southern Region against his 23% in the Centre and 7% in the North. *Daily Times,* 20 May 1994.

[27] See, e.g., *Daily Times,* 19 May 1994; *The Enquirer,* 21-24 May 1994.

[28] See, e.g., *The Monitor,* 29 June 1994; *The New Express,* 30 June 1994.

[29] Deborah Kaspin correctly observes that, strictly speaking, it is regionalism rather than ethnicity proper which guided voting behaviour. Deborah Kaspin, 'The Politics of Ethnicity in Malawi's Democratic Transition," *The Journal of Modern African Studies,* Vol. 33/4 (1995), pp. 595-620 [602].

political order providing the means for the formation and sharpening of policy on such critically important issues, it all revolves around a divisive and sterile struggle between the leaders of competing regional/ethnic fiefs. It is worth recalling that it was the divide-and-rule potential of promoting ethnic identity that made it such an attractive proposition to the colonial state.[30] It is difficult not to regard this as a strategy more or less cynically adopted by the ruling elite to create politico-economic borders which make control easier. Wiseman Chirwa, e.g., has suggested that in Malawi ethnicity and regionalism are, in fact, ideological tools used by "the country's bourgeoisie and petit bourgeoisie to inherit the state as a class for purposes of accumulating political power and economic resources."[31]

As indicated in chapter eight, the churches have an ambiguous history in relation to ethnicity and nationhood.[32] While the missionaries played a crucial role in the "creation of tribalism,"[33] they also "imagined" the nation. They gave people pride in a particular history, language and tradition while at the same time relativizing ethnic differences. As Thole sang: "Redemption done by God's right hand is breaking forth through all the land." Geographical distances and historical differences were broken down, as people discovered a sense of belonging together, united by the momentous event of the coming of the gospel of Christ. The ambiguity remains, however,

---

[30] See Mamdani, *Citizen and Subject,* pp. 8-24.

[31] Wiseman C. Chirwa, 'The Politics of Ethnicity and Regionalism in Contemporary Malawi," *African Rural and Urban Studies,* Vol. 1/2 (1994), pp. 93-118 [94].

[32] For a discussion of such ambiguity on a global level, see Theo Tschuy, *Ethnic Conflict and Religion: Challenge to the Churches,* Geneva: WCC, 1997, pp. 138-141.

[33] See Leroy Vail, "Introduction: Ethnicity in Southern African History," in Vail ed., *The Creation of Tribalism in Southern Africa,* pp. 11-13; see also Aidan Campbell, "Ethical Ethnicity: a Critique," *The Journal of Modem African Studies,* Vol. 35/1 (1997), pp. 53-79.

and at every moment of crisis the churches are tested as to whether regional/ethnic loyalty or evangelical unity will prove decisive. Church leaders are often trapped by loyalty to their own ethnic and cultural community and can easily end up legitimating ethnic conflict. Yet, as the experience of the Public Affairs Committee demonstrates, they can also act as a rallying point for national unity.

An important crucible in which this struggle is worked out is the General Synod of the CCAP. It is more than coincidence that the Blantyre, Nkhoma and Livingstonia Synods are identified with the regional power-blocs which have brought a dangerous political fragmentation to Malawian national life. For reasons of mission history, the southern Blantyre Synod is ethnically composed of predominantly Yao and Mang'anja, the central Nkhoma Synod is composed of predominantly Chewa, and the northern Livingstonia Synod is composed of predominantly Ngoni and Tumbuka. Presbyterian Christians have to face the question of how far these tribal and geographical divisions inhibit the development of a real centre of ecclesiastical unity in the General Synod, which is widely considered to be "very ineffective."[34] It may be that the CCAP can give a lead to the nation by implementing the recent recommendation of the visiting team from the World Alliance of Reformed Churches: "The process of closer cooperation and unity among the Synods calls for the writing of a constitution for the General Synod which will make it effective and empowering it in the life and mission of the CCAP."[35] It is regrettable to observe, however, that at the very time when inter-regional tension is at its height the three member Synods of the General Synod are drawing further apart rather than closer together. The long-drawn out Dwangwa border dispute between Livingstonia and Nkhoma Synods has flared up to such an

---

[34] See, e.g., comments of Synod representatives to WARC representatives, July 1995, Report of Pastoral Team Visit to the Church of Central Africa Presbyterian (CCAP), Malawi, 30 June-3 July 1995, Geneva: World Alliance of Reformed Churches, 1995, p. 3.

[35] Ibid, p. 5.

extent that Livingstonia has suspended its active participation in the work of the General Synod. By settling for a federalism which is based on inter regional suspicion the CCAP has failed to achieve a unity which could withstand political pressures which play up ethnic and regional differences. The struggle within the CCAP at this point may prove to be the make-or-break of Malawi's endeavour to sustain a viable sense of national identity and unity. If the CCAP were able to discover and put into practical effect a spiritual unity, then it would act to counter the tendency for regionalism to inhibit the formation of a truly democratic outlook. Common allegiance to the coming king would enable people to transcend ethnic and regional differences and open up the political process to another set of criteria altogether.

Indeed, a focus on Christ crucified raises profound questions as to how "otherness" is being accommodated in the Second Republic. Not only is a regionalistic form of ethnicity a definitive factor shaping the political process but also attitudes to those who are "other" in terms of race, religion or culture, such as the Asian community, often reveal a tendency to exclude and scapegoat. This is most marked of all in relation to the "otherness" of gender. Even when the government, for example, accedes to pressure to promote women, it does so in terms which suggest that the male-dominated establishment will accommodate women strictly on its own terms. When President Muluzi appointed Stella Kamwendo to be District Commissioner of Phalombe, he commented: "I promote women when they work hard. Mrs Kamwendo ran around *like a man* the moment this disaster hit and made sure she looked after the people."[36] What has been absent, by and large, from the Second Republic has been a willingness on the part of men to re-negotiate *their* identity by readjusting it to the identity of the "other," i.e. the women. The coming of God's kingdom arises out of the event of the crucifixion of Jesus where God has decisively made space for

---

[36] *The Nation,* 2 February 1998, my italics.

humanity in God's self. What this means for human society, as Miroslav Volf suggests, is that "the very *identity* of each is formed through relations to others; the alterity of the other enters into the very identity of each."[37] As the central citadel of human life is yielded to Christ crucified, one outcome is that "this de-centered center of self-giving love - most firmly centered and most radically open - is the doorkeeper deciding about the fate of otherness on the doorstep of the self."[38] In this perspective identity is not lost but rather discovered and deepened through a radical loving openness to "others." The diversity of race, language, culture, religion, tradition and gender found in Malawi's Second Republic gives the opportunity for immeasurable mutual enrichment. The king, who embodies in his own life and history the most radical openness to others, breaks down the destructive logic of exclusion and brings the promise of a society united not in homogeneity hut in joyous appreciation of multiple diversities. As people are led in the direction of the kingdom, the Second Republic can begin to fulfil the hopes of all those who expected that it would give them a place where they could truly belong.

Indigenization of Democracy

Where churches and other religious institutions may have a particularly critical contribution is in the "indigenization" of democracy. The democratic system will have limited impact so long as it is confined to language and structures imported from elsewhere. As Edge Kanyongolo remarks: "the regulatory authority of the constitution ultimately depends on the degree of autochthony of its liberal democratic tenets."[39] There is need to make connections with the vernacular understanding, to find for the new democratic

---

[37] Volf, *Exclusion and Embrace*, p. 154, author's italics.

[38] Ibid, p. 71.

[39] Kanyongolo, "The Limits of Liberal Democratic Constitutionalism," p. 364.

institutions points of resonance with the African tradition.⁴⁰ Otherwise democracy, paradoxically, becomes the mechanism by which the educated elite entrench their supremacy and alienate the rural majority. The need for a reappropriation of the African tradition is heightened by the way in which "culture" was manipulated by Kamuzu Banda as a source of legitimation for his regime.⁴¹ Peter Forster has observed that whereas Banda focused on the authoritarian elements in African tradition, the "rebel" ministers who split with him in the "Cabinet crisis" "were prepared to some extent to take pride in traditions, but where they saw virtue in the past, it was in terms of egalitarianism rather than hierarchical authority."⁴² Now is the time to recover these very powerful currents in traditional Malawian life on which a democratic ethos and consciousness may be developed.

David Clement Scott, one of the early Scottish missionaries at Blantyre made the observation in 1881 that: "The African if he is anything is constitutional - no change or step of importance is taken without first open *mlandu* in which *the opinion of all is fully sought and expressed.*"⁴³ Having identified this strongly democratic tradition among the people of Malawi, Scott moved quickly to incorporate it into the life of the church. In 1894 he ordained seven deacons from among the early converts and these formed the effective governing council of the young church. Scott had no hesitation about their capacity to fulfil this responsibility by drawing on the resources of

---

⁴⁰ In addressing the question of "the role of the church in the formation of democratic assumptions and behaviour" in the South African situation, both Stanley Mogoba and Caesar Molebatsi begin with the African tradition. See Klaus Nurnberger ed., *A Democratic Vision for South Africa,* Pietermaritzburg: Encounter Publications, 1991, pp. 567-584.

⁴¹ See Peter G. Forster, "Culture, Nationalism, and the Invention of Tradition in *Malawi,*" *The Journal of Modem African Studies,* Vol. 32/3(1994), pp. 477-497.

⁴² Ibid,, p. 489.

⁴³ *Life and Work in British Central Africa* (Blantyre Mission newspaper), November 1891, my italics.

their own tradition: "One could wish for no weightier justice than that of native *mlandu-power* Christianized into a Church Court."[44] An important question for the church is how far the indigenous democratic traditions which it incorporated in its own life from this early period have survived sufficiently to be reappropriated by the state at a time when it is emerging from a period of despotism and striving to find solid foundations on which to build a democratic order. The potentially strategic role which the churches occupy at this point is that they have been engaged in a long-running indigenization project as their once-exotic faith has been planted in African soil. It is instructive to compare the current expansion of the churches which is popular, vernacular and spontaneous with the democratization which appears elitist, foreign and contrived. Could the powerful drive behind the indigenization of Christianity be tapped as a means of enabling the Malawian people to discover the democratic norms and values which will provide the true foundation for a viable democratic political order?[45]

Church Life and Civil Society

In the democratization process, as we have seen, many of the functions of civil society fell to the churches. Integral to the success of the Public Affairs Committee was the fact that it gathered together surviving fragments of civil society. Its membership was made up not only of the churches themselves but also the Malawi Law Society, the Associated Chambers of Commerce and Industry, the Muslim Association, and the emerging pro-democracy political parties. This alliance covered a sufficiently broad range of nongovernmental associational life to embrace a truly national constituency and to be

---

[44] Ibid, November 1894.

[45] For an exploration of what this might mean for civic education, see James Tengatenga, "Singing, Dancing and Believing: Civic Education in Malawi Idiom," in Kenneth R. Ross ed., *Faith at the Frontiers of Knowledge,* Blantyre: CLAIM-Kachere, 1998.

able to negotiate with government on that basis. At this point the churches could be seen to be galvanizing civil society and injecting a totally new dynamic into Malawian political life simply by bringing into play groups and associations which were outside the party/government structures. PAC's mobilizing of civil society, however, was undermined, paradoxically, by the success of the pro-democracy movement which took many of the lawyers, business people and putative politicians into government. The situation then tended to revert to one where associational life was very much concentrated in the churches. A series of British and American researchers passing through the University of Malawi have gone out looking for civil society and have found nothing but church life! Likewise, a recent study of Non-Governmental Organizations in Malawi concluded that, in the main, it is the church-related NGOs which "have a rooting in their own constituencies and can rely on sustainable links with partners in Europe and the USA."[46]

The churches occupy this influential position partly by default. The one-party system which prevailed from 1964 to 1992 systematically suppressed or co-opted all other organizations which might play a positive role in civil society. The churches, on the other hand, though restricted in their witness, had grown prodigiously during this period, both in numerical strength and in public confidence. In the absence of other forms of associational life, the churches were the only nationally organized institutions which could mount a challenge to the one-party system. However, the fact that they were able to do so to such remarkable effect cannot be explained entirely by negative factors. Neither the prophetic power of the Catholic Bishops' Pastoral Letter of 1992 nor the organizational genius behind the Public Affairs Committee can be explained without reference to the vitality of contemporary Christianity in Malawi. There was a moral and spiritual force in the pro-democracy

---

[46] Manfred Glagow et al., *Non-Governmental Organisations in Malawi: Their Contributions for Development and Democratization*, Hamburg: Lit Verlag, 1997, p. 158.

movement which drew deeply on Christian convictions regarding justice, truth and human dignity. This gave resonance to its message amongst a predominantly Christian population and broke through the web of deceit woven by the propaganda of the one-party system so that a new political dispensation became possible.

In post-1994 Malawi, the churches have continued to play an important civil society role in a situation where almost all initiative comes from government. They have attempted to make clear their distance from government, e.g. in August 1995 when PAC sent an open letter to the President criticising the government for being accountable to international institutions rather than its own people and, in particular, for resisting World Bank recommendations to trim the cabinet while agreeing to remove the subsidies on fertilizers;[47] or when the Catholic Bishops issued a Pastoral Letter in September 1996 which offered critical analysis of the problem of government corruption.[48] Other distinctive contributions of PAC included playing a key role in persuading the opposition to return to Parliament after a long-running boycott;[49] and mediating between Government and the Civil Servants Trade Union to settle a damaging strike.[50] At the same time, powerful forces operate to secure the churches' collusion with government and they will not retain their independence without a struggle, especially since government patronage will always hold a strong appeal for impoverished church leaders. Jande Banda has astutely noted that "Critics of those in power, so necessary for the realization of a healthy democracy, do not survive for long. They are silenced not by state weaponry but by state patronage."[51] Yet the experience of

---

[47] *The Nation,* 24 August 1995.

[48] *Walking Together in Faith: Our Journey Towards the Year 2000,* Pastoral Letter from the Catholic Bishops of Malawi, September 1996.

[49] Int. Rev Misanjo Kansilanga, 9 April 1997.

[50] *The Nation,* 25 April 1997.

[51] Banda, "The Constitutional Change Debate," p. 326.

having been compromised and silenced has sharpened the sensitivity of church leaders to the importance of maintaining critical distance in relation to government. The churches are preparing themselves to play the role of watchdog in relation to national political life, exposing any corruption which creeps into the exercise of government and detecting any imbalances in the separation of powers. The challenge for government is whether it will be prepared to tolerate and encourage such critical engagement in the interests of healthy democracy or whether it will act out of narrower self-interest to subvert it by means of patronage.

Church Congregations and Grassroots Democracy

Malawi may be a model of democratization so far as the formal constitutional and political structures are concerned but anyone expecting that these automatically lead to a flourishing democratic society will be disappointed. With rare exceptions, the vast rural population remains passive so far as the political process is concerned. The churches, with their parish networks and their record of success in mobilizing the rural population for electoral participation, may be the only means of promoting pro-active participation on the part of the people at large. This is a challenge which the churches must meet not primarily in their upper echelons but, rather, at a much more grassroots level. In the watchdog function of the church, the top leadership is necessarily prominent. Committees, Councils, Conferences, Synods and Assemblies have access to the public arena and top church leaders can address national issues through the mass media. This gives the opportunity to engage with national politics when required. It was through statements issued at this level that the churches were effective as the midwives of democracy. When it comes, however, to the consolidation and deepening of democracy, attention turns to the church at the level of the local congregation or base community.

Peter von Doepp has observed that most consideration of the political role of the churches in Malawi has focused on their "external" face - the meeting of the organs of the churches with the organs of the state in the public realm, typified in the PAC-PCD dialogue in the early days of the democratic transition.[52] By comparison, very little attention has been paid to the "internal" face of the churches - "the manner in which the clergy routinely engage and relate to the larger body of the faithful within the institution" which "shapes political life at the deeper level of social organization and culture."[53] Given that the churches constitute by far the most popular and influential form of associational life in Malawi, the forms of social organization, modes of discourse and behavioural patterns which are nurtured in church life have profound long-term political significance. A pertinent question here is whether the churches are part of the solution or part of the problem? John Minnis has observed that: "By developing an 'economy of affection' as a buffer against the state, Malawians learned to look increasingly inward for enjoyment and intimacy, and to Christianity, local customs and traditions for identity and self-contemplation. As a result, even today, Malawians have no culture of looking outward onto a wider public to which 'private' problems could be transposed into 'public' issues. In fact, it could be argued that within the context of colonial socialization processes, politics was defined as a field of endeavour reserved only for those who ruled."[54] Does church life, in fact, inhibit the development of pro-active democratic participation?

To take a particular case, we may consider the formation at Nkhotakota of the Tobacco Tenants and Allied Workers Union. In a front-page report The Saturday Nation commented: "Like the pastoral letter which started the process of political change in Malawi, the tenants' union is the brainchild of Catholic Church

---

[52] See chapter five above.

[53] Peter von Doepp, "The Kingdom beyond *Zasintha:* Churches and Political Life in Malawi's Post-authoritarian Era," in Phiri & Ross ed., *Democratization in Malawi*, pp. 102-126 [105].

[54] Minnis, "Prospects and Problems for Civil Society," pp. 137-138.

leaders. Two priests, Fr Clyde Maclew (English) and Fr Jim Green (Irish), who were stationed at St Paul's Parish in Nkhotakota, sensitized the tenants to the possibility of forming a union after trying in vain to fight for the tenants' rights."[55] Such cases show the impact which the churches can have in giving people the confidence to form and pursue a political agenda. However, the rarity of such reports suggests that these are the exceptions which prove the rule that, by and large, church life is characterized by what Peter Walshe has described in another context as "timid local clergy and phlegmatic parishes."[56] How much the disturbing message of the coming kingdom of God is allowed to penetrate church life is a question that has to be faced. What is certain is that there are very few other groups which are "able to manage and steer communal anger," as Celestin Monga defines the function of civil society.[57] Indeed, the question must be asked, how far church life simply reflects prevailing social and political trends rather than challenging them? There is, according to the findings of Peter von Doepp, "an extensive informal transcript carrying numerous accounts of clerical corruption.... The stories are widespread and contribute to the perception that the clergy are engaged in their own process of 'eating' to consolidate their status as part of the self-indulgent elite. Accompanying the accounts of corruption are stories concerning the use and abuse of women."[58] The 'hidden' informal transcript has by now entered the public realm. In late 1997 *The Nation* published a leader column entitled "The Church needs soul-searching" which, after mentioning several cases of corruption and sexual immorality, concluded: "It is a worrying development that we should see signs of discord or moral bankruptcy in the Church, with the people we

---

[55] *The Saturday Nation,* 3-9 May 1997.

[56] Peter Walshe, *Prophetic Christianity and the Liberation Movement in South Africa,* Pietermaritzburg: Cluster Publications, 1995, p. 143.

[57] Celestin Monga, *The Anthropology of Anger: Civil Society and Democracy in Africa,* Boulder & London: Lynne Rienner, 1996, p. 149.

[58] Von Doepp, The Kingdom beyond *Zasintha,"* p. 120.

look to for our spiritual salvation in the forefront. We think it is time the churches collectively went into soul-searching to find out why they are so scandal-ridden and find solutions which will restore public confidence in their role as the spiritual guides of society."[59] The outcome of such behaviour on the part of church leadership is that "vertical patron-client ties remain the dominant form of social problem solving" and "bit by bit, the civic credibility of the churches is undermined - thwarting their own ability to address widespread social anomie or abuses of power within the state."[60]

It may be that the next stage in the democratization process will depend to a significant extent on the form of associational life which prevails in parish churches. In so far as the churches simply mirror a hierarchical, authoritarian and exploitative political ethos they will tend to inhibit civil society activism rather than promoting it. On the other hand, in so far as the churches are open, participative and justice-oriented they will be likely to have a "knock-on" effect in the life of the community at large which is positive in terms of promoting civil society. An encouraging note is our finding that most church members see a clear difference between church leaders' exercise of power and that of political leaders.[61] On the other hand it must be acknowledged that people's participation in church life has not, by and large, given them the spiritual vision and moral impetus necessary to achieve a meaningful participation in the political process. The critical ecclesiological question is whether the prevailing model will be the church "from above" or the church "from below." This question of polity reaches deep into the identity of the church and, depending on the kind of answer it gives,

---

[59] *The Nation*, 15 December 1997. Public interest in matters of church discipline suggests that the church is regarded as having a key role to play in the construction of a viable civic order. See, e.g., *The Nation*, 10 January 1997; *The Weekend Nation*, 11-17 January 1997.

[60] Von Doepp, "The Kingdom beyond *Zasintha*," p 121.

[61] See p. 82 above.

determines the extent to which it can be a significant force in Malawi's democratization at the deeper level of promoting a vibrant civil society.

Indeed, the question must be asked, how far church life simply reflects prevailing social and political trends rather than challenging them? There is, according to the findings of Peter von Doepp, "an extensive informal transcript carrying numerous accounts of clerical corruption.... The stories are widespread and contribute to the perception that the clergy are engaged in their own process of 'eating' to consolidate their status as part of the self-indulgent elite. Accompanying the accounts of corruption are stories concerning the use and abuse of women."[62] The 'hidden' informal transcript has by now entered the public realm. In late 1997 *The Nation* published a leader column entitled "The Church needs soul-searching" which, after mentioning several cases of corruption and sexual immorality, concluded: "It is a worrying development that we should see signs of discord or moral bankruptcy in the Church, with the people we look to for our spiritual salvation in the forefront. We think it is time the churches collectively went into soul-searching to find out why they are so scandal-ridden and find solutions which will restore public confidence in their role as the spiritual guides of society."[63] The outcome of such behaviour on the part of church leadership is that "vertical patron-client ties remain the dominant form of social problem solving" and "bit by bit, the civic credibility of the churches is undermined - thwarting their own ability to address widespread social anomie or abuses of power within the state."[64]

---

[62] Von Doepp, The Kingdom beyond *Zasintha"*, p. 120.

[63] *The Nation*, 15 December 1997. Public interest in matters of church discipline suggests that the church is regarded as having a key role to play in the construction of a viable civic order. See, e.g., *The Nation*, 10 January 1997; *The Weekend Nation*, 11-17 January 1997.

[64] Van Doepp, "The Kingdom beyond *Zasintha"*, p 121.

It may be that the next stage in the democratization process will depend to a significant extent on the form of associational life which prevails in parish churches. In so far as the churches simply mirror a hierarchical, authoritarian and exploitative political ethos they will tend to inhibit civil society activism rather than promoting it. On the other hand, in so far as the churches are open, participative and justice-oriented they will be likely to have a "knock-on" effect in the life of the community at large which is positive in terms of promoting civil society. An encouraging note is our finding that most church members see a clear difference between church leaders' exercise of power and that of political leaders.[65] On the other hand it must be acknowledged that people's participation in church life has not, by and large, given them the spiritual vision and moral impetus necessary to achieve a meaningful participation in the political process. The critical ecclesiological question is whether the prevailing model will be the church "from above" or the church "from below." This question of polity reaches deep into the identity of the church and, depending on the kind of answer it gives, determines the extent to which it can be a significant force in Malawi's democratization at the deeper level of promoting a vibrant civil society.

Beyond Freedom: the Politics of Love

For democracy to be effective it is not enough to establish a certain legal and constitutional system. There is need for the inner drive and motivation to make the system work. It is when democracy is considered at this deeper level that religious considerations arise, especially in a context where the worldview and behaviour of the people is greatly influenced by religion. Democratization will remain superficial if it fails to take into account the religious understanding

---

[65] See p. 65 above.

of political power and authority which prevails in African societies.[66] Where there are issues of democratization to be addressed, it is unlikely that these will be fully understood without reference to the underlying religious understanding of politics and power. Hence the churches as religious communities engaged with their social reality at a religious level have a considerable influence - for good or ill - on the evolution of the political order around them. It is not coincidental, then, that the churches were integral to the democratic transition in Malawi nor that the struggle for religious legitimation was at the heart of the political contest. It is a pattern to be expected where the political order is understood to repose, ultimately, upon religious realities. The challenge for the churches is whether they allow themselves to be used as ideological support for a predetermined political agenda or whether they can relate their biblical message to the political life of the nation in a critical and creative way.

It is as the churches represent the non-dominating, serving love of Jesus that they have their deepest impact upon the process of democratization. Inasmuch as the churches can enable the "love of power" to be replaced by the "power of love"[67] at the heart of political behaviour, they are in a position to give to a young democracy the moral and spiritual impetus which it requires if it is to succeed. "This," as John de Gruchy notes, "is not something which democracy itself can produce; it is a spiritual value of redemptive love which no political system can manufacture."[68] The

---

[66] See Benezet Bujo, *African Theology in its Social Context,* New York: Orbis, 1992, pp. 18-21; and Martin Mandew, "African Traditional Decision Making," in Nurnberger ed., *A Democratic Vision,* pp. 319-330 [319-321]; see also Placide Tempels, *Bantu Philosophy,* Paris, 1959, p. 63; and Bediako, *Christianity in Africa,* pp. 234-251.

[67] See Jan Milic Lochman, *The Faith We Confess: An Ecumenical Dogmatics,* Edinburgh: T. & T. Clark, 1985, pp. 96-97.

[68] John W. de Gruchy, *Christianity and Democracy,* Cambridge: Cambridge University Press, 1995, p. 244.

challenge here to the church is one which cuts much deeper than the issue of whether it can raise a prophetic voice in relation to the politics of the day. For it reaches to the heart of the church's own life and calls it to be the community which manifests such outgoing and redemptive love. Here we return to the point with which we began - the discipline under which the Nicene Fathers did their theology. It is a matter of rooting and grounding our whole being, word and action on the given reality of Jesus Christ. Insofar as this is achieved and the church reflects the authentic life of the risen Jesus, so far does the church fulfil her own identity and become a true sign of hope for the nation. To walk the way of Jesus, at the heart of contemporary history, is to bring to expression the love which alone can heal the nation and release the dynamics of viable democracy.

After a lifetime of costly struggle for justice, Vera Chirwa has stated her conviction that "Malawi's greatest need today is the need for love."[69] Perhaps she has discovered, as Reinhold Niebuhr did, that "anything short of love cannot be perfect justice."[70] The quest for democracy, for a system of social organization in which everyone is respected, everyone has a stake, and everyone has a say, will always remain an elusive business until it has got down to the fundamental issue of love. Many Malawians today are disillusioned with freedom. Oppression has been overthrown, liberation has been achieved, people are free to speak, to move, to publish, to associate. Yet what is the value of all this if poverty deprives people of their human dignity and they have no power to be the artisans of their ow destiny? For freedom to reach its goal, it needs the love which sustains, empowers and builds a true humanity. Hence Gustavo Gutierrez, in

---

[69] At the Ku Chawe Consultation of the Theology of Life Programme, Department of Theology and Religious Studies, University of Malawi, 3-5 August 1995.

[70] Reinhold Niebuhr, "Christian Faith and Natural Law," in D.B. Robertson ed., *Love and Justice: Selection from the Shorter Writings of Reinhold Niebuhr,* Cleveland: The World Publishing Company, 1967, pp. 46-54 [50].

the introduction to the revised edition of *A Theology of Liberation*, observed that: "It is not enough that we be liberated from oppressive socio-economic structures; also needed is a personal transformation by which we live with profound inner freedom in the face of every kind of servitude.... Finally, there is liberation from sin, which attacks the deepest root of all servitude; for sin is the breaking of friendship with God and with other human beings, and therefore cannot be eradicated except by the unmerited redemptive love of the Lord whom we receive by faith and in communion with one another. "[71]

For the patterns of privilege, exclusion and exploitation which are entrenched in Malawi's social structure to be uprooted and replaced with sharing, inclusive and participatory patterns, there can be no substitute for encounter with the transforming love of God. "Without a 'politics of the pure heart'," Miroslav Volf recently remarked bluntly, "every politics of liberation will trip over its own feet."[72] Is this where Malawi's peaceful revolution has come unstuck? Has insufficient attention been paid to what Volf calls, "creation of the kind of social agents that are shaped by the values of God's kingdom and therefore capable of participating in the project of authentic social transformation"?[73] Where such deep structural injustices and such profound distortions of community have become as entrenched as they have in Malawi, the only way forward is through the love which breaks out of self-interest and enters into the kind of self-giving which was pioneered by Jesus when he went to the cross. "For whoever wants to save his life will lose it, but whoever loses his life for me and for the gospel will save it."[74] It is for the church to live out and interpret this paradoxical way of Jesus, the king who has come and who is coming. For only as this

---

[71] Gustavo Gutierrez, *A Theology of Liberation,* rev. ed., London: SCM, 1988, p. xxxviii.

[72] Volf, *Exclusion and Embrace,* p. 119.

[73] Ibid, p. 118.

[74] Mark 8:35.

scandalous logic moves people to give themselves in love, that the justice and freedom aimed for in Malawi's Second Republic will begin to be achieved.

Bibliography

Appiah-Kubi, Kofi & Sergio Torres eds., *African Theology en Route*, Maryknoll: Orbis, 1979.
Athanasius, *Contra Gentes and De Incarnatione* (ed. and trans. R.W. Thomson), Oxford: Clarendon Press, 1971.
Banda, Jande, "The Constitutional Change Debate of 1993-95," in Kings M. Phiri & Kenneth R. Ross eds., *Democratization in Malawi: A Stocktaking*, Blantyre: CLAIM-Kachere, 1998, pp. 316-333.
Bandawe, Lewis Mataka, *Memoirs of a Malawian*, ed. Bridglal Pachai, Blantyre: CLAIM, 1971.
Barth, Karl, *Church Dogmatics*, Vol. 11/1, Edinburgh: T. & T. Clark, 1957.
Bauman, Zygmunt, *Postmodern Ethics*, Oxford: Blackwell, 1993. Bediako, Kwame, *Christianity in Africa: The Renewal of a Non-Western Religion*, Edinburgh: Edinburgh University Press & Maryknoll: Orbis, 1995.
Bediako, Kwame, *Theology and Identity: The Impact of Culture upon Christian Thought in the Second Century and Modern Africa*, Oxford: Regnum, 1992.
Bismarck, Joseph, "A Brief History of Joseph Bismarck," *Occasional Papers* (Malawi Government, Ministry of Local Government, Department of Antiquities, Publication No. 7), Zomba: Government Press, 1969, pp. 49-54.
Boulaga, Eboussi, *Christianity without Fetishes*, Maryknoll: Orbis, 1984.
Bujo, Benezet, *African Theology in its Social Context*, New York: Orbis, 1992.
Carpenter, H.J., "Popular Christianity and the Theologians in the Early Centuries," *Journal of Theological Studies*, NS Vol. 14 (October 1963), pp. 294-310.
Chiphangwi, Saindi D., "Why People Join the Christian Church: Trends in Church Growth in the Blantyre Synod of the Church of Central Africa Presbyterian 1960-1975," Ph.D., University of Aberdeen, 1978.
Chirwa, Wiseman C., "The Politics of Ethnicity and Regionalism in Contemporary Malawi," *African Rural and Urban Studies*, Vol. 1/2 (1994), pp. 93-118.
Clutton-Brock, Guy, *Dawn in Nyasaland*, London: Hodder & Stoughton, 1959.
Cullen, Trevor, *Malawi: A Turning Point*, Edinburgh: The Pentland Press, 1994.
Davidson, Basil, *The Black Man's Burden: Africa and the Curse of the Nation-State*, London: James Currey, 1992.
De Gruchy, John W., *Christianity and Democracy*, Cambridge: Cambridge University Press, 1995.

De Gruchy, John W., "From Cairo to the Cape: the Significance of Coptic Orthodoxy for African Christianity," *Journal of Theology for Southern Africa*, No. 99 (November 1997), pp. 24-39.

De Gruchy, John W., *Liberating Reformed Theology: A South African Contribution to an Ecumenical Debate*, Grand Rapids: Eerdmans & Cape Town: David Philip, 1991

Dickson, Kwesi, *Theology in Africa*, London: Darton, Longman & Todd, 1984.

Dickson, Kwesi A. & Paul Ellingworth eds., *Biblical Revelation and African Beliefs*, London: Lutterworth Press, 1969.

Domingo, Charles, *Letters of Charles Domingo*, ed. Harry Langworthy, Zomba: University of Malawi, Sources for the Study of Religion in Malawi No. 9, 1983.

Dulles, Avery, *Models of the Church*, Dublin: Gill & Macmillan, 2nd ed., 1988 [1974].

Dzimbiri, Lewis B., "Democratic Politics and Chameleon-Like Leaders," in Kings M. Phiri & Kenneth R. Ross eds., *Democratization in Malawi: A Stocktaking*, Blantyre: CLAIM-Kachere, 1998, pp. 87-101.

Fasholé-Luke, Edward et al ed., *Christianity in Independent Africa*, London: Rex Collings, 1978.

Fiedler, Klaus, "Joseph Booth and the Writing of Malawian History: an Attempt at Interpretation," *Religion in Malawi*, No. 6 (1996), pp. 30-38.

Fiedler, Klaus, "Power at the Receiving End: the Jehovah's Witnesses' Experience in One-Party Malawi," in Kenneth R. Ross ed., *God, People and Power in Malawi: Democratization in Theological Perspective*, Blantyre: CLAIM-Kachere, 1996, pp. 149-76.

Forster, Peter G., "Culture, Nationalism, and the Invention of Tradition in Malawi," *The Journal of Modern African Studies*, Vol. 32 No. 3 (1994), pp. 477-497.

Forster, Peter G., *T. Cullen Young: Missionary and Anthropologist*, Hull: Hull University Press, 1989.

Gifford, Paul ed., *The Christian Churches and the Democratization of Africa*, Leiden: E.J. Brill, 1995.

Glasgow, Manfred et al., *Non-Governmental Organisations in Malawi: Their Contributions for Development and Democratization*, Hamburg: Lit Verlag, 1997.

Gunton, Colin E., *The One, the Three and the Many: God, Creation and the Culture of Modernity*, Cambridge: Cambridge University Press, 1993.

Gunton, Colin, "Proteus and Procrustes: A Study in the Dialectic of Language in Disagreement with Sallie McFague," in Alvin F. Kimel ed., *Speaking the Christian God: The Holy Trinity and the Challenge of Feminism*, Grand Rapids: Eerdmans, 1992, pp. 65-79.

Gutierrez, Gustavo, *A Theology of Liberation,* rev. ed., London: SCM, 1988.
Hastings, Adrian, *African Catholicism: Essays in Discovery,* London: SCM, 1989.
Hastings, Adrian, *The Church in Africa 1450-1950,* Oxford: Clarendon Press, 1994.
Hetherwick, Alexander ed., *Robert Hellier Napier in Nyasaland,* Edinburgh & London: Wm Blackwood & Sons, 1925.
Hilary, *Saint Hilary of Poitiers: The Trinity,* trans. S. McKenna, Washington: Catholic University of America Press, 1954.
Hinga, Teresa M., "Jesus Christ and. the Liberation of Women in Africa," in Mercy A. Oduyoye & Musimbi R.A. Kanyoro eds., *The Will to Arise: Women, Tradition and the Church in Africa,* Maryknoll: Orbis, 1992, pp. 183-194.
Huntington, Samuel P., *The Third Wave: Democratization in the Late Twentieth Century,* Norman: University of Oklahoma Press, 1992.
Idowu, Bolaji, *Towards an Indigenous Church,* London: Oxford University Press, 1965.
Idowu, E. Bolaji, "Introduction," in Kwesi A. Dickson and Paul Ellingworth eds., *Biblical Revelation and African Beliefs,* London: Lutterworth Press, 1969.
Jackson, Bill, *Send us Friends,* np, nd[1996].
Kannengiesser, Charles, "Athanasius of Alexandria vs. Arius: The Alexandrian Crisis," in B.A. Pearson & J.E. Goehring eds., *The Roots of Egyptian Christianity,* Philadelphia: Fortress, 1986, pp. 204-215.
Kannengiesser, Charles, "Athanasius of Alexandria and the Foundation of Traditional Christology," *Theological Studies,* Vol. 34 (1973), pp. 103-113.
Kannengiesser, Charles, *Arius and Athanasius: Two Alexandrian Theologians,* Hampshire: Variorum, 1991.
Kanyongolo, F.E., "The Limits of Liberal Democratic Constitutionalism in Malawi," in Kings M. Phiri & Kenneth R. Ross eds., *Democratization in Malawi: A Stocktaking,* Blantyre: CLAIM-Kachere, 1998, pp. 353-375.
Kaspin, Deborah, "The Politics of Ethnicity in Malawi's Democratic Transition," *The Journal of Modern African Studies,* Vol. 33/4 (1995), pp. 595-620.
Kelly, J.N.D., *Early Christian Doctrines,* (5th rev. ed.), London: Adam & Charles Black, 1977.
Kibicho, Samuel G., "The Continuity of the African Conception of God into and through Christianity: a Kikuyu Case Study," in Edward Fasholé-Luke et al. ed., *Christianity in Independent Africa,* London: Rex Collings, 1978, pp. 370-392.
Kirche und Gesellschaft in Malawi: Die Krise von 1992 in historischer Perspektive, Hamburg: EMW Informationen No. 98, February 1993.
Kolie, Cecie, "Jesus the Healer," in Robert J. Schreiter ed., *Faces of Jesus in Africa,* London: SCM, 1992, pp. 128-150.

Langworthy, Harry, *"Africa for the African": The Life of Joseph Booth,* Blantyre: CLAIM-Kachere, 1996.
Lewis, Joanna, Peggy Owens & Louise Pirouet eds., *Human Rights and the Making of Constitutions: Malawi, Kenya, Uganda,* African Studies Centre, University of Cambridge, 1995.
Living our Faith, Pastoral Letter from the Catholic Bishops of Malawi, Lent 1992; later published under the title *The Truth Will Set You Free,* London: CIIR, 1992 (Church in the World 28).
Livingstone, W.P., *A Prince of Missionaries: Rev Alexander Hetherwick,* London: James Clarke, n.d.
Lochman, Jan Milic, *The Faith We Confess: An Ecumenical Dogmatics,* Edinburgh: T. & T. Clark, 1985.
Lwanda, John L., *Kamuzu Banda of Malawi: A Study in Promise, Power and Paralysis,* Glasgow: Dudu Nsomba Publications, 1993.
Lwanda, John L. C., *Promises, Power, Politics and Poverty: Democratic Transition in Malawi (1961-1999),* Glasgow: Dudu Nsomba, 1996.
Mackintosh, H.R., *The Doctrine of the Person of Jesus Christ,* Edinburgh: T. & T. Clark, 1912.
Macpherson, Fergus, *"Sumu za Chifipa:* Christian Songs in Malawi," *Bulletin of the Scottish Institute of Missionary Studies,* 6-7 (1990-91), pp. 36-53.
Malawi: A Moment of Truth, London: CIIR, 1993.
Malawi: Human Rights Violations 25 Years After Independence, London: Amnesty International, 1989.
Malawi: Prison Conditions, Cruel Punishment and Detention Without Trial, London: Amnesty International, 1992.
Maluleke, Tinyiko Sam, "Black and African Theologies in the New World Order: A Time to Drink from our Own Wells," *Journal of Theology for Southern Africa,* Vol. 96 (November 1996), pp. 3-19.
Mamdani, Mahmood, *Citizen and Subject: Contemporary Africa and the Legacy of Late Colonialism,* Princeton: Princeton University Press, 1996.
Mbiti, John S., "The Biblical Basis in Present Trends in African Theology," *Africa Theological Journal,* Vol. 7/1 (1978), pp. 77-85.
Mbiti, John S., *Bible and Theology in African Christianity,* Nairobi: Oxford University Press, 1986.
McCracken, John, "Church and State in Malawi: The Role of the Scottish Presbyterian Missions, 1875-1964," in Isabel A. Phiri, Kenneth R. Ross & James L. Cox ed., *The Role of Christianity in Development, Peace and Reconstruction: Southern Perspectives,* Nairobi: All Africa Conference of Churches (African Challenge Series No. 8), 1996, pp. 48-73.
McCracken, John, "Democracy and Nationalism in Historical Perspective: the Case of Malawi," paper presented at Conference on Historical Dimensions

of Democracy and Human Rights in Zimbabwe, University of Zimbabwe, 9-16 September 1996.

McCracken, John, *Politics and Christianity in Malawi 1875-1940*, Cambridge: Cambridge University Press, 1977.

Minnis, J.R., "Prospects and Problems for Civil Society in Malawi," in Kings M. Phiri & Kenneth R. Ross eds., *Democratization in Malawi: A Stocktaking*, Blantyre: CLAIM-Kachere, 1998, pp. 127-145.

Monga, Celestin, *The Anthropology of Anger: Civil Society and Democracy in Africa*, Boulder & London: Lynne Rienner, 1996.

Mphaisha, C.J.J., "Retreat from Democracy in Post One-Party State Zambia," *The Journal of Commonwealth and Comparative Politics*, Vol. XXXIV/2 (July 1996), pp. 65-84.

Mphande, Lupenga, "Dr Hastings Kamuzu Banda and the Malawi Writers Group: The (un)Making of a Cultural Tradition," *Research in African Literatures*, Vol. 27/1 (Spring 1996), pp. 80-101.

Msiska, Stephen Kauta, *Golden Buttons: Christianity and Traditional Religion among the Tumbuka*, Blantyre: CLAIM-Kachere, 1997.

Mufuka, K.N., *Missions and Politics in Malawi*, Kingston, Ontario: Limestone Press, 1977.

Mugambi, J.N.K. & Laurenti Magesa eds., *Jesus in African Christianity*, Nairobi: Initiatives Publishers, 1989.

Mugambi, J.N.K. & Laurenti Magesa eds., *The Church in African Christianity: Innovative Essays in Ecclesiology*, Nairobi: AACC, 1990 (African Challenge Series No. 1).

Musopole, Augustine C., "A Theological Vision for Malawi," *Religion in Malawi*, No. 6 (1996), pp. 3-8.

Mwasi, Yesaya Zerenji, *My Essential and Paramount Reasons for Working Independently*, ed. John K. Parratt, Zomba: University of Malawi, Sources for the Study of Religion in Malawi No. 2, 1979.

Ncozana, Silas S., *Sangaya*, Blantyre: CLAIM-Kachere, 1996.

Newbigin, Lesslie, *Foolishness to the Greeks: The Gospel and Western Culture*, Geneva: WCC, 1986.

Newell, Jonathan Q., "A Moment of Truth?' The Church and Political Change in Malawi, 1992," *The Journal of Modern African Studies*, Vol. 33/2 (1995), pp. 243-62;

Newlands, George M., *Hilary of Poitiers: A Study in Theological Method*, Bern, Frankfurt am Main, Las Vegas: Peter Lang, 1978.

Nurnberger, Klaus ed., *A Democratic Vision for South Africa*, Pietermaritzburg: Encounter Publications, 1991.

Nyamiti, Charles, "African Christologies Today," in Robert J. Schreiter ed., *Faces of Jesus in Africa*, London: SCM, 1992, pp. 3-23.

Nyamiti, Charles, "Contemporary African Christologies: Assessment and Practical Suggestions," in R. Gibellini ed., *Paths of African Theology,* London: SCM, 1994, pp. 62-77.

Nyamiti, Charles, *Christ as our Ancestor - Christology from an African Perspective,* Gweru: Mambo, 1984.

Nzunda, Matembo S. & Kenneth R. Ross eds., *Church, Law and Political Transition in Malawi 1992-94,* Gweru: Mambo Press, 1995.

O'Donovan, Oliver, *Resurrection and Moral Order: An Outline for Evangelical Ethics,* Leicester: IVP, 1986.

Owens, Peggy ed., *When Maize and Tobacco are not Enough: a Church Study of Malawi's Agroeconomy,* Edinburgh: Centre for Theology and Public Issues & Blantyre: CLAIM-Kachere, 1997.

Pachai, Bridglal, *Malawi: The History of the Nation,* London: Longman, 1973.

Parratt, John, *Reinventing Christianity: African Theology Today,* Grand Rapids: Eerdmans & Trenton: Africa World Press, 1995.

Pauw, C. Martin, "Mission and Church in Malawi: The History of the Nkhoma Synod of the Church of Central Africa Presbyterian 1889-1962," DTh, University of Stellenbosch, 1980.

Phiri, Isabel Apawo, "Marching, Suspended and Stoned: Christian Women in Malawi 1995" in Ross ed., *God, People and Power,* in Kenneth R. Ross ed., *God, People and Power in Malawi: Democratization in Theological Perspective,* Blantyre: CLAIM-Kachere, 1996, pp. 63-105.

Phiri, Isabel Apawo, *Women, Presbyterianism and Patriarchy: Religious Experience of Chewa Women in Central Malawi,* Blantyre: CLAIM-Kachere, 1997.

Phiri, Kings M. & Kenneth R. Ross eds., *Democratization in Malawi: A Stocktaking,* Blantyre: CLAIM-Kachere, 1998.

Pobee, John S., *Toward an African Theology,* Nashville: Abingdon Press, 1979.

Quinn, Anne-Lise, "Holding on to Mission Christianity: Case Studies from a Presbyterian Church in Malawi," *Journal of Religion in Africa,* Vol. XXV/4 (1995), pp. 387-411.

Ross, Andrew C., *Blantyre Mission and the Making of Modern Malawi,* Blantyre: CLAIM-Kachere, 1996.

Ross, Andrew C., "Forty-five Years of Turmoil: Malawi Christian Churches, 1949-1994," *International Bulletin of Missionary Research,* Vol. 18/2 (1994), pp. 53-56, 58-60.

Ross, Andrew C., "Some Reflections on the Malawi 'Cabinet Crisis' 1964-65," *Religion in Malawi,* No. 7 (1997), pp. 3-12.

Ross, Andrew C., "The African - 'A Child or a Man': the Quarrel between the Blantyre Mission of the Church of Scotland and the British Central Africa Administration 1890-1905," in E. Stokes & R. Brown, eds., *The Zambesian*

Past: Studies in Central African History, Manchester: Manchester University Press, 1966, pp. 332-51

Ross, Andrew C., "The Blantyre Mission and the Problems of Land and Labour 1891-1915," in R.J. Macdonald, ed., *From Nyasaland to Malawi,* Nairobi: East African Publishing House, 1975, pp. 86-107.

Ross, Kenneth R. ed., *Christianity in Malawi: A Sourcebook,* Gweru: Mambo Press, 1996.

Ross, Kenneth R., "Does Malawi (Still) Need a Truth Commission?," in Kings M. Phiri & Kenneth R. Ross eds., *Democratization in Malawi: A Stocktaking,* Blantyre: CLAIM-Kachere, 1998, pp. 334-352.

Ross, Kenneth R. ed., *God, People and Power in Malawi: Democratization in Theological Perspective,* Blantyre: CLAIM-Kachere-Kachere, 1996. Ross, Kenneth R., *Gospel Ferment in Malawi: Theological Essays,* Gweru: Mambo Press, 1995.

Ruether, Rosemary Radford, "The Liberation of Christology from Patriarchy," in A. Loades, *Feminist Theology: a Reader,* London: SPCK, 1990, pp. 138-148.

Sanneh, Lamin, *Translating the Message: the Missionary Impact on Culture,* New York: Orbis, 1989.

Schoffeleers, J. Matthew, "Folk Christology in Africa: The Dialectics of the Nganga Paradigm," *Journal of Religion in Africa,* Vol. XIX/2 (1989), p. 157-183.

Setiloane, G.M., "How the Traditional World-View Persists in the Christianity of the South-Tswana" in in Edward Fasholé-Luke et al ed., *Christianity in Independent Africa,* London: Rex Collings, 1978, pp. 402-412.

Shepperson, George & Thomas Price, *Independent African,* Edinburgh: Edinburgh University Press, 1958.

Shepperson, George A., "External Factors in the Development of African Nationalism, with Particular Reference to British Central Africa," *Phylon,* Vol. XXII/3 (Fall 1961), pp. 207-225.

Shorter, Aylward, "Folk Christianity and Functional Christology," *AFER,* Vol. 24 No. 3 (June 1982), pp. 133-137.

Smout, T.C., *A Century of the Scottish People 1830-1950,* London: Collins, 1986.

Storrar, William, *Scottish Identity: A Christian Vision,* Edinburgh: Handsel Press, 1990.

Tengatenga, James, "Singing, Dancing and Believing: Civic Education in Malawi Idiom," in Kenneth R. Ross ed., *Faith at the Frontiers of Knowledge,* Blantyre: CLAIM-Kachere, 1998; Reprinted Mzuzu: Luviri Press, 123-141.

Tengatenga, James, "Young People: Participation or Alienation? An Anglican Case" in Ross ed., *God, People and Power,* in Kenneth R. Ross ed., *God, People and Power in Malawi: Democratization in Theological Perspective,*

Blantyre: CLAIM-Kachere, 1996, pp. 107-23. Reprinted Mzuzu: Luviri Press, 2018, pp. 107-124.
The Kairos Document. Challenge to the Church: A Theological Comment on the Political Crisis in South Africa. Braamfontein: The Kairos Theologians & London: CIIR/BCC, 1985.
The Referendum in Malawi: Free Expression Denied. Article 19 Issue 22 (April 1993).
Thompson, T. Jack, *Christianity in Northern Malawi: Donald Fraser's Missionary Methods and Ngoni Culture,* Leiden: E.J. Brill, 1995.
Torrance, Thomas F., *Space, Time and Resurrection,* Edinburgh: Handsel Press, 1976.
Torrance, Thomas F. *The Trinitarian Faith: the Evangelical Theology of the Ancient Catholic Church.* Edinburgh: T. & T. Clark, 1988.
Torrance, Thomas F., *Theology in Reconciliation,* London: Geoffrey Chapman, 1975.
Tschuy, Theo, *Ethnic Conflict and Religion: Challenge to the Churches,* Geneva: WCC, 1997.
Turner, Harold W., "The Contribution of Studies on Religion in Africa to Western Religious Studies," in Mark Glasswell & Edward Fasholé-Luke eds., *New Testament Christianity for Africa and the World,* London: SPCK, 1974, pp. 169-78.
Vail, Leroy and Landeg White, "Tribalism in the Political History of Malawi," in Leroy Vail ed., *The Creation of Tribalism in Southern Africa,* London: James Currey & Berkeley and Los Angeles: University of California Press, 1989, pp. 151-192.
van Dijk, Rijk A. "Young Malawian Puritans: Young Puritan Preachers in a Present-day African Urban Environment," Ph.D., University of Utrecht, 1992.
van Donge, Jan Kees, "Kamuzu's Legacy: the Democratization of Malawi," *African Affairs,* Vol. 94 (1995), pp. 227-57.
van Donge, Jan Kees, "The Mwanza Trial as a Search for a Usable Malawian Political Past," in Kings M. Phiri & Kenneth R. Ross eds., *Democratization in Malawi: A Stocktaking,* Blantyre: CLAIM-Kachere, 1997, pp. 21-51.
Volf, Miroslav, *Exclusion and Embrace: A Theological Exploration of Identity, Otherness, and Reconciliation,* Nashville: Abingdon Press, 1996.
Von Doepp, Peter, "The Kingdom beyond *Zasintha:* Churches and Political Life in Malawi's Post-authoritarian Era," in Kings M. Phiri & Kenneth R. Ross eds., *Democratization in Malawi: A Stocktaking,* Blantyre: CLAIM-Kachere, 1998, pp. 102-126.
Walking Together in Faith: Our Journey Towards the Year 2000, Pastoral Letter from the Catholic Bishops of Malawi, September 1996.

Walls, Andrew F.. *The Missionary Movement in Christian History,* Edinburgh: T. & T. Clark & New York: Orbis, 1996.

Walshe, Peter. *Prophetic Christianity and the Liberation Movement in South Africa,* Pietermaritzburg: Cluster Publications, 1995. *Where Silence Rules: The Suppression of Dissent in Malawi,* Washington and London: Africa Watch, 1990.

Zizioulas, John D., *Being as Communion: Studies in Personhood and the Church.* London: Darton, Longman & Todd, 1985.

Index

Adoptionism, 48
Aford, 118, 127, 204-05
Africa Watch, 135, 184, 232
African Methodist Episcopal Church, 116, 171
African Traditional Religion, 49, 79
Ambrose of Milan, 48
Amnesty International, 120, 135, 227
Amos, 166, 190
Ancestor(s), 42-43, 58, 85, 229
Anderson, Benedict, 177-78
Anglican Church, 116, 171
Antony, 19
Arabs, 88
Arden, Donald, 146
Arianism, 18, 24, 36
Athanasius, 18-24, 30-31, 35-36, 224, 226
Banda, Hastings Kamuzu, 13, 74, 101-02, 107, 109-11, 114, 124, 126-27, 133-43, 145, 147, 152-63, 165, 167-70, 174, 183-89, 195, 200, 204-05, 210, 227-28
Banda, Jande, 200, 213, 224
Bandawe, Lewis Mataka, 92, 182, 224
Baptist Convention, 92, 116, 127
Barmen Declaration, 103

Barth, Karl, 203-04, 224
Bauman, Zygmunt, 198, 224
Bediako, Kwame, 25, 35, 59, 68, 72, 105, 220, 224
Bible, 8, 16, 20-21, 23, 25, 27-29, 36, 40-41, 43, 49, 53, 58, 68, 72, 84, 94, 104, 189, 227
Bismarck, Joseph, 89, 95-97, 224
Blantyre, 12-13, 74, 81, 87-88, 90-95, 97-105, 108-09, 114, 119-20, 126-27, 131, 135-37, 139-41, 145, 148-49, 153, 155-57, 159-62, 165-68, 170, 173-74, 177-80, 187, 199, 207, 210-11, 224-31
Blantyre Mission, 87-88, 90-91, 92-93, 95, 98, 108, 139, 177-78, 210, 229-30
Blantyre Synod, 12, 87, 99-105, 109, 126-27, 136, 155-57, 160, 162, 168, 173-74, 207, 224
Booth, Joseph, 97, 127, 225, 227
British Protectorate, 88, 90, 108, 177-78
British South Africa Company, 90, 178
Bruce, Alexander Livingstone, 93

233

Bujo, Bénézet, 14, 16-17, 30-31, 85, 220, 224
Bwanausi, Harry W., 139, 143-44, 159
Cabinet Crisis, 110, 183, 229
Carpenter, H.J., 20, 224
CCAP, 13, 28, 51, 64, 87, 99, 103, 109-10, 114, 116, 120, 124, 131, 141, 144-45, 152-53, 155-56, 166, 171, 202, 207
Chalker, Baroness, 146-47
Chewa, 81, 183-86, 188, 195, 204, 207, 229
Chief, 42-43
Chihana, Chakufwa, 113, 118, 170, 205
Chilembwe, John, 92-93, 95, 97-98, 126-27
Chinkwita, Emmanuel, 120, 127
Chinula, Charles, 182
Chinyika, 39
Chipembere, Henry Masauko, 173, 182-84
Chiphangwi, Saindi D., 87, 162-65, 169, 174, 224
Chirwa, Orton, 140, 169, 173, 182-83
Chirwa, Vera, 140, 169, 173, 221
Chirwa, Wiseman, 195, 206, 224
Chisiza, Yatuta, 173
Chitalo, Edda, 139
Chitipa, 39

Chiume, Kanyama, 183-84
Chokani, Willie, 159
Choosing our Future, 122
Christian Council, 116, 128, 149, 171
Christopher, Robin, 146-47
Church of Scotland, 13, 90-91, 94, 100, 102, 108, 119, 124, 131-41, 143-53, 169, 229
Churches of Christ, 116, 171
Civil Society, 130, 199, 211, 215-16, 228
Clergy, 64, 76
Clutton-Brock, Guy, 180, 224
Colonialism, 199, 227
Conference of European Churches, 146
Conqueror, 42-43
Constitution (Malawi), 107
Council of Churches in Britain and Ireland, 150, 153
DanChurchAid, 150
De Gruchy, John W., 25, 157, 220, 224-25
Democracy, 118, 123, 132, 139, 143, 147, 150, 157, 200, 203, 209, 214, 216, 220, 224, 227-28
Devil, 45, 125
Diamond, Larry, 132
Discipleship, 54
Discipline, 64
Docetism, 48

Doig, Andrew B., 99, 140, 169
Dwangwa, 207
Dzimbiri, Lewis, 201, 225
Ecumenism, 79
Egypt, 18, 35, 190
Environment, 167, 231
Federation of Rhodesia and Nyasaland, 99, 144, 158, 179, 183, 185
Forster, Peter, 181, 210, 225
Gender, 51
General Election, 56, 107, 124, 128, 146, 150-51, 175, 186, 199, 205
Green, Jim, 34, 216
Gunton, Colin, 34, 194-95, 225
Gutierrez, Gustavo, 221-22, 226
Hanson, R., 32
Hastings, Adrian, 71, 133, 134, 138, 226, 228
Healer, 16, 42, 43, 226
Hepburn, Hamish and Anne, 139
Hetherwick, Alexander, 90, 91, 93-95, 136, 226-27
Hilary of Poitiers, 19, 21, 226, 228
Hinga, Teresa, 33-34, 226
Holy Spirit, 50, 57, 194-95
Hood, Stanley, 136, 151
Hymns, 11
Identity, 59, 85, 175-76, 186, 191, 198, 204, 224, 230-31

Idowu, E. Bolaji, 14-15, 85, 226
Independence, 109, 135, 154-55, 187, 227
Indigenization, 66, 209
Initiation, 63
Jehovah's Witnesses, 161, 173, 225
Johnston, Harry, 90
Justin Martyr, 50
Kadzamira, Cecelia, 135, 158
Kaferanjira, Rondau, 89
Kairos, 86, 138, 231
Kaleso, Peter, 127, 141, 165-68, 174
Kamwendo, S., 180, 208
Kannengiesser, Charles, 18-19, 21, 23-24, 226
Kansilanga, Misanjo, 116-17, 120-21, 129, 137, 145, 149, 155, 171-72, 213
Kanyongolo, Fidelis Edge, 199, 203, 209, 226
Karonga, 39, 61
Kaunda, Kenneth, 147
Kibicho, Samuel, 31-32, 226
Kolie, Cecie, 16, 226
Kufa, John Gray, 93
Laity, 76
Lamya, 39
Lehmann, Paul, 198
Lesotho, 144
Living our Faith, 73, 102, 110, 112-13, 137, 188, 202, 227
Livingstone, David, 93, 98, 177, 227

Livingstonia Mission, 139
Livingstonia Synod, 11, 51, 119, 127, 148, 207
Local Government, 95, 199, 224
Lomwe, 91, 185
Longwe, Aaron, 119, 127, 148
Luxembourg, Rosa, 198
Lwanda, John Lloyd, 138, 154, 186, 197, 200-01, 227
Lyon, David, 136
Mackintosh, H.R., 18, 227
Maclew, Clyde, 216
Macmillan, W.B.R., 59, 134, 225
Macpherson, Fergus, 133, 142, 144, 147, 181-82, 227
Malawi Chamber of Commerce, 188
Malawi Congress Party, 101, 107, 109-10, 114, 138, 158, 176, 180
Malawi Law Society, 116, 171, 188, 211
Malota, Donald, 89
Mamdani, Mahmood, 199, 206, 227
Mang'anja, 88, 207
Mapanje, Jack, 164
Matecheta, Harry Kambwiri, 89, 98
Mbiti, John, 25, 28-29, 86-87, 227
Men, 90, 140, 183
Messiah, 28, 42, 48, 58

Mihecani, 92
Missionaries, 93, 227
Mozambique, 91, 127, 141, 167, 183
Mpakati, Attati, 173
Mphande, Lupenga, 133-34, 228
Msiska, Stephen Kauta, 101, 228
Muluzi, Bakili, 126, 164, 200, 205, 208
Mumba, Levi, 182
Muwamba, T. Jake, 116, 128, 139
Mwanza, 111, 122, 126, 141, 165, 166, 167, 168, 231
Mzimba, 39, 61
Napier, Robert, 89, 90-91, 95, 226
Nation, 3, 8, 89, 99, 102, 110, 114, 129-30, 145, 147, 152, 177, 179, 189, 191-92, 194, 200, 202, 208, 213, 215-17, 224, 229
National Assembly, 199
National Constitutional Conference, 200
National Consultative Council, 128
National Referendum, 117, 122, 124, 126, 150
Nationalism, 99, 176, 178-79, 183, 189, 210, 225, 227, 230
Native Associations, 179

Ncozana, Silas S., 88, 114, 116, 140, 148-49, 158-61, 168-74, 228
Netherlands, 145
Newman, John Henry, 16
Ng'oma, Joyce, 135
Ngoni, 181-82, 185, 207, 231
NGOs, 212
Niebuhr, Reinhold, 221
Nkhata Bay, 39, 111, 122
Nkhoma Synod, 124, 188, 207, 229
Nkhonde, 39
Nkhotakota, 215
Ntcheu, 89
Nyamiti, Charles, 15, 24, 32, 37-38, 43, 85, 228-29
O'Brien, J., 146
O'Donovan, Oliver, 33, 229
Owens, Peggy, 132, 151, 227, 229
Pobee, John S., 14, 85, 229
Portugal, 88, 108, 177
Portuguese, 88, 91, 177, 183
Poverty, 138, 185, 197, 227
Preaching, 28, 73
Presidential Committee on Dialogue, 117, 173
Providence Industrial Mission, 92, 116, 171
Public Affairs Committee, 13, 73, 102, 107-08, 113, 116-17, 119, 121-22, 128-30, 139, 145, 150-51, 154, 171, 175, 188, 199, 203, 207, 211-12

Ranger, Terry, 17, 140
Rhodes, Cecil, 90, 178
Robertson, Charles, 134-35, 221
Roman Catholic Church, 117, 171
Ross, Andrew C., 87-88, 90-91, 108-10, 139, 144, 156, 177, 180, 183, 229,
Rumphi, 39, 61
Sangaya, Jonathan, 88, 155, 157-64, 169, 174, 228
Sanneh, Lamin, 27, 68, 105, 230
Santer, Mark, 146
Saviour, 18, 28, 42, 48, 50, 181, 182
Scott, David Clement, 88-93, 178-79, 210
Second Republic, 12-13, 149, 152, 197, 202-03, 205, 208, 223
Seton-Watson, H., 176
Seventh Day Baptist Church, 116, 171
Sharpe, Alfred, 90-91
Shorter, Aylward, 16, 221, 230
Siwale, Donald, 179
Smout, T.C., 100, 230
State of Emergency, 158
Steel, David, 147
Storrar, William, 191-93, 230
Sudan, 18
Sukwa, 39
Swanwick Conference, 150

Swaziland, 141, 167
Symmachus, 48
Tembo, Mawelera, 116-17, 120, 126, 171, 181
Thole, Peter, 11, 182, 197, 206
Tonga, 39, 185
Torrance, Thomas F., 19, 22, 30, 231
Tumbuka, 11, 39, 68, 181, 185, 207, 228
Turnbull, Bill, 146
Turner, Harold, 35, 231
United Democratic Front, 107, 118, 125, 176
University of Malawi, 4, 8, 10-11, 38, 61, 64, 66, 113, 152, 169, 179, 197, 203, 212, 221, 225, 228
USA, 92, 145, 151, 212
Vail, Leroy, 175, 184-86, 189, 195, 204, 206, 231
Vilikazi, A., 27
Volf, Miroslav, 198, 209, 222, 231
Von Doepp, Peter, 216-17, 231

Walshe, P., 216, 232
Westminster Foundation for Democracy, 151
White Fathers, 146
White, Landeg, 175, 204, 231
Wigglesworth, Chris, 131-32, 137, 143-44, 147
Wilkie, James L., 119, 134, 137, 143-44, 146-50
Witchcraft, 45
Women, 34, 52, 53, 81, 226, 229
World Alliance of Reformed Churches, 102, 114, 144-45, 153, 170, 202, 207
Yao, 88, 184-85, 207
Young, Thomas Cullen, 74, 123, 181, 224-25
Youth, 81
Zambezi Evangelical Church, 116, 171
Zambia, 140, 147, 159, 183, 200, 228
Zeleza, Paul, 152
Zizioulas, John, 194, 232
Zomba, 5, 9-10, 66, 95, 113, 139, 159, 179, 224-25, 228

www.ingramcontent.com/pod-product-compliance
Lightning Source LLC
Chambersburg PA
CBHW050533300426
44113CB00012B/2067